MW01675888

BORNEO

The Stealer of Hearts

Frontispiece.

BORNEO
The Stealer of Hearts

Oscar Cook

(Late District Officer, North Borneo Civil Service)

Opus Publications
Kota Kinabalu
2007

To

MY FATHER AND MOTHER

PREFACE

If the personal pronoun is predominant in the following pages I would ask forgiveness, and the reader to remember that this record is personal. I would also ask him to believe that it in no way constitutes, or is intended to be, a criticism of the Administration of North Borneo, or a treatise on the various " 'ologies " beloved of the serious-minded. The record is actually the outcome of the urgings of several friends, so upon them, rather than upon the writer, must rest the responsibility for its presence in type.

O. C.

June 10th, 1923.

Published by

Opus Publications Sdn. Bhd. (183100-X)
A913, 9th Floor, Wisma Merdeka Phase 1
P.O. Box 15566
88864 Kota Kinabalu, Sabah, Malaysia
Tel: 088-233098 Fax: 088-240768
e-mail: info@nhpborneo.com

BORNEO: The Stealer of Hearts
by Oscar Cook

ISBN-10: 983-3987-10-9
ISBN-13: 978-983-3987-10-8

First published 1924 by Hurst and Blackett. Ltd., London.

Reprinted 2007 by Opus Publications Sdn. Bhd., Kota Kinabalu.

Printed in Malaysia

CONTENTS

LIST OF ILLUSTRATIONS

Borneo: The Stealer of Hearts

CHAPTER I

JOINING THE SERVICE—TENOM MY FIRST DISTRICT

I AM afraid I must admit to a strain of insubordination running through my nature. Be this as it may, June 1912 found me in disagreement with the Manager of Woodford Estate of the Beaufort Borneo Rubber Company, who gently yet firmly intimated to me that he would put no obstacle in the way of my resignation. These were the days of prosperity among Rubber Estates. Assistants were as thick as the proverbial thieves and in greater demand, but to my disgust all the Estates seemed just to have filled up their vacancies. So there I was, nearly 9,000 miles from home, not overburdened with wealth, and faced with unemployment!

At this juncture one who has always been a good friend to me during my ten years in Borneo came to the rescue, and suggested that I should join the North Borneo Civil Service. I acted on his advice and sent off an application to His Excellency the Governor marked "Personal and Private." I do not know whether these magic words carried any weight, but, to my great delight, I was requested to visit Jesselton to be interviewed by him.

The interview will always remain a vivid memory. The Governor, who had been a Postmaster-General in the Ceylon Civil Service, was an Irishman, and his methods were rather unusual. I had previously met him at a social function, but I must admit it was with a distinct feeling of trepidation that I was ushered into his presence. He was the Governor, I was very small fry, and, furthermore, in quest of a job.

When I entered he was seated at a big table in the middle of his office. Overhead a punkah waved lazily. At the end of the table sat the Government Secretary, tall and thin, with prominent teeth, and eyes hidden behind enormous tortoiseshell-rimmed glasses. His Excellency looked up from some papers, stared at me but said nothing. I waited for him to speak. At last, to break the ice, I ventured a halting "How d'ye do, Sir ?" In reply he pushed his glasses up onto his forehead and jerked out, "Sit down, young man." I obeyed. He then went on with his papers. The silence began to worry me, and I felt I wanted to fidget, when a question came hurtling across to me in a broad Irish brogue :

"So ye want to join the Service do ye ? Why ?"

I replied to the best of my ability. Then silence again. The Government Secretary blew his nose, and answered a call on the telephone. His Excellency picked up a pen and began writing.

I was almost off my guard when another question was hurled at me : "And ye know something about Customs you say ?" I answered in the affirmative. "Very well, ye may go, Mr. Fraser will write ye." With a smile His Excellency held out his hand and dismissed me.

In due course a letter came enclosing official regulations and such like. If I approved them I could join the Service. I did approve, and so, on August 1st, 1912, I duly became a Cadet on the princely salary of $140.00 a month. But what did I care about pay ! I was young and unmarried; opportunities for promotion were many, and I was a member of the Civil Service of North Borneo, a British Protectorate, and a country the size of Ireland, owned and governed by a Chartered Company.

I have always been extremely grateful to that Governor for giving me my chance. He was eccentric and abrupt, but both he and his wife were really the soul of kindness and hospitality, as many a young and junior married officer knows. It was with real regret that many of us learnt that he would not complete his full term of office.

The following anecdote will furnish a good example of his brusquerie. The occasion was an official one of some importance, and His Excellency's staff was augmented for the occasion by an A.D.C. in full regalia of spiked helmet, red sash, etc. Suddenly the Governor saw the A.D.C., looking exceedingly imposing, standing close by.

"Who is that young man?" he asked of someone, and was told he was his A.D.C. For a moment His Excellency looked puzzled, then he burst forth in his broadest brogue:

"A.D.C.! A.D.C.! a most useless post and generally the most useless man in the service! Young man, take my bag." And he handed the flushed and embarrassed youngster a little black bag, in which he always carried a spare vest for purposes of changing should the one he was wearing become damp from perspiration. So the procession moved off with the A.D.C. carrying a drawn sword in one hand and a little black bag in the other! His military instinct was outraged, yet he had to obey orders. But that evening he was dining at Government House.

August 4th found me in the train *en route* from Beaufort for Tenom, which was to be the scene of my first official labours. Incidentally there is no Customs work at Tenom, which is 86 miles up the railway, and the Headquarters of the Interior Residency!

We made a merry party on the train meandering along the side of the Padas river from Beaufort to Tenom, as opportunity had been taken of the Bank Holiday week-end to play a series of Inter-district Football, Tennis and Cricket matches. So, though going to new work and fresh scenes, I was not among total strangers. In fact, a curious and kindly Fate ordained that my first Resident should have been District Officer at Beaufort when I first arrived in the County, while, as Assistant District Officer at Tenom, I was taking over from Mr. Anson Cowie, son of the late Mr. W. C. Cowie, practically the founder and guiding spirit of the British North Borneo Co., and against whom, some years previously, I had scored a goal when he was goalkeeper for Westminster School.

In 1912 there was a daily train service—since discontinued—up and down between Tenom and Beaufort. At least it was scheduled as daily, but frequently earth slips and landslides due to the heavy rains would block the line for a day or so at a time.

Normally the journey of about 30 miles took three hours, but one always considered it lucky to reach one's destination only an hour late. Though tedious and tiring, the route in places ran through some magnificent scenery, with the Padas river on one side and high hills on the other, while the train twisted and turned to such an extent, as the line followed its precarious course along the river bank, that it resembled an elongated worm wriggling along the ground, and passengers in the front

Tenom Barracks, Gaol and Stores from the D.O.'s House.

p. 18

portion could almost put their hands out of the windows and shake those of passengers in the rear.

On wet days up certain grades passengers have even been known to descend and help push the train over the most slippery and steepest gradients, while at one watering place chocks of wood were invariably put under the engine wheels to prevent the train from slowly slipping backwards !

Tenom being the Headquarters of the Residency, though not large, was a busy and important centre. The *deus ex machina* was of course the Resident, whose tentacles reached out over the districts of Rundum (District Officer), Tambunan (District Officer) and Kaningau (Assistant District Officer), while he immediately controlled Tenom itself. As Assistant District Officer I was in charge of the Treasury, and this comprised my main duties while I was learning Malay and Law and getting accustomed to administrative routine. The various official titles I bore even in these early days of my career may perhaps be interesting. I was Acting Assistant District Officer, Postmaster, Coroner, Official Administrator, and Assistant Protector of Labour. By November I had added the title of Magistrate of the IIIrd class to the above.

The first case I took as Magistrate was both a terrifying and an amusing affair. By ill luck it was a civil suit between two Chinamen, and if any reader has had the necessity, or temerity, to open the ordinary book of Indian Civil Procedure Code he will know how impossible it seems for a beginner to find any information he may require.

The Process Server came to my office bringing a "Minute" from the Resident. It was as follows: "Mr. Cook, will you take this civil suit ?" To this bombshell I replied with the stereotyped " Resident, noted," and proceeded to the Court House.

On my entrance of course everyone stood up until I was seated at the Bench. On the table I found a sheet of foolscap paper on which was written " Lee Ah Fook and Chun Yun San 25^{oo} and costs." At a table below me stood Lee Ah Fook and Chun Yun San, and at the side of the daïs stood the Court Clerk and interpreter. I picked up a pen, coughed, and looked at the latter. He said something in Chinese to one of the Chinamen—I never knew which—who answered. The other nodded his head and said something, also in Chinese. The Court Clerk then addressed me. " Defendant admits the debt. I presume your Worship will give judgment for Plaintiff." I nodded. " And costs ? " he asked. " Oh certainly," I answered. The Clerk said something to the parties concerned, who then immediately trooped out. I was about to follow when the Clerk informed me that the law required the record to be filled up in my own fair hand. So under his guidance and in the proper spacing I wrote the facts as recorded above.

It is to be supposed that the most important personage in the Residency is the Resident, but I often wondered if this was so in the days of which I am writing. The fame of the various Residents had not reached Singapore when I passed through in 1911, whereas the fame and power of a certain manager of an estate five miles distant from Tenom, had certainly done so ! I well remember with what surprise I listened to comments about this gentleman in the Singapore Cricket Club. " You going to Beaufort ? Then you'll probably meet L—— ! " " Who's L—— ? " " Oh, Manager of Sapong Estate and his own Magistrate ! No, I don't mean he holds that official position, but—well he always gets just what he wants."

It was, then, in a very curious frame of mind that I sat as Magistrate on some cases against coolies whom this "notoriety" was prosecuting in person for various breaches of the Labour Ordinance. Behind his perfect manner in Court I could feel a relentless determination; underneath his suave courtesy I could detect his opinion of my utter insignificance. From this moment I knew we were antagonists, and would cross swords on every possible occasion.

The Resident had gone home on leave and another had been appointed in his place.

The new Resident was the direct antithesis of the old, loving "red-tape" and officialdom as much as the other had hated it. Coupled with this trait he had an unfortunate and frigid manner, a mordant humour, the gift of repartee, and the faculty of always being in the right. It was this nature that inspired a certain member of the Service, now dead, and who was author of a "Borneo Alphabet," to pen the following lines:

> "F stands for F——, of whom it is said
> His hats are now all too small for his head."

Red-tape is undoubtedly necessary in the Administration of a country, but this man carried it to the extreme limits of pedantry, as an example will show:

I asked in person for permission to attend a Sports week-end at Beaufort during the Easter holidays of 1913, and was told to write an official application. I did so. The reply came back, "Yes, if your work permits." On Wednesday in Holy Week I minuted, "Resident, work permits, may I go to Beaufort on Thursday?"

He replied, " Yes ; when do you expect to return ? " I answered, " On Tuesday."

As arranged, I returned on Tuesday and carried on for two weeks or more while the Resident was away on tour. On his return I met him every day for a week. Then, one day, his orderly brought me the minute paper. On it was written, " Mr. Cook, have you returned ? " I was tempted to reply, " Resident, no ! " but checked the impulse, and merely gave the date of my return.

Throughout 1913 life at Tenom was decidedly strenuous, for the Resident was one of those restless and energetic persons who never allowed himself or his officers much leisure, and apart from my daily duty I was 'sweating' for my Higher Malay and Second Law Examinations. Cricket, football and tennis also took up a good deal of time.

As an alternative occupation to head-hunting the Murut possesses a fondness for getting drunk, indulged in on every possible occasion.

Tapai, or pengasai, as the Murut calls it, is not a nice drink. In fact, to my thinking it is the very reverse, for it is chiefly made from fermented rice, or sweet potatoes, is very potent, and generally sour and possessed of a pungent and nauseating odour. Births, marriages, deaths, sowing, harvesting, and any occasion that comes to mind is made the excuse for a debauch.

The liquor is generally kept in jars and drunk through straws straight out of the jar. The jar will be filled nearly to its brim with tapai. Then large leaves are placed on the top just under the lower edge of the rim. These leaves are pierced with straws for sucking up the liquid and the intervening space between the leaves and the top of the jar is filled with water. Etiquette demands that one drinks till the water has been drained off the leaves. They are then flooded again and the process repeated.

It is customary for Muruts to show respect to the white man by producing their very best tapai, and pitting the oldest and ugliest women of the village against him in a drinking competition. Both drink from the same jar simultaneously, each sucking through a straw and each holding that of the other so as to make sure of no deception, for by pulling up the straw one would be drinking the less potent liquid, and this is not considered a "square deal." In my early days, and later, when transferred to Kaningau, I had to employ an "official drinker." The applicants for the post were many!

Tapai drinking has always been a source of worry to the Government, for not only do the natives consume a very large portion of their potential food-crop in its manufacture, but many senseless crimes are committed by them when under its influence. Also, to a certain exent, it accounts for the high rate of infantile mortality, since fond mothers frequently give babies at their breasts a long suck at the straw, with a remark such as, "Poor baby, of course he wants his tapai too!"

About the middle of 1913 a policy of Land Settlement was inaugurated by the Government. This became the occasion for many meetings by the Muruts, and consequently the consumption of much tapai. A Settlement officer was sent up to enquire into and define the boundaries of individual native land. He shared my house, which had been especially constructed in order to allow two officers to live under one roof, yet at the same time could be entirely separated if they so wished.

The Muruts, most conservative of all people, were

opposed to the settlement, and the task was uphill work. The natives resented the idea of paying a small land-tax on their holdings, especially as they never utilised more than a quarter of their land each year, and only planted over the same area in rotation every fourth year. But the reason for this system was their extreme laziness and refusal to plough the land, since the only attempt at ploughing was to puddle the selected area in the wet season by driving buffaloes round and round. Had they tilled their land the whole holding would easily have supported an annual crop.

To enable him to visit some of the outlying villages the Settlement officer bought a young pony. But the brute refused to gallop, and, in the hope that he might follow my animal's example, I rode with him one morning and sent my pony off at top speed. It was a foolish thing to do, as heavy rain had fallen over night, and the path was intersected with wooden bridges. A rain-sodden wood bridge does not give very secure footing, and I paid the penalty of my foolishness. My pony slipped, and, before I could get free, had fallen and rolled over my left leg, pinning me down on the near side. Had we rolled or slipped a yard further the pony and I would have been pitched into a very turbulent and rock-strewn stream! The immediate upshot of the accident was that I was carried home and unable to put my foot to the ground for ten days, and have ever since suffered from a flat left foot. This was annoying, but subsequent happenings were little short of scandalous.

The accident happened a few days prior to Hari Raya, the great Mahomedan festival. This festival was kept with éclat by the neighbouring estates which employed Mahomedan labour, and on Sapong especially it was a time of much feasting, for the " notoriety " was prodigious

VIEW OF BARRACKS. SHOPS AND STATION IN THE DISTANCE.

p. 24

in his hospitality. I was, therefore, rather surprised on Hari Raya to be rung up by the doctor, and informed that he proposed visiting me that evening about 5 p.m. I gathered, however, that one reason chosen for the visit on this particular day, and at the hour mentioned, was a desire to avoid attending a big dinner at the manager's that night, though, curiously enough, he refused my invitation to dine *à deux*. However, he never came, but, as my injuries were quickly mending, I did not worry.

I rather expected him over the next day, and, about 8 a.m., he rang me up. But it was a very excited and almost incoherent doctor who spoke, or rather spluttered, at the other end. I managed, however, to make out that he wanted me to send one of my police down to the ferry at the Padas river, which must be crossed on the journey between Sapong and Tenom, to make certain of his being able to reach me. Wonderingly I did as requested, and then sat down to possess my soul in patience.

In due time he came, and I do not think I have ever seen a man so angry, excited and incoherent. I gathered, as the gist of his story, that, on the previous evening, he had set out to visit me and also a private case in the town, had reached the ferry and then proceeded no further. At first there was no sign of the ferryman, but when, after much calling, he appeared, it was merely to tell the doctor in a most truculent manner that the *Tuan Besar* (manager) had given him orders on no account to ferry the doctor across the river that night.

This was rather an astounding piece of news, but something even more extraordinary was to follow, for it transpired that the doctor stated the literal truth, and that the manager's action had the cognizance of the

Resident ! It was almost unbelievable that such a thing could happen.

The doctor took the matter up with the Government and also with the Medical authorities in England, but he never obtained any real satisfaction, excepting that of a forced apology from the Resident. Against the manager the Government said they could take no steps, since the ferry was the private concern of Sapong Estate, and the ferryman an Estate coolie. This, despite the fact that in my office safe lay a contract signed between the ferryman on the one part and the Resident for and on behalf of Government on the other part !

At this same ferry, which was situated a mile from Tenom, a somewhat gruesome tragedy had occurred a little while before. A large raft had been built on two native dug-outs and travelled from bank to bank by means of a wire fixed to its bows, and fastened to a pulley, which ran on a steel hawser that was stretched high in the air across the river. By setting the rudder against the stream the force of the current propelled the raft across the river. It was then possible to take ponies and traps across quite easily.

As some repairs were necessary to the overhead wire I had sent some prisoners to do this work prior to obtaining a new raft. The river, as it happened, was in flood, but this was a matter of no consequence to the work in hand, and I was in no way troubled as to the safety of the prisoners. The shock I incurred can, therefore, be imagined when I suddenly received a message that all the prisoners had been drowned in crossing the river, and their bodies carried down-stream. I immediately proceeded as fast as possible to the scene of the disaster, but halfway there received another surprise, for I met the prisoners under their police guard returning quite normally to their mid-day meal! They had mended the wire and had not even crossed the river. Though a load had been lifted from my mind since the prisoners were safe, I was frankly puzzled by the message, so, in a less hurried manner, I continued my journey to the ferry, with the intention of inspecting the completed work.

My path ran through thick jungle, and only on rounding the last of many twists and turns did the river come suddenly into view. And there, clinging in midstream to the travelling wire suspended from the overhead hawser, was a Chinaman. As I watched spell-bound, he slipped a few inches nearer to the swollen torrent beneath, and as he slipped he uttered a piercing cry of fear.

Unconsciously I had reached the river bank and stepped into the water up to my chest without any clear idea of what I meant to do. I suppose instinct prompted the idea of attempting to swim to the falling wretch and trying to bring him to the bank. But a hand was placed on my shoulder and a voice spoke close to my ear, "Come back, you d——d young fool! You'll never reach him. You can't swim against that flood." I turned and found the speaker to be the Assistant Manager of Sapong.

In a flash I realised the truth of his words. It was utterly impossible for any swimmer starting from where we stood to live in that flood. Whoever tried to do so would be simply courting death by being carried down stream to be dashed to pieces among the rapids half a mile below!

On the opposite bank were boats, but nobody to man them, and we could not reach them. We shouted to the terrified man to pull himself up the wire and essay to reach the bank by pulling himself hand over hand along the hawser. But fear had paralysed him. He could not, or would not, understand, or make the attempt. And all the while he slipped lower and lower. And all the while I cursed myself for a coward, yet realised the utter madness of such an attempt at rescue.

Another slip and the water would lap his feet ; a little longer and his strength would give out. Someone shouted, " Look, Tuan, look ! " and pointed up-stream, to where, rounding a bend, we saw a boat containing a solitary occupant coming rapidly down-stream. Nearer and nearer it came. Could the helmsman possibly get close enough ? Could he hold the wire for just long enough to allow the poor wretch to drop into the boat ? And if he did would the boat stand the sudden strain ?

Breathlessly we watched and waited. . . . Yes ! he was holding the wire ; the nearly fainting man was in the boat and the final struggle to reach the bank began. Slowly, slowly—at last, a hundred yards below where we had been standing, our eager hands caught the gunwale of the boat and pulled it into safety.

The strain over, my mind swung back to official enquiries. " How had the affair happened ? " " Was anyone drowned ? " I was soon told. A number of Chinese, coming from Sapong, wished to cross the river, and the ferryman had conceived the idea of fastening the ferry raft-wire from the overhead hawser on to the open " dug out " in use at the time to save himself the trouble of paddling against the flood. At any time such an idea would be risky, but under flood conditions it was madness and suicidal, as he found out when in midstream, for the boat, caught by the conflicting pulls of the flood and wire, capsized.

Of the eight persons—a number far in excess of safety —in the boat I think only two were saved. He who had clung to the wire, and his saviour, who happened to be the ferryman and his brother. Somehow he had managed to reach the shore, and knowing of the boat up-stream had made his plucky rescue.

But his troubles were not over, since he was prosecuted by Government for causing death by a rash and negligent act, convicted of the offence and sentenced to pay a fairly stiff fine.

It was customary for the Sergeant of Police to make a final report at 8 p.m. each night to the Resident. In the Resident's absence the report would be made to me. I remember on one occasion, among other minor details, the Sergeant reported that P.C. Aing's wife had returned to him from a visit to her relations. I saw no special need to take any particular notice of the fact, and by the time I went to bed had quite forgotten the affair. But I was not to be rid of Mrs. Aing so easily.

About 2 a.m. I was awakened by voices—I recognised one as that of the corporal—calling "Tuan! Tuan!" (Tuan is the mode of address to a white man.)

"What's the matter?" I grunted sleepily.

"Aing's wife has a bad stomach-ache," came the reply.

"Well, give her some Epsom salts," I answered rather tartly.

There was a pause, followed by an apologetic cough, then the voice continued:

"We gave her that, Tuan, but it is no good."

"Well, try castor oil," I replied in a distinctly cross tone.

This time the pause was longer, and the cough more apologetic, but the corporal insistent.

"It would be best for the Tuan to come and see for himself. Aing's wife is really very ill, and the stomach-ache very bad."

I realised there was nothing for me to do but to

accompany him to the barracks As we neared these I saw signs of great commotion. Every woman in the place seemed to be in attendance, or running in and out of doors. Young children, who should have been asleep, were squatting in groups on the verandah playing and crying just as they pleased. Every room was lit up and the whole place radiated a suppressed excitement. In one corner only was there a total disregard of the prevailing atmosphere, and here four policemen were unconcernedly playing a game of "Main Trop" (a form of whist).

At the top of the steps the Sergeant met me.

"Susah betul, Tuan," he said, "susah skale." (Most unfortunate indeed.)

I entered Aing's room, pushed my way through a ring of deeply interested and much chattering females, and saw the patient stretched on a mat before me. At each side of her knelt an old woman, each of whom was vigorously massaging the suffering woman's abdomen.

"Apa Sakit ?" (What's the matter?) I enquired as the sufferer groaned heavily and tried to turn on her side.

"Ah, Tuan," one of the old women replied, "it's most troublesome—the child will not be delivered."

For a moment I was speechless with anger ; then the humour of the situation came uppermost. This, however, faded quickly when the sufferer groaned again. I put some pertinent questions and received reassuring answers. Everything was going on well but they were anxious ! I told them I would telephone for the doctor, and immediately crossed from the barracks to the office. As I was taking down the receiver I was startled by a terrific yell and clapping of hands. I hesitated for a moment, and the Sergeant came running up.

" It's all right, Tuan," he panted, " the child is born." I put back the receiver.

" Good," I said ; " but what the devil was all that noise for ? "

" That," answered the Sergeant, " was to startle the child and make it take a breath."

If brevity is the soul of wit, contrast is the savour of life, but the savour was a little too strong when a few days after the birth of P.C. Aing's daughter I heard of the death of a Chinese coolie at Sapong Estate in rather unusual circumstances.

The Padas river runs through the Estate and at one spot there is a large lake or backwater—a kind of overflow of the river—on the bank of which was built a large Kongsi (coolie lines) inhabited by about one hundred Chinese coolies. Regularly night and morning coolies bathed in this backwater, the more venturesome frequently swimming to the farther bank, where, jutting out from the rank vegetation of the jungle, was a small sandy spit, which was the favourite haunt of an enormous crocodile, who would lie there for hours sleeping and basking in the sun.

The coolies had no fear of him. In fact they called him by a pet name, used to talk to him, and when he was absent from his haunt would swim across and place tit-bits of fowl, pig or monkey on the sand. For several years this happy state of affairs had existed, and on visits to the Estate I had often seen the crocodile. Then suddenly came a change. A new *tandil* (overseer) came into residence in the Kongsi, and on the very evening of his arrival, while bathing, he saw the " croc " crawl slowly out of the water and stretch himself upon the sand.

With a cry of " Buaya, Buaya " (crocodile), he hastily scrambled out of the water, and running to the

Kongsi picked up his rifle. In a minute he was at the water's edge again, and about to shoot, when several coolies came running up imploring him to desist.

The crocodile was their friend they told him ; he had been there for years and never taken anyone ; he knew them and they him, and they understood each other ; there was no need to shoot : he would do no harm ; to shoot would cause bad " joss " and make the crocodile angry. To all of which the *tandil* turned a deaf ear. He would shoot, and shoot to kill the filthy, loathsome brute. Heedless of the coolies' remonstrances he raised his rifle and fired. A splash of sand rose into the air. With a slow, silent glide the crocodile slipped into, and under, the water. The coolies, though still fearful, breathed a sigh of relief. The *tandil* had missed.

The next evening the coolies as usual were bathing—some were swimming far out across the backwater ; the *tandil* was standing on the bank watching them. Suddenly he cried out " Buaya," and some of the coolies, being still nervous from the previous evening's occurrence, began to swim for the shore. A long, thin snout could be seen just floating on the water—floating apparently calmly and carelessly. In a second, the tragedy was over. An agonised yell ; a disturbing of the water ; the disappearance of the snout ; a thin wake of water ; some air bubbles ; a reddening rising to and colouring the surface, and the crocodile was revenged for that wanton shot.

The body of the unfortunate man was never regained, but, as an outcome of the affair, the *tandil's* authority over the coolies was lost for ever. I could have found it in my heart to punish him severely, but there was nothing in law that could be brought against him. Everyone heartily wished that it had been he and not an innocent coolie whom the crocodile had taken. His act had been so wanton and so unnecessary that he alienated all sympathy. For it is in respecting beliefs and superstitions, which, though possibly foolish and non-understandable in themselves, are yet not inimicable to administration or control, that success lies in a country like British North Borneo.

By the end of August I had passed my Higher Standard Malay and 2nd Law Examination, and so was more or less eligible to be placed in charge of a district under the supervision of a District Officer. Kaningau was mooted as my destination, but just when it appeared likely the transfer would take place a decision was made to retain me in Tenom, at the Resident's special request.

This was a compliment to my official capabilities, but events were about to happen which upset " the best laid schemes of mice and men." The long approaching storm between the " notoriety " and myself was about to break, and it finally did so in no uncertain manner.

Information reached me from an unimpeachable source that the " notoriety " had again taken the law into his own hands by causing two of his Chinese coolies to be flogged in his presence for some minor offence, and then by leaving them incarcerated for some days in the Estate lock-up, a flagrant abuse of the system which allowed Estates to keep a lock-up for the purpose of having some suitable place in which to detain recalcitrant or violent coolies pending, but only pending, their removal, under suitable escort, to the nearest Government office at the very earliest possible moment.

As A.D.O. I laid the information before the Resident, who instructed me to hold an enquiry into the matter in my capacity of Assistant Protector of Labour. The enquiry was duly held, with the result that a criminal case had to be brought against the culprit in the Magistrate's Court. The date of the case was fixed, but, unfortunately, just prior to the hearing, the Resident before whom as District Magistrate the case would have been tried had to undergo an operation, so a postponement was ordered. Eventually, after much correspondence, official and otherwise, a Magistrate of the 2nd class was especially granted 1st class powers and duly sent to Tenom to try the case.

The result I knew was a foregone conclusion, but the interest to me lay in two points (*a*) the defence and (*b*) the sentence. The former, though it failed to obtain an acquittal for the accused—who, if I remember rightly, ultimately pleaded guilty, but claimed extenuating circumstances—would have done credit to any of our leading counsel of to-day. The latter awarded fines amounting to $50.00 for each flogging and $25.00 for each wrongful confinement, making a total fine of $150.00.

Such is the bald outline of the events which led to a reversal of the policy of retaining me in Tenom. I was not, therefore, surprised when I received orders to hold myself in readiness to proceed on transfer to Kaningau. Personally I was pleased at the prospect, for, since his trial, the "notoriety" introduced an official atmosphere into every private occurrence of daily life. On December 11th, 1913, I was duly gazetted Acting Assistant District Officer, Kaningau.

CHAPTER II

KANINGAU AND LAND SETTLEMENT

KANINGAU is thirty miles from Tenom, with which it is connected by a bridle path. The first ten miles of the journey, however, are generally accomplished by using the train which runs from Tenom to Melalap Estate, the final and furthest point of the ninety-six miles of railway in N. Borneo.

By using the railway one reached Melalap about 4.30 p.m., partook of the hospitality of the Estate that night and could start off on the twenty mile journey to Kaningau early the next morning. Thus the traveller easily reaches his destination before the heat of the day becomes too burdensome. All luggage and personal effects are carried by coolies—the average load being about 50 lbs.

Except when travelling on the railway or by steamer, or along the main rivers that intersect the country, porterage is almost entirely done on the backs of the natives.

The providing of the necessary coolies when duly requisitioned is one of the duties of Government chiefs, or, in their absence, of village Headmen. Payment per day, or journey, is of course made on a fixed official scale. A chief or headman who fails to provide coolies when called upon to do so is liable, under the Village

Administration Ordinance, to prosecution and would be convicted, unless he proved his failure to be due to slackness or disobedience of his orders by the various coolies detailed off by him.

To ensure an equitable distribution of this necessary labour, which I must admit is generally most uncongenial to the natives, a register is kept in each District Office, under the supervision of the Native Sergeant of Police, who details the dates of requisition, and numbers supplied from each Kampong (village).

It is a curious and interesting fact that a native, though long winded and circuitous to a degree in telling a story or giving evidence, will always take the most direct route when on the road, and shows, upon every occasion, an intense dislike to following the frequent and lengthy windings of a bridle path, cut along the contours of hills, and graded not more than 1 in 15, when he can shorten the route by going straight up and down the steep sides of a hill. Here again another curious fact is noticeable. A native, carrying on his back a load of from 40 to 50 lbs. and ascending or descending a hill, will set a pace that the average European will find hard to equal. But let the route be upon a level path and the native will travel so slowly that a European can with ease out-distance him.

In the Kaningau district practically all transport is done on the natives' backs. Here, as in other parts of the territory where transport is of a similar nature, the native has evolved a perfectly simple yet equally efficacious method of carrying his goods with the utmost ease to himself, combined with protection from the sun or rain.

A " Basong " or " Bongon," as the receptacle is called, is cylindrical in shape, with a circumference at the top about twice that at the bottom. It is usually made of the

BASONGS.

A JUNGLE SCENE, SILOMPOPON.

p. 36

bark of Sago trees ; has a thin wooden bottom, and a lid, the top of which is thin wood, with the over flap made of the bark of a tree.

There is not a nail in the whole contrivance, all joints being fastened together with rotan. None the less, when completed, and if well and properly made, it would be hard to find any suitcase or kit-bag so water-tight and weather-proof as a Basong ; while, since its shape is designed with the idea of fitting comfortably on the human back so as to allow the weight to be borne on the shoulders by the shoulder-straps, no surprise need be occasioned at finding some half-dozen Basongs or so among a District Officer's regular up-country outfit.

On leaving Tenom for Kaningau the Resident informed me that one of the principal tasks before me was the inculcation into the native mind the blessings and necessity of Land Settlement. The method of procedure was left to me. I was glad of this, as I held strong views on the subject.

As the actual settlement work was not to start for some weeks I determined on a policy of conciliation and persuasion, rather than one of reliance on the terrors of the law with which to break down the Muruts' passive resistance.

With this end in view I particularly sought out and cultivated the acquaintance of Ambidau, son of the Government Chief Gunsanad. There was good and sufficient reason for this action. Ambidau was a Christian ; that is to say he accepted the Christian teaching and was a member of one of the Missions in the territory. He therefore knew a smattering of English, and could also read and write a little. His official wife (I think he had three others unbeknown to the Mission Authorities) was also a Christian. Consequently, he was looked up to among the younger generation of the district as a personage of some importance, and one of no little acumen and ability. He also derived glamour and importance from the fact of his birth, and the belief that he would in turn succeed his father as paramount chief.

Gunsanad, a loyal and capable chief, was pro-Government; Ambidau was outwardly the same, but actually the leading spirit against the Settlement policy. On account of his advancing age, his fondness for opium and consequent disinclination to any sustained effort, Gunsanad frequently utilised Ambidau as his deputy. The result, of course, can easily be imagined. It was obvious, therefore, that Ambidau was the hinge upon which to turn native resistance.

So at Ambidau I set my cap. Nowhere would I go without him! He was indispensable! My guide, philosopher and friend. In short, my complete pocket "vade mecum"! Through him I arranged a tour of all the neighbouring villages; with a stay at each village as long as he liked; with mass meetings to hear me expound the blessings of Land Settlement and to enable every individual, who so wished, to air his grievance, and, having done so, to quench his thirst with copious draughts of tapai.

I could have thought of nothing more pleasing to the natives, for my visits to their villages and my sojourn in their houses provided a legitimate excuse for the making, production and consumption of much tapai. At the third village I visited I had a happy thought. I formally appointed Ambidau my official Tapai Drinker, a post he accepted with delight and alacrity.

In return, and knowing the results of properly and assiduously fulfilling the duties of this post, he appointed his wife, Miang, as A.D.C. to me. At first I felt embarrassed, and pointed out the irregularities of the position, but he was adamant. In drinking on my behalf he would frequently become hopelessly drunk, and, if not drunk, then so sleepy as to be utterly incapable of paying proper attention to me or my wishes. Nothing would move Ambidau, and as Miang herself seemed hurt by my objections to the appointment I gave way, and the good lady was attached to my staff! I fancy that in the Mission school they must have recently told her the story of Ruth, for certainly her motto was, " Whither thou goest, Lord, I go also " !

Actually my stay in Kaningau was limited to three months, but before I left I had the satisfaction of informing the Resident that all opposition to Settlement was at an end, and that no one was keener on it than Ambidau.

Ambidau came to me one day, about a week before my departure, and confessed to having seen the error of his ways, and that he realised it was no good continuing to kick against the pricks. He would therefore like to work, not only for Government, but in Government service, and asked for my good offices in helping him to obtain some post. I readily promised assistance, but felt bound to point out that, at first, he would probably have to leave the district while learning his new duties, whatever they might be. He readily agreed to this, but expressed the hope that after his probationary period was over work might be found for him in Kaningau.

In a flash the Resident saw the full possibilities of the situation, and realised how completely Ambidau had delivered himself into our hands, for the only possible work that he could be given in the district was that of Assistant Demarcator, whose duties it would be to survey with plane-table and compass, under the supervision of the District Officer, the native holdings then due for determination under the Land Settlement.

The irony of the situation tickled the Resident's humour immensely. None the less, Ambidau was sincere in his protestations, and eventually returned to Kaningau to measure those very lands against the demarcation of which he had previously fought so strenuously.

With the idea of lessening the calls upon natives to turn out as porters, and also to reduce the expenditure under transport, Government had decided to try and utilise cattle ; and among other special duties that fell to my lot while in Kaningau was the supervision of the breaking-in of some young animals as pack-bullocks.

The immediate task was in the hands of the Government herdsman—a particularly obnoxious, obsequious and slimy Pathan—and the work did not progress to my satisfaction. This was not to be wondered at considering my frequent absences from Headquarters, but it was nevertheless distinctly annoying.

In the end I gave " Mr. Herdsman " an ultimatum. The three bullocks would be completely broken in to pack-work by a certain date, or, at the end of the month, he could seek other employment.

Two days before the stipulated date I was seated in my office, wrestling with some refractory accounts, when my obnoxious and obsequious friend limped in. He rolled his eyes, breathed heavily and painfully, and pressed his left hand to his heart, while, with his right hand, he alternately caressed and massaged his right shin and foot.

After a while I looked up at him but said nothing.

" Sahib " (this class of man always uses " Sahib " instead of the more general " Tuan " in Borneo when he wants something for nothing), " Sahib," he continued, " the devil is in those bullocks."

" Perhaps," I answered, " but that's just your job—to eradicate the devil."

" I have tried to, Sahib," he replied, " but it is no good ; they're too much for me. Why, the little red one, with the four white feet, that your Honour likes so much, and that I have fed with my own hands, is the worst of the lot, and to-day—ah ! oh, my chest ! "

He pressed his hand tighter over his heart, limped impressively to the window and began to cough—a great, rasping, sonorous, spitting cough.

When he had finished he came back and picked up his story.

" The devil is in him to-day. He butted me twice in the chest, and kicked and trampled on my feet and shins. My chest is one great bruise and I can hardly breathe ! Will the Sahib give his servant some medicine ? "

And the coughing and limping performance began again.

I waited for silence before speaking, then in my silkiest tones I addressed him,

" I'm sorry you are so hurt, Alif Din, and I will give you some medicine. But I seem to remember that when I engaged you you said you were an expert with cattle . . . "

" But, Sahib—— "

" Silence ! " I shouted, then continued quietly. " You have two more days in which to break them in, or at the end of the month you go. You understand ? "

" Tuan," he answered, and forgot to press his hand to his heart, cough, limp or stroke his injured shin. " And the medicine, Tuan ? " he asked.

I turned to a shelf near my desk. On it were a number of bottles covered in the dust and grime of years. I cleaned one so that I could just read the label. I deciphered the words " Dysentery Mixture " and the date

"1908." The mixture looked unappetising. At the bottom of the bottle was a dirty yellow sediment about an inch in depth ; on top was a pale green oily liquid. I shook the bottle, poured the contents into a glass and passed it over to Alif Din.

"Drink," I commanded, and he obeyed, with many splutterings and grimaces. Then he limped out, coughing and repeating his previous performance.

I went back to my accounts quite unconcernedly, for I was certain that the mixture, though extremely unpalatable, was perfectly harmless ; also I knew that Alif Din had the previous evening ridden the little red bullock to a neighbouring village to attend a "drunk." His ailments were not the outcome of the animal's viciousness, but the award of the hefty Murut maiden who went by the courtesy title of "Alif Din's wife." She rightly objected to being awakened at 5 a.m. by the return of her drunken "husband," and shewed her displeasure in no uncertain manner.

Alif Din, of course, wanted the day to sleep off the effects of his night's outing. Hence his visit and the story he told me. I was not, therefore, surprised when, the next morning, he presented himself, smiling and well, at my office.

"Tuan," he said, "I hear from the Sergeant your Honour is going on tour to-morrow ; is that so ?"

I answered it was so.

"Then," he continued, "the bullocks are quite tame and broken in. How many will the Tuan require ?"

"All three," I answered.

"Tuan !" he replied, "and I will accompany your Honour as they are in my charge and accustomed only to me."

"But your chest and wounds——" I began.

" Are nothing, Tuan," he broke in quickly. " The Tuan's medicine has cured me—it is wonderful—and I am a little weary of my wife."

But though I got rid of Alif Din I was not destined to remain undisturbed, for a few minutes later I heard the telephone ringing and my orderly duly announced that, " The doctor wanted to speak."

I went to the instrument, which was placed in the office verandah, and, picking up the earpiece, spoke.

" Hullo ? "

" Yes," came back the reply, " is that Cook ? "

" Yes," I answered.

" Can you hear ? I've got some news for you."

" Right-oh—carry on—you're quite clear."

" Well—listen—don't shout, but you're going to be transferred again."

" How do you know ? "

" It's a fact—and official too."

" Where to ? "

" A place with a block-house."

" Ranau ? "

" No, not Ranau—it's what they call the penal station for ' naughty boys.' "

" Oh, you mean Semporna."

" Yes, that's it. Where is it ? "

" On the East Coast, miles from anywhere ! "

" Well, you're going there ! "

" But how do you know ? "

" I overheard the ' notoriety ' saying so."

" If he says so, of course it's official. But what did he say ? "

" ' Thank God that young blighter, Cook, is getting shifted ! He is being sent to Semporna.' "

" Splendid. I'm fed up with the Interior."

" It's pretty rotten ; but don't let on you know about it, as I don't know when the move is coming off."

" Right-oh, Doc, and thanks for the news—cheerioh."

I went back to my work, with a rather preoccupied mind.

Three weeks later, when in the course of a telephone conversation with the Resident, he gave me the official confirmation of the doctor's news. I could not refrain from letting him know I was expecting it, and that I was delighted at the idea of going to Semporna.

" But how did you know ? " he asked.

" The doctor told me three weeks ago," I answered

" The doctor told you ! " and his voice betrayed his surprise.

" Yes," I replied, smiling into the telephone, " he heard —— talking about it with great delight. It's wonderful the amount of official information that comes out of Sapong ! "

However, before the transfer took place I was honoured with a visit from His Excellency the Governor, who was making his first tour of inspection of the Interior. He was accompanied on the trip by a Superintendent of the Constabulary.

I remember the Resident was supposed to join the party at Tambunan, the next district to Kaningau, but for some reason of his own elected to await His Excellency at Kaningau.

The visitors, who were spending the previous night at Melalap Estate, were expected to arrive about 12 noon, so midday found the Resident and myself, resplendent in Civil Service uniform, pacing up and down the lawn awaiting the " vice-regal " party. Our wait proved a long one, for His Excellency actually arrived at 5.45 p.m.

Apparently, the party had been late in leaving Melalap, and found the charms of the rest-house at Senaggong —a half-way halt—so enticing that it had decided to " lie-up " during the heat of the day. The idea was sensible but possessed one drawback, viz., there was no means of informing us at Kaningau of the change of plans.

I do not think the Resident was best pleased at being kept waiting all day—" booted and spurred "—in official uniform, especially as he foresaw the habit of late starts being continued throughout the trip, for if he was possessed of one obsession above others it was for early rising and early starting when on tour.

Dinner was quite a jovial meal, for His Excellency was an easy guest to entertain and a good conversationalist ; I could, however, see storm-clouds beginning to gather on the Resident's brow when, as coffee was being passed round, His Excellency turned to me and asked :

" What time can we have breakfast to-morrow, Cook ? "

" Any time you like, Sir," I replied.

" About eight ? " queried His Excellency.

" Yes, Sir," I answered.

Then as an after-thought he turned to the Resident.

" Eight o'clock suit you, or is that a little late ? "

" Just as you like, Sir," was the Resident's rather stiff reply.

So I gave orders for breakfast at eight sharp, and added explicit instructions to my " boys " that early tea was to be ready in the verandah at 5.30 a.m. for the Tuan Resident, as he always wakened early.

When I turned out in the morning about 6.30 I was not therefore surprised to find the Resident, fully dressed and equipped for the journey, pacing up and down the verandah like a caged tiger, and every minute or so looking at his watch. How he managed to control his rising impatience till eight o'clock I cannot conceive, and then, unfortunately, when he appeared, His Excellency nearly put spark to tinder when he enquired of me,

" What on earth was all that noise and banging about round about 5 a.m., Cook ? "

" I don't know, Sir," I answered, " unless it was the 'boys' getting the Resident's early tea according to orders."

" Well, they made enough noise about it, and I hope you enjoyed it when you got it, Resident," His Excellency grunted.

" That's the trouble, Sir," I couldn't help saying, " for the Resident got no tea after all. The 'boys' put the kettle on the fire and then went back to bed ! "

His Excellency smiled, but to help to hide his amusement he asked the Superintendent of Constabulary to pass him the marmalade.

It is perhaps curious that the two people who had, in their small way, caused rather a disturbance in the Interior, should both leave it almost together. But whereas I was only transferred to another district, the doctor gave up his position as Medical Officer of Sapong Estate and returned to England.

His departure was prior to mine, and attended with a rather unpleasant incident.

Previous to leaving he wished to visit Kaningau for personal reasons, and I was looking forward to his visit and the pleasure of putting him up, especially as mine was the only European's house in the district. My disappointment can then be imagined when the Resident ordered me to go a small trip to a place called Mesopo, where there was a police station and a native clerk, at the very time when the doctor was coming to Kaningau. I readily admit the need for the trip, but why at that exact date ?

My disappointment was later turned to disgust when, as I was about to start for Mesopo, I received implicit orders not to allow the doctor the use and hospitality of my house under any consideration. The excuse given for such an order was that as the doctor was anti-Government in his sentiments he should not be allowed the use of a Government building !

I had naturally to obey orders, and so cancel the offer of my house during his visit, but I left my cook in charge, and, in his possession, the key of a well-filled store-cupboard. It wasn't much, but it was the most that could be done.

There is a sequel to the doctor's visit that is perhaps worthy of record.

He was expected to return to Tenom on a Monday evening, and the Resident and the "notoriety" had booked in their names, and for their use, all the rooms in the Rest-House as from Monday morning, with the avowed intention of preventing the doctor obtaining a room.

Early on Monday morning the two conspirators forgathered on the rest-house verandah, loudly congratulating each other on what promised to be "a tremendous score off the doctor." But they were counting their chickens before they were hatched, as they realised when a bedroom door at the back of them opened, and the doctor's towsled head appeared in the opening, shouting to the boy for tea !

He had returned on Sunday evening, and, from his bed, had listened to the conspirators' openly expressed delight. He afterwards told me that the expression on their faces was more than ample payment for any annoyance he had suffered at their hands.

Thus, my stay in the Interior came to an end, and

during the remainder of my years in the Service I never re-visited it.

On my way to Tenom to the Coast I stayed again at Melalap Estate. Great changes had taken place since my previous visit, as a manager and an assistant had been murdered by a gang of Javanese coolies. I knew them both very well for I had frequently accepted their hospitality during my tenure at Tenom. The memory of their unhappy death cast a gloom over the whole Estate, and was poignantly in my thoughts as I made my way to Jesselton *en route* for Semporna.

After the remoteness of the Interior, Jesselton, with its Club and other social amenities, seemed a busy centre of civilisation and luxury. But an echo of the past and of my friends in Tenom and Kaningau reached me when, late that evening, my Murut "boy," Imbul, brought me a note from my little friend Miang, wishing me "bon voyage," and good luck in my new district.

CHAPTER III

SEMPORNA

THE journey from Jesselton to Semporna is accomplished by sea. In 1914 steamers of the North German Lloyd Company maintained communication between British North Borneo and the outer world, steaming round the territory's nine hundred miles of coast line. These were, however, augmented by the Sabah Steamship Company, which ran a service of two purely coastal steamers. It was in one of these, the s.s. "Sabah," that I made the journey.

Granted fine weather the trip is one of sheer delight, and constitutes a splendid four days' holiday of rest and ever-changing interest. The steamer calls at Usukan, Kudat, Sandakan and Lahad Dato, before landing the traveller at what, in my days, was an island wharf planted among the coral reefs, deep blue seas andc oconut islands that go to the making of Semporna.

I know my first and greatest sense of delight and relief during the trip arose from the realisation that I had no safe or Treasury keys to worry about, as, for the time being, I had no money under my charge. Relieved of this responsibility every minute of the trip was one of sheer pleasure. I basked in the sun and inhaled deep breaths of the ocean wind. I keenly studied the ever-changing, and, to me, new coast-line, and I enjoyed the company of my two fellow passengers.

The trip was a replica in miniature of my first voyage out to the East in 1911, and just as "Gib," Port Said, Colombo and Penang filled me with expectancy and delight so the small ports of call, each in turn, seemed the very Mecca of the cruise.

The first streaks of dawn breaking across the sky found me on deck at a quarter to six to catch my earliest glimpse of Lahad Dato, the headquarters (since removed to Tawao) of the Residency.

As my feet touched the deck I became conscious of the absence of any roll or movement. I looked around, but could see nothing—a thick mist enveloped us. As I walked along the small deck I could feel a distinct lift to starboard and experienced a curious sense of rigidity about the boat.

A light was burning in the engineer's cabin. I knocked and entered. He was dressed and drinking coffee but was not in the best of tempers, since, in the dark and mist, the serang (native helmsman) had missed the channel of approach, and piled the "Sabah" up on a coral reef on the wrong side of one of the beacons that marked the entrance to the harbour.

There was, however, no fear of very much damage having been done, but the delay was annoying as we should have to wait for the high tide before there was any chance of getting off.

While I was commiserating with him the rising sun dispelled the mist and a hail reached our ears. On looking over the taffrail we saw the Customs boat approaching. In her stern were seated the Resident, my old friend, and the Treasurer, who was also Superintendent of Customs and Harbour Master.

After a couple of "gin-slings" and the retailing of the latest news from up and down the coast, the Customs boat

" pushed off " taking me with it as the guest of the Resident, till such time as the " Sabah " should be ready to continue her voyage, which, as a matter of fact, was seven o'clock the next morning.

I was immensely pleased to meet the Resident again, and to find that I should be working under him ; for, apart from being one of the best of Residents to work for, he was also a very real, personal friend.

To my surprise I found I was not immediately to take up my duties at Semporna, but to proceed beyond, to Tawao, and relieve the acting District Officer, the latter having been seconded for special duty on Sebattik island in connection with the final settlement of the Dutch Boundary.

So, after giving my heavy luggage into the care of the Pathan police Sergeant, and a hurried run ashore to look at my new quarters and the shops, while the Semporna cargo was being unloaded, I continued my journey to Tawao, where we arrived just before 6 p.m.

The arrival was rather hectic. Chance willed that the District Officer and his Dutch colleague were in the town collecting stores. A Government Surveyor was staying with the Manager of Tawao Rubber Estate, and both had come in to meet the D.O. The acting D.O., of course, was, so to speak, in residence. All five, according to immemorial custom, came down the wharf to meet the " Sabah." Then, greetings and news over, we all adjourned to the Rest House, which acted as a kind of Club House too.

The " Sabah's " arrival had interrupted a " sitting " of dicing for a five dollar pool. I joined in readily, and as the last thrower had " Five Kings to beat." There were shouts of encouragement and the usual cry of " One tie, all tie " as I took up the box and shook the dice. A flip and they all rolled out. Everyone looked ; then a pause, then a gasp and then a great shout. I had thrown " Five Aces " in " one cold flop." The pool was mine, and so were the drinks ! They were " on " me and custom ordained champagne !

In those days Tawao was devoid of telephone or telegraphic communication, and one lived in a splendid isolation, only broken by the regular visits of the steamers. This isolation, and consequent peacefulness, was further augmented by the attitude of the Secretariat, which, for some reason best known to itself, always considered the East Coast unworthy of much attention. It was an axiom that once a man was stationed on the East Coast he was forgotten till such time as he chose to remind the Authorities of his existence !

However this may be, both Tawao and Semporna, in my time, were delightful stations. There was a sufficiency of work to keep one interested ; an efficient staff of clerks to attend to it ; good shooting, bathing, and fishing ; and in Tawao tennis and football and occasionally cricket. The steamers brought ice, and there was no telephone ! What more could a District Officer desire.

But even during my short sojourn these halcyon days were numbered, for a wireless installation was in course of being erected.

England's complete unpreparedness for the War had its counterpart in North Borneo, for, when the storm clouds broke in August 1914, the only people who knew anything about the wireless were the Germans erecting the stations, and communication with the outside world was in the hands of a German Steamship Company !

After I had taken over from the acting D.O., he proceeded to the Cowie Harbour Coal Company's mine

GOVERNMENT OFFICES, GAOL AND BARRACKS, TAWAO.

p. 52

at Silompopon for the purpose of making and submitting a report.

He knew no more about a mine and its workings than I did, but as a " makan angin " (Malay for " a holiday ") the visit was nearly all that could be desired. The Manager and his assistants were sportsmen ; there was a club, a hard tennis-court, and last but not least three exceptionally charming white women.

The Europeans at Silompopon lived a rather lonely life, they were, therefore, always glad to see a new face, and as the A.D.O. was always a cheery person, his visit was a welcome event.

Shortly after my arrival in Tawao I received a request from the Manager of the Mines to visit Silompopon in an official capacity. There were some cases to be tried which were beyond the A.D.O.'s jurisdiction, and some indentured coolies to be " signed on contract." Between the lines of the request I could read a pressing social invitation. Duty, of course, compelled me to go aboard the company's launch, and in due time I reached Silompopon.

I intended to pay only a short visit, but, in the end, stayed a week, as, directly after my arrival, the launch went into dock for repairs. I, therefore, made the best of a bad job, ceased to worry over my enforced absence from Tawao, and proceeded to enjoy every minute of each day.

In the mornings the A.D.O. and I would accompany the Manager or an Assistant round and down some part of the mine, emerging to light about midday to congregate with other members of the staff at the club. There we essayed to slake an unquenchable thirst with iced drinks. Then came tiffin (lunch) followed by an afternoon siesta. Tea and a bath invigorated us for the ensuing tennis, and a dinner-party and impromptu dance would bring the day to a close.

At Silompopon fever was practically unknown, and though the labour force was a large one the health of the coolies was particularly good. The doctor gave it as his opinion that this was due to the tremendous heat experienced underground, which induced such copious perspiration that most impurities of the body were sweated out.

On my return to Tawao I found a quantity of official mail awaiting my attention. Among other items the Resident had passed on a " Minute " from the Government Secretary enquiring rather plaintively if any news could be given as to the A.D.O.'s whereabouts. In true official style and in keeping with the rest of the paper the Resident minuted to me, " Mr. Cook (Officer-in-charge Tawao), can you say ? I think he is at Silompopon." I replied, " Resident, Mr. —— is at the mines, making his report."

In due course the A.D.O. was re-called from the mines and asked to explain his unwarrantably lengthy stay there. In his reply he merely quoted his instructions which were more or less as follows : " Mr. —— will proceed to Silompopon to make a report on the mines. He will remain there until further notice."

Truly the East Coast was the best place in the world in which to become lost and forgotten !

Shortly afterwards the D.O. finished his work on the Boundary Commission and returned to Tawao, thus allowing me to proceed to my proper duties at Semporna.

I have already said that Semporna was dubbed the " Penal Station." Why I cannot think, unless on account of its loneliness. Certainly it was blest (?) with neither telephone nor telegraph and was forty and sixty miles respectively from Lahad Dato and Tawao, but these considerations were not sufficient to earn it so unenviable a reputation. Personally I always had, and still have, a great liking and affection for Semporna, and consider it one of the most beautiful districts in the Territory; while, to my thinking, the East Coast Natives are the most interesting and courteous of the various tribes which comprise the polyglot population of North Borneo.

It is a fascinating district, with a broken, indented coast-line, sometimes fringed with shell-strewn sandy beach; sometimes bordered with vast stretches of nipah palm, or the grotesque shapes of the Bakau forests; with an expanse of sea dotted and studded with sandy coral islands, edged with native houses, and backed with coconut trees and ubi-kayu (tapioca) gardens; with coral reefs and winding channels; with storm and sunshine; ever-beating gongs and sharp tap-tap of the busy cloth weavers; with the ever-coming and going of natives in their bright clothes and beautifully carved Lipa-Lipa, Sapit or Dapang (classes of boats).

In 1914 I wrote the following description of it for the "Borneo Herald":

"To many Semporna is but a name; to others it is, I believe, synonymous of that warm place to which most of us will hereafter go; and to a few it is, so I have gathered, a pestilential memory, a very night-mare of a dream. But why? Aye, there is the rub!

"Semporna—Perfect—and from a panoramic view it probably is perfect of its kind. Stand on the verandah of the Block House and gaze seawards. In the foreground is the 'trusan' backed with Bum Bum Island—a trusan always alive with craft, bright with the long narrow sails, often vary coloured, of the Lipa-lipa, or the squarer, almost lug-shaped, sails of the Dapang, intermingling with the bright coloured clothes of the natives. A little to the left is the bay, the water always varying in its colour from sapphire blue to pea-soup green, from pale green to faintest pink as the coral reefs catch the rays of the sun. Carry your gaze further afield and your eye will be caught by the mighty cone-shaped peaks of Timbu-Mata and Pulau Gaya, rising sentinel like out of the sea—islands these that conjure up in your brain nemories of 'The Impregnable City' and 'Treasure Island' and fill you with the romantic visions of boyhood's dreams.

"Or yet again there is a storm, the wind is howling round the house, the rain driving in through the cracks in the 'chicks,' but you do not care : you are watching a storm-caught prahu making for port ; you are fascinated with the cloud effects rolling and unfurling themselves round the triune peaks of Pulau Gaya ; you are unconsciously keeping time with your foot to the tom-tom-tom of the gongs across the water.

"But you cannot live on a view, I hear someone say. Quite true. There are, however, other interests as well. For half the month at least you travel—none too comfortably perhaps—visiting the islands and each visit brings a fresh surprise and unnoticed beauty, a new point of view ; each Kapala Kampong (Head of a village) has his little eccentricities, his curious foibles. One always wants—and oft succeeds—to cadge your cigarettes ; another loads you with coconuts ; while a third thrusts, unconsciously (?) rotten eggs upon your boy for your honour and consumption. And the children. How they love the impromptu races upon the stretches of sand, the long jump and French cricket ; how they revel in the bathing and diving.

"And the few days each month you are in Semporna do not hang heavy on your hands. There is always something to be done either in Office or out; a steamer in, a mail to be answered, a broken 'jem-batan' (wharf) to be repaired or a towkay to be induced to paint his Kedei (shop). In the evening?—Rest from the struggle with refractory and disappointing Customs figures. At 5.15 p.m. the populace turn out almost 'en masse' and on the bumpy stony coral 'padang' (field) play with all their energy a strenuous game of Football. Or if, as often happens, the football is 'hors-de-combat' then 'Rounders' is the order of the day. Seven out of every ten players mishit the ball, but that does not matter, the shrieks of laughter are only longer and louder when by mistake the ball is really hit, the delight of the striker is unbounded and a 'rounder' scored an event memorial.

"'How about the smell?' I fancy someone murmurs. Well, you get used to that, in fact doubtless it is as healthgiving as 'Sanatogen.' It is an integral part of Semporna, as much as its gongs and cloth-weaving. Semporna, Bajaus, Smells: they are all one and summed up in their different yet respective ways they are Semporna—Perfect."

But in thinking of Semporna I shall always remember the two men with whose names the district will always be associated—Pang Eng Guan who was chief clerk, and Panglima Udang, Government chief.

The former was a very perfect Chinese gentleman who earned the respect and affection of every officer, from Residents to cadets, whose good fortune it was to work with him. In the earlier days of the Chartered Company's régime, when European officers were scarce, and piracy and Suluk raids of frequent occurrence, he had borne the burden of maintaining the Government prestige.

Udang was always reputed to be the son of a slave, and of low caste. Be that as it may, he became the one person of consequence in the district, and, in reality, often of more value to Government than an European officer.

He was of enormous bulk, with a face like that of an orang-hutan, with tiny eyes that were perpetually screwed up and blinking. He possessed a habit of always falling asleep, but of waking up at the very moment his decision on any point, or answer to any question, was required.

His word was absolute law over the whole district, and he was held in respect and fear by all. This, no doubt, was partly due to the fact that superstition credited him with the gift of "Kabal," *i.e.*, immunity from sword, spear or bullet wound—an immunity which he himself absolutely believed in, and frequently, though vainly, asked me to test.

Udang in Malay means a shrimp, but anything more unshrimp-like than the portly and unwieldly Panglima it would be hard to imagine.

The Government buildings in Semporna were neither spacious nor large, and, with the exception of the customs office and wharf, were all grouped in a compound of about seventy-five to one hundred yards square, enclosed by a high barbed-wire fence, the gates of which were generally closed at 8 p.m.

This precaution had been necessary in former days on account of the raids frequently made by the Suluks or Obians from the neighbouring outlying islands of the Phillipines. But though in my time the possibility of such danger had practically ceased to exist, the old conditions and orders were still maintained.

This state of affairs contributed largely, no doubt, to the unpopularity of the station. I must admit that there are certain drawbacks in having one's quarters confined to two rooms situated over the office and barracks; while it is not all joy having one's bathroom in a separate building at some small distance from the house. These conditions were such as should have been altered by Government. In fairness, however, I must concede that that Block House was in most excellent condition, its timber throughout being of Billimu (the Borneo Iron Wood) which is almost indestructible.

It had never been deemed wise to keep any prisoners sentenced to gaol in the district; consequently there was no proper lock-up, and prisoners (when there were any, which was not often) whilst awaiting transfer to the gaol at Lahad Dato were detained in one or other of the store-rooms.

On one occasion, a few weeks after my arrival, two deserters from one of the Timber camps, of which there were four in the district, had been caught by the police, and, pending their trial, were lodged in the store-room adjoining the barracks. It happened that Empire day fell due while they were on remand, and I was somewhat concerned as to a fitting way, besides the official holiday, of celebrating the event.

I was discussing the matter the previous evening with the Pathan Corporal. At first he had no suggestions to make, then was suddenly seized with an idea, but was obviously shy of suggesting it, so I gave him a lead.

"Out with it, Corporal," I said, "you've got an idea I can see."

"Yes, Tuan," he said, "but don't be angry with me."

"That's all right," I answered.

So, relieved by my reply, he launched forth into the

suggestion of a conjuring performance for the evening of Empire Day, finishing up with satisfaction, " Everyone likes to witness a good conjuror."

I agreed that the idea was excellent, but asked where the conjuror was to be found.

Then only, and right at the end of all our talk, as is always the way of a native, the corporal stated his real case. The conjuror was in the lock-up ; he was one of the two deserters, a hefty, strapping Javanese.

The humour of the idea immediately took hold of me, yet, for the sake of official appearances, I made a pretence of weighty consideration. At length I agreed and sent for the prisoner. He was a pleasing rogue, and entered fully into the spirit of the idea. He was also immensely pleased when I informed him that after he had served his sentence I would give him ten dollars as a present.

The next morning, under the care of one of the police, he went to the shops to purchase a few necessities for the show.

Evening came and the compound, hung with lanterns, was encircled with every available native in the station, and many from the adjoining islands. The seat of honour was mine ; on my right sat Panglima Udang, blinking and winking his eyes as usual ; on my left was Pang Eng Guan.

The conjuror, assisted by his fellow prisoner, was naked save for a pair of trousers. He had no stage and no background, for the performance was in the open, whilst the audience sat and stood round in a ring.

Never have I seen such conjuring ! The man was a marvel. As each trick was performed the last proved better and more surprising than its predecessor. Udang, however, did not quite appreciate the conjuror's patter.

The third trick was to do with a ring, and the conjuror, after showing it to me, and asking if it really was there, and other stock questions, did likewise to members of the audience. This proved too much for Udang. He lifted his ponderous body from his chair and in a stentorian voice cried out,

" Enough ! if the Tuan has seen the ring, we have all seen it."

Then he sat down and blinked himself to sleep. But the conjuror was not impressed, nor did he cease his patter.

The final trick was the most wonderful I have ever seen, and curiously enough in a way presaged an actual occurrence that eventually took place.

The conjuror was tied up with rope. His feet and hands were tied, and then his body wound round and round with cords which we knotted as much as we liked. He was then wrapped up in a sheet, which in turn was also tied up. Over the sheet we tied a blanket. Then the performer lay on the ground ; on his chest was placed an old and dried coconut and finally he was covered with a large straw mat.

After the space of two or three minutes we were requested to remove the matting. We did so. The coconut was completely husked ; the fibre lay about in shreds, yet the conjuror was still tied up in the blanket !

He was then covered over with the mat again. Three minutes of silence followed, broken only by a wriggling noise from under the mat. Then a voice asked for the mat to be removed. The request was promptly complied with. The blanket and the cords with which it had been tied lay in a huddled heap on the ground. Beside them, still bound in the sheet, was stretched the conjuror. The same performance took place with the sheet.

Gasps of surprise and wonder escaped from an almost awe-struck audience as the bound figure was covered, for the last time, with the matting. The air was tense; the atmosphere electric; even Udang sat up and ceased to blink. Everyone was craning forward, holding their breath and watching the wriggling mass of humanity under the mat.

After a more pronounced wriggle than any previous one the mat seemed to bunch up. Then, of a sudden, it spread out and collapsed like a deflated bladder, and was still. From under the mat came a faint chant or incantation; then, fainter still, a request that the mat should be removed.

For a second there was a hesitation, fear gripping the audience. It passed and someone stepping forward lifted the mat away.

There was a long silence, so acute that it was almost articulate; then a mighty gasp, half cry, half sigh; then pandemonium broke loose among the audience, for there was nothing, absolutely nothing, under the mat save the bare earth. The Corporal's eyes met mine, and even his swarthy skin had paled. Udang swore a Bajau oath. Then a voice spoke in my ear. "Tabek, Tuan," it said, and turning I saw the conjuror. He was standing directly behind my chair!

It is frequently said that coming events cast their shadows. However that may be I must acknowledge that, in spite of his cleverness as a conjuror, I never expected the Javanese and his fellow prisoner (a Suluk) to effect an escape from the block house. But this is exactly what they did accomplish. Luckily for me, from the official point of view, the escape took place during my absence from Semporna.

I had gone to Lahad Dato to sit for my final Law examination, and the morning after was talking to the Resident in his office when a letter was placed in my hand. It was marked " *Urgent.*" I opened it, and to my horror read of the escape of the two deserters. This was bad enough, but worse was to follow. They had taken with them one police rifle, a box containing eight hundred rounds of ammunition, a waterproof cape, and a few other odds and ends. The letter concluded with saying the men were still at large, but known to be on the mainland.

Silently I handed the epistle to the Resident. His only response was a long-drawn whistle. We sent for the natives who had brought in the letter. They had been nearly a day getting into Lahad Dato, so their news was not very recent and amounted to little more than the letter.

Then the Resident kept the telegraph line from Lahad Dato to Sandakan busy. First he wired for the immediate return of the G.S.Y. " Silam," which unfortunately was in Sandakan. Then he informed the Commandant of the Constabulary, and Resident of Sandakan, that watch might be kept in the event of the escaped men trying to get away across country.

Having done this there was nothing further for us to do but to await the return of the " Silam." Owing to the monsoon that was blowing, and the set of the tides, the possibility of our reaching Semporna under sail was ruled out. The journey would have taken nearly two and a half days.

In due course the " Silam " came in, and we set out for Semporna, arriving at 11 a.m. An ashamed, frightened and voluble corporal was curtly told by the Resident to make himself and his police as scarce as possible. In short, they were told there was nothing for them to do beyond carrying on the daily routine. (The Resident shared with me a distinct antipathy for the average low-caste Pathan who was to be found in the Constabulary.) Then, from Panglima Udang, Pang Eng Guan and the Imam (a clever and intellectual Bugis) we learned the latest news.

The men were still on the mainland, and in hiding close by. This was obvious, as the want of water and the necessity of stealing food would compel them to remain near the station and village.

Previous to our arrival there had been a pitched battle between the hunted and the hunters. Honours were easy and casualties nil, but about a hundred rounds of ammunition had been expended! There are bullet marks on the block house to-day. But best of all the two men had quarrelled and separated, and the majority of the stolen ammunition had been recovered.

In this report the police did not show up well. They had deliberately missed an opportunity of shooting and capturing the Javanese, but, scared to death of him, they had given their rifles to the Natives, and sent them out as a protecting screen when searching for the prisoners.

The Resident, as usual in affairs of action, was prompt and decisive. He placed the whole matter in Udang's hands. The natives were to watch the boats day and night. They would guard the shops during darkness, and a reward of fifty dollars for the capture of each escaped man was offered.

Then we lunched and went fishing during the afternoon. That night, about 11 p.m., just as we were "turning in," there was a commotion outside the compound, and cries for the gate to be opened. From the verandah we could see a medley of natives, a waving and flickering of torches. A hum of voices sounded vibrant on the still air and then became drowned by the shrill shrieking of the Pathan police. The Resident turned to me.

"They've caught one of them," he said, and we went down into the compound.

He was right. What a sight met our gaze! Slung on two long poles, borne on the shoulders of four Suluks, trussed like a pig being taken to market, with his clothes torn and his face black and grey from a spattering of ashes, was none other than the Javanese—my friend the conjurer!

A word from the Resident and he was untrussed, but handcuffed and leg-chained instead. And then we listened to the story of his capture.

Driven by hunger and rain he had called at a native house. The inhabitants had pretended sympathy and friendship, but even so he was watchful and distrustful, and never allowed anyone to pass behind him. He asked for food and drink and was given rice, fish and coffee, yet he always kept on the alert. But the odds were against him, and it was only a question of time before the food and warmth took effect and his watchfulness slackened. He asked for a cigarette, stretched out his hand for one, turned to look at a young girl who came out of an inner room and . . . a handful of ashes hit him in the face, they got in his mouth and eyes and up his nose; he put his hands to his eyes and . . . four men pounced upon him. He was overpowered in spite of his struggles, bound up and carried to the station.

His original offence of desertion was trivial, but his escape and subsequent resistance were serious. Still I was sorry for him. He was a pleasing and cheerful rogue. As I saw him safely locked up and stationed a sentry over the store-room, he smiled at me through the bars of the door, remarking quite resignedly, " Fate's against me this time, Tuan ! "

Pleased with the night's work the Resident and I returned to our waiting beds, comfortably assured that in good time the other capture would be effected. And, sure enough, the next morning, while we were at breakfast, one of the two native (Murut) police whom the Resident had brought with us, led in a rather battered, sulky and disconsolate prisoner. He had been caught trying to steal from the bakery, had put up a fight and had been worsted.

One good effect resulted from the episode. The Pathan police, whom I never liked, were transferred, and their place filled with Sikhs. Curiously enough no action was taken against them by the Commandant. His reason was, I believe, that as no particular man was on sentry duty, no one was particularly to be blamed. Possibly his attitude was correct. But what about the policemen who locked the prisoners up at 5 p.m. each night and obviously omitted to search them and the store-room, thus allowing them to smuggle in a " parang " (knife), with which they cut away the bars ?

As matters turned out the Sikhs proved little better than the Pathans, for a few months later they allowed a Bajau, who had been convicted of cheating and had been sentenced to three months r.i., to escape also.

I was really more perturbed over this escape than the former ones because the prisoner, named Simamankau, was a local native, and I foresaw the possibility of his receiving support and sanctuary from friends and relatives.

The corporal did not know at what time the man had escaped. All he knew was that the relieving sentry had seen him in the lock-up at 6 p.m., but he had not tested the door or lock. When, in his turn, he was relieved at 8 p.m. his relief tried the door. It opened! He looked inside. The store-room was empty!

A census of boats on the mainland proved none to be missing. Clearly, then, the escaped man was close by, or had swum across the channel that divided Semporna from Bum Bum Island, on which were several villages, among them his own. Udang sent across to Bum Bum to warn all the village headmen, and search parties hunted in vain till driven in by heavy rain.

Morning found Simamankau still at large and the search parties completely baffled. The Imam, Imbul and I conducted a search on our own. Our efforts were fruitless, so on the Imam's advice we went across to Simamankau's village. The villagers, one and all, denied his presence. Somehow I felt sure he was hiding in the village. The Imam and Imbul were certain too. I had no proof but I acted on instinct, backed by the Imam's advice, and gave the village twenty-four hours' grace in which to produce him or suffer divers grievous penalties.

That evening at 6 p.m. Simamankau gave himself up. To the end he denied having swam the channel or having hidden in his village, and even went to the length of showing me the spot, not a hundred yards from my house, where he had lay hidden. But there were no traces of trampled grass. Further, rain had fallen nearly all night and he showed no signs of fever; nor, when given food, would he eat; and yet he had eaten nothing (officially) for twenty-four hours!

With the worry of Simamankau's escape off my mind I became curious over the Imam's and Imbul's insistence that he was hiding in his village. By chance I saw them conversing together. I joined them, intent on satisfying my curiosity.

"Why were you so sure Simamankau was across the Trusan (channel)?" I asked.

"Because of the Angai Bird," the Imam answered.

"Angai Bird?"

"Yes, Tuan. Does the Tuan remember just before we turned back he turned round and spoke to me?"

"Yes."

"And does the Tuan remember a bird on his right whistling twice?" Imbul impatiently asked.

"Yes," I answered; "what of it?"

"It was an omen—a good omen too—the bird was on the Tuan's right; Simamankau's village was on the right. Therefore Simamankau was in his village; therefore the Tuan would re-capture him—is it not so, Imbul?" and the Imam appealed to my boy.

"Yes," Imbul answered.

"The Angai bird is never wrong, Tuan," the Imam continued, "but the omen may be good or bad. To-day it was good, so Simamankau is back in gaol."

I had come across many of these superstitious beliefs in signs and animals during my term in the Interior, but I could not help being struck at finding a Bugis of the Celebes (an educated Mahomedan to boot!) and a Murut from the interior of Borneo holding so firmly to a similar superstition.

The Bajaus and Suluks of Semporna are pre-eminently a sea-faring people. They are skilled in the art of boat-building and sail-making. They have names for the stars and use them for navigation, yet they all believe in the efficacy of "calling the wind up" when the breeze is either light or entirely absent, and not one of them would ever dream of doing so unless he were aft of the mast for fear that a head wind might arise.

Another curious superstition forbids the bringing into a boat of any part of the Kayu Aru (Casuarina) tree. The penalty for so doing is to incur either a storm or head wind.

If superstition is closely woven into the daily life of the native, religion also plays a considerable part. Nowhere in Borneo did I find a stricter attention to Islamic tenets than in Semporna, nor Mosques in a better state of preservation.

The Native Court—comprised of the Imam and Panglima Udang, and frequently strengthened by the presence of some village headman—rarely sat, while work in the Magistrate's Court was extremely light. These conditions point to a morality above the ordinary.

The penalty for the offence of Incest, if left to the Native Court, as also among the Pagan races, would be death to both offenders. This, however, Government would not countenance, though the Court was allowed complete and undivided control in the matter of assessing and awarding " Sagit " (Reparation and recompense).

There was one case of Incest that had been brought before the Native Court three times in as many years and yet had not finally been settled. Any untoward incident, such as bad weather, poor fish catches, or an epidemic, was always put down to the fact that this particular offence had never been satisfactorily punished. It cropped up again in my time, and though really triable only by the Native Court, being a breach of Sexual Law (and not an un-natural offence triable under the Indian Penal Code), I decided to settle the matter one way or another in an administrative capacity.

The crux of the matter, I remember, rested in the

opening of a grave and exhuming the remains of an infant, buried on Omadal Island. This child, reported to be the offspring of the supposed guilty parties, was credited with having been born with head and face of a rat on a human body.

The situation of the grave was supposed to be well known, and the accusing parties were most insistent on the fact of incest having been committed, and the birth of this half human, half animal child.

The contending parties, therefore, met in my office, and in the presence of myself, Panglima Udang and the Imam, agreed on oath that the opening of the grave and the disclosure of the remains should once and for all decide the issue. If the skull of a rat were found among other bones then the offence had been committed and the accused were to be punished. If the remains were normal, or none could be found, then the whole charge and accusation fell to the ground, never to be made again.

News, of course, travels fast in native countries, and I should think nearly a third of the local population had congregated at Omadal to witness the exhumation, so great was public interest in the matter. But, though expectancy ran high, hopes of sensationalism were doomed to be disappointed. After much wrangling as to the exact site of the grave I was forced to order an area of twenty-five feet square to be dug up. In this area it was conceded the remains must be.

The task was long and wearisome, but in the end completed. Every foot of that twenty-five feet square was dug and turned ; but never a bone was discovered !

So a base calumny was at last, after three long years, laid by the heels, and stigma, shame and suspicion removed from an aged man and his rather youthful daughter.

Their gratitude was touching to witness. Tears

sprang into the old man's eyes as he raised my right hand in both his, carrying it, according to custom, to his chest and then released it that he might press his own against his forehead in token of his homage and respect.

Throughout this brief episode his daughter had stood perfectly still; her large dark eyes, I noticed, were riveted on me; her young and rounded breasts rose and fell quickly as if some strong emotion were overmastering her normal respiration; her lips trembled; her hands twisted and untwisted a cheap silken pocket handkerchief. Then—in a flash she was on her knees before me, her hands seized mine and her lips smothered them with kisses. Hurriedly, yet gently, I tried to draw them away, but she would not slacken her grasp, till I spoke with sharp disapproval in my voice. She obeyed and throwing back her head her eyes met mine for the briefest second. Then, with what seemed a single instantaneous movement her lips just touched the uppers of my shoes and she was gone, fleeing, fleet as a doe, to hide between the purdahs of her father's boat.

Because of episodes such as this it always makes me angry when I hear anyone refer to "the ingratitude of these damned natives" or deny them decent sensibilities or feelings.

Morality and clean living such as I saw and experienced while in Semporna make me wonder at the audacity of those whose one idea is to "Christianise" the native.

The ability, intellectuality and craftsmanship of the Bajaus and Suluks are great, so much so that, though annoyed, one can smile when one hears talk of the darkness and abysmal ignorance of "the poor black man."

Just such an annoying person as I describe came, of all people, to settle in Semporna.

He was a "Plymouth Brother." He had been in the

Navy (according to him a veritable sink of iniquity), was young and—had been "saved." The world lay at his feet, a quagmire of sin and ignorance ! Semporna was at his finger tips—a brand to be plucked from the burning. The Islamic Faith—rotten, insidious, cruel, and degrading—must be rooted out, and he was the chosen instrument. He had seen Borneo in a dream, and his feet had been led to Semporna.

He was actually employed by the North Borneo Trading Company, and his duties consisted in taking charge of the Company's four timber camps in the district. I am afraid neither his employers nor the labour force under him were much the better for his presence or efforts. It was not so much the man himself as his type that was at fault. He certainly was not a success with his coolies, for natives, like Tommy Atkins, really have little use or respect for anyone who is not a gentleman.

Still, he meant well, and, in his misguided and enthusiastic attempts at proselytising, did his best.

To me he was always a source of endless interest ; and of an evening I would spend many an hour discussing philosophy and religion with him, till, one day, with set look and firm lips, he refused further discussion.

"No," he said, "I won't argue any more with you. It is the Devil in you arguing. You are not humbly and truly seeking knowledge. You are not a Christian, for there is no true humility and love in your thoughts."

To all of which I had no answer. What could I say ?

But months later, on the night before I left Semporna on transfer, at the close of a five months' cholera epidemic, he came to me in the Block House, and, putting out his hand, said with a rather winning smile,

" I want to say I think—in fact I know—you're a better Christian than I am."

I was surprised and a little touched, and I suppose my surprise showed in my face for he continued,

" Yes, I mean it ; I do really. I talk an awful lot about the Lord, but you—you, well you do things, and look after your natives and the district and—and—— "

" Have a stengah (whiskey and soda) ? " I interpolated quickly, and handed him a glass.

So my " heathen " Mahomedans are still unregenerate and sunk in the error of their ways. They still build boats, collect sea produce, fish and go hunting ; still marry and wear clothes handwoven by their wives, of which, if they are rich enough, they may possess four ; still love to dance and beat their gongs ; are still tee-totallers and have not learnt to lie and steal. And I like to think that they are none the worse for my sojourn among them. But I took no personal pride in the man's epitaph upon me, for actually mine was just the everyday work of any officer in the Service.

I do not think the man realised the depth of truth hidden in his remark " your natives and the district." For that's just it. They become " your " natives ; the district grows into " your " district ; not in the sense of personal possession and power, but in a sense of personal trust and affection. It is " your " help and advice ; " your " decisions and judgments ; " your " enthusiasm and ideas that are sought for and accepted every day.

And in August 1914 when the Resident I worked under was transferred from the Residency I felt just such a personal loss. He may have been a " wild mad Irish-man " but he was a very true, loyal and lovable friend, and I, for one among many others who knew him better and longer than I, felt sad and lonely at his untimely death a few days later at Papar.

The appointment of the new Resident almost coincided with the greatest event in history—the European War. News came to Semporna slowly. The Empire was at war and we in our district knew it not. The days passed on and still no news reached us. All we knew was that trouble was brewing in Europe ; that the German Lloyd steamer was long overdue ; that our rice supply was running low.

Then one afternoon, over the distant edge of Pulau Larrapan (Larrapan Island) arose a faint column of smoke. All in Semporna watched it eagerly. Round the corner of the island it moved and under it was a smudge. Gradually the smudge grew larger, took shape and, at last, became distinguishable. It was the " Silam " travelling under full steam.

Down to the wharf the populace went, an excited, curious, questioning, gaily dressed crowd, the T head at the wharf was crammed.

Someone official was aboard the " Silam " for the " D.O.'s " flag was flying astern. From the funnel tube a jet of white steam rose in the air ; then three long blasts from the siren drowned the clamouring voices on the wharf.

In a few minutes more I was aboard and shaking the District Treasurer by the hand.

Yes—we were at war with Germany ; our troops were in Belgium and France ; we had retreated ; no steamers had come from Singapore ; one German boat (the s.s. " Marudu ") had escaped just in time from Sandakan. Rice was getting short ; he was on his way to find out the state of things in Tawao. No, no orders had been received from the Government ; prices were rising ; act on your own ; if necessary commandeer and control the rice ; damn the profiteers. Yes, there were many Germans in the Philippines, and they possessed steamers too ; he must push on so as to get past the Lehnert Reef before dark. Oh, there was a small official mail for me, nothing much, just routine stuff. Irving sent chin-chins and Fawcett of the Tobacco Estate was down with fever ; he would call in on the way back to-morrow or the next day ; cheerioh and " so long."

Such was the hurried news I collected. But it was tremendous enough, and filled all my being as I walked slowly back to the block house.

That evening the price of rice rose from 30 cts. a gantang (a measure) to 50 cts., and then slowly to 75 cts. As the D.T. had said, " Damn the profiteers ! " It was time I took control.

So in the morning I gathered all the Chinese shopkeepers into my office and gave them, in silken tones, my ultimatum. " The price of rice was to be fixed at 50 cts. a gantang. They were to keep a register of all purchasers, and only sell a stipulated quantity to each individual a week, or—I should seize all the rice in their shops, and pay them only their invoice prices."

A Chinaman is one of the best business men in the world. He knows when to argue and haggle and when not. With one dissentient voice my first proposition was quickly accepted.

" Listen," I said to the dissenter, " I haven't time to argue with you, and I wouldn't if I could. If you don't agree I shall seize your rice. And remember this, my friend, if I don't act the natives will. Your looted and burnt shop will be a poor return for your years of trading in Semporna. But it will be what you deserve, and what you'll get if you try to profiteer, for I swear I won't give you police protection."

There are more ways than one of killing a cat, and if Mr. Chinaman failed to see the justness of the suggested action he at least saw the force of the reasoning.

To Panglima Udang, the Imam and other influential natives, I explained the situation, and sent Udang on a trip round the islands to spread the news, and calm the people's fears.

Then to my official mail! There was little in it. An approval of an application for five acres of land by a native, two Magistrate's Court cases passed and approved by the Judicial Commissioner, a query from the Commissioners of Customs in regard to some figures in the July Customs report, two bottles of "Cough Mixture" from the Sandakan Hospital—and a notification that the Empire was at war.

Attached to this last were various instructions. I could not restrain a smile as I read, "You will stop and board any suspicious steamers that you may see, and satisfy yourself in regard to them before allowing them to proceed." I! and presumably in a native sailing boat, dependent on wind and oars!

Yet in the end I actually boarded one, and she was a T.B.D. and British!

One evening I was setting sail for home after an afternoon's fishing, when, in the dusk, I espied two columns of smoke. Rapidly they came closer, and, as the light of day died out, I could just discern two shapes—a Destroyer and a great big Tramp,—a collier perhaps.

Then, at the moment darkness descended, they turned hard to starboard. What were they, and what was their destination? British, French, or German? Such were the questions my boatmen asked me as we gave chase!

In the end, out of the darkness loomed a big and a lesser shape. That night I slept in " the bandstand " on board H.M.S. " Jed," and in the morning, at fifteen knots an hour, she gave me tow half-way into Semporna ; then with her collier went her way.

Hardly had I set my foot on the wharf when the inevitable question was asked me, " Was that a ' Kapal prang ' (man o' war) on which you slept last night, Tuan ? " And I had been asked, practically commanded, to say nothing of the vessel's doings and whereabouts !

But, though Europe was in conflagration, though England was stirred to its very depths, Borneo remained as undisturbed and aloof from the outer world as ever, and life in Semporna rolled on its quiet uneventful way.

One event, however, stirred and roused me to a white-heat of anger, for once again officialdom raised its head and from the " sanctity " of the Secretariat the Government Secretary thought fit to be insulting.

I may have been impetuous and absurdly impulsive ; my action and request may have been even thoughtless, but a request for " leave " that I might volunteer and join up did not call for such a " minute " as I received.

For many years no European officer had been regularly stationed at Semporna ; official regulations required an application for leave to be accompanied with the name and proposition of an officer who could attend to the applicant's work during his absence. I complied with this regulation and suggested the District Treasurer should, as in the past, periodically visit Semporna.

And the answer ?

" Leave not approved. Further, please inform Mr. Cook, that, judging from his opinion of his duties as a

Government officer I fail to see what use he would be to his country as a soldier. However, there is nothing to prevent him resigning should he be so foolish as to do so.

"F. W. F."

I was stupefied and astounded! That such words could be written at such a time. But as I could not afford to pay a passage home there was nothing for me to do but to "grin and bear it."

But how anxiously I awaited my mails; with what eagerness I scanned my letters, and then turned to the papers! England was at war with Germany! And only a month before a well-known American Financier, who passed through Semporna and breakfasted and lunched with me, had said war was utterly impossible.

"Why do you want to fight Germany?" he asked me. "Why do you hate the Germans?"

"Why do you instinctively dislike a certain man? Why do two dogs fight?" was my answer.

"You mean?" he queried.

"It's human nature," I replied.

"Perhaps," he murmured, and then continued in his crisp tones, "But the financiers of the world will never allow it—it would mean ruin, utter ruin."

I was young and conceited enough to burst forth with, "I'll bet you, Mr.——"

He stopped me with a gesture, then said with a whimsical smile, "Human nature—'out of the mouths of babes and sucklings'—perhaps you're right—I hope not—we couldn't allow it—and yet—it's human nature."

I've never met him since, though I read in the papers of his presence in England. But in the days that followed August 4th, 1914 I often wondered whether he remembered his stay in Semporna, and the frustrated bet.

The major portion of my duties in Semporna consisted of travelling round the district—visiting all the villages and islands. The people were always pleased to see the D.O., and showered hospitality upon me, but fresh excitement was now added to my visits for I brought the illustrated papers with me, and told stories of the war.

Turkey had not yet entered the arena, so matters were not complicated by any questions touching the Caliphate and the Islamic Faith. Later, with Turkey fighting against us, the Bajaus and Suluks readily accepted such statements as " Turkey's action was suicidal and mad, and basely ungrateful."

After all the war hardly touched the natives. Constantinople was far away and but few had made the pilgrimage to Mecca. Their daily life—the collecting of the produce, fishing, a little planting, births, deaths and marriages—was a matter that touched them more closely, and the Prentah (Government) was very real. They lived under the shadow of its wing, experienced its benefits. And, like all orientals, they were Fatalists. " What was to be, would be." Also true to their creed and hereditary training they held an exaggerated belief in the inevitableness and permanency of Authority, so the idea of the Prentah's defeat never really entered their thoughts.

But in the Timber camps matters did not run so smoothly for there war conditions were more quickly felt. Money was scarce. Strained finances did not permit the Company to grant the usual presents and advances to the Mahomedan coolies at their annual festival of Hari Raya, and the superintendent had foolishly given preferential treatment to the Chinese, which added fuel to the fire.

The subsequent business was really none of mine, but when the office was besieged by about sixty excited Javanese, Malays and other Mahomedans, the time seemed ripe to take a hand.

I sent for " my Plymouth Brother," who came full of woes and explanation. The fault was not his, but his clerk's. The money had been paid to the Chinese—it was a mistake—but what could he do ?—There was no more.

I knew all the coolies ; knew their wives and families, just as, in a small district like Semporna, I knew the wives and families of " my " natives ; knew the names of their dogs and the age of their cats—and I was sorry for them. Hari Raya meant much to them—it was their Christmas, Easter and August Bank Holiday rolled into one. They had no money to spend or gamble, and the shops would give no credit.

What was to be done ? There was only one course open to me. I took it and advanced the Plymouth Brother the money on behalf of the Company. I took one precaution, however, for I paid it out to the coolies myself.

A football match was also fixed up for the afternoon, Semporna v. the Trading Company, and in the evening, and far into the next morning, there was to be a Main Dindang (dancing).

I have always thought that Malay dancing is somewhat tedious to watch, though the lightness of foot and necessary " time " of the performers is wonderful. But there is something soothing and fascinating in the slow, rhythmic, snakelike movements of the Bajaus and Suluks—the women in their silken, tight-fitting coats, edged with small silver or brass bells ; with silken slack trousers of wondrous colour ; with a flaming scarf thrown over one shoulder and golden combs rising out of their coal black hair ; with long golden or brass finger-nails added to the fingers of each hand ; with faces often whitened with lime out of which shine their splendid dark-brown eyes ; with an occasional smile caressing their lips and spreading across the general immobility of their faces ; with the light, silent movement of their feet on which tinkled and jingled gold and silver anklets ; with the slow rising and falling, circling and swaying of their arms and hands heavy with bracelets and rings.

No lighting or scenic effects here ; no stagecraft to assist : only a bare platform, often only the greensward or a *coral* beach and the hidden personality of the dancer ; a few spluttering, indifferent lamps and sometimes the glorious, wonderful moonlight ; no orchestra or organ, but the beating of gongs ; the soft tones of the "guling tangan" (instrument of eight small gongs) and the boom and thunder of the "gandang" (drum or tom-tom) ; the lap of the sea on the beach ; the sigh of the breeze in the coconut trees ; the scent of the tropic flowers and palms ; the myriad stars ; the pale silver moon and . . .

The dance is over ; the dream woman is no more ; in her place is a man astride a wooden horse ; his head is grotesquely dressed in a monkey's mask ; from his spine protrudes a long curling tail ; his feet resemble those of a cock ; he postures and capers and rides about to the accompaniment of patter and shrieks of laughter and many jests. His horse won't go ; he beats it and belabours it with a twisted, gnarled and bent black sea-weed ; it prances and rears and . . .

He is gone ; in his place is a tiny mite of four or five, robed in silk, with high combed hair and whitened face and golden finger-nails ; studiedly, self-consciously, she dances ; correct yet stilted ; striving, trying so hard to please. She stumbles, slips ; her little feet have become entangled in her flowing heavy folding sarong and . . .

Sweet and low comes the rhythm and strain of " Salāmun "—the one great Love-song of the district—gently the voices hum its refrain ; a hundred feet just faintly beat its languorous time and . . .

The woman of my dreams is dancing again.

Years ago in one of the Drury Lane pantomimes Harry Fragson sang a song called " In Dreamland." In " Dreamland " only the most wonderful and beautiful things ever happened. But though for a time one may live in " Dreamland " yet sooner or later one must come back to earth.

So it was in Semporna, for on my return from a visit to some of the islands I found awaiting me a report of a suspicious illness at Pulau Danawan, the most outlying island in the district.

One man had died in a few hours; others on the island were in great pain, and the symptoms pointed to cholera. There was, as it happened, no medical handbook in Semporna, and only a rough and ready supply of medicines—quinine, salts, castor oil, asperin, cough mixture, iodine, iodoform, and a few ointments and disinfectants—so what to take with me I knew not. In the end I decided to take my own private " Red-Cross " case, also milk and brandy.

If my surmise was correct and the illness was cholera—so easily brought in from the outlying islands of the Philippines or from Dutch Borneo—I realised how serious matters might easily become in a scattered and divided district like Semporna, and with a nomadic population like the Suluks and Bajaus. The islands were open to intercourse, with a limited water supply, frequently only obtainable from a few wells, which were unavoidably the supply for several villages or adjoining islands!

But before leaving for Danawan there were two very necessary arrangements to make. First I sent a letter to the District officer at Tawao asking that the District Surgeon (Dr. Lau Lai—a Chinaman) might be sent to me. This letter went by one of the " Straits " steamers which fortunately was passing through, and on which vessel Dr. Lau Lai was to return to Semporna. At the same time I sent a letter to the Resident at Lahad Dato by the s.s. " Sabah," which, by good luck, was also in Semporna, requesting the " Silam " to be despatched at once to await the doctor's arrival in Semporna.

For the doctor I left instructions that if, on his arrival, I was not in Semporna, he was to come by a certain route to Danawan, where he would find me trying to combat the disease.

Then in my Lipa-lipa I set sail for the island.

According to wind and tide the journey may be accomplished in one to three days in a sailing boat. Fortune stood by me on this occasion for I reached Danawan on the evening of the same day.

I had never seen anything more peaceful and beautiful than Danawan as I approached it that night. Far away on the horizon a faint silver light was slowly growing in the sky and gradually gilding the sea. Noiselessly we approached the island, borne along by a faint but steady breeze. Over the edge of the sky came a tiny segment of the moon ; larger and larger it grew till the whole shining ball was poised, as it seemed, a few feet above the sea. The water sparkled and glittered like a million diamonds. Higher rose the moon, and, for a while, became lost—hidden behind the peak of St. Amil, an island just behind Danawan, and separated only by a narrow and deep channel—then over the top of the island-hill it burst, shedding its silver light on the village of Danawan, built on a stretch of sand on the very water's edge. The long fronds of the coconut trees behind the houses rustled faintly in the wind ; shadows of impish, freakish fancies danced upon the hardened earth, lights flickered in the houses and peeped from the cracks in the walls ; across the space came the soft notes of "guling tangan." Gently, slowly, almost silently we drew closer. The spell of the night had woven itself into our consciousness and speech would have been a desecration. In silence our sail was furled and taken down. Noiselessly the paddles met the water. Closer and closer we crept. Peace in a coral island in the Pacific, and . . . perhaps, death in a hideous form was stalking through its glades.

A dog barked ; then another and another. Doors opened quickly and heads appeared. The "guling tangan" ceased. Voices came across to us. "Siapa itu ?" (Who's that ?)

"Tuan," I answered.

The cry was taken up and passed from house to house. "Ada Tuan ! Ada Tuan ! Tuan sudah, datang bagus, banyak bagus." (The Tuan has come, that is good, all will be well now.)

There was a splash, our anchor dropped and we lay some fifty fathoms from the shore. A boat put out from the largest house—that of Panglima Besari the headman—and came alongside us. From Panglima I learnt that—as I expected—the dead man had been buried ; that there were no more deaths. Best news of all, the sick people were getting better and there were no new cases. But, for safety's sake, I allowed no one on shore, and the next morning, accompanied only by my serang, I landed.

I paid a house to house visit giving special attention

to the house in which the death had occurred. Everything and everybody in the house was either bathed in disinfectant or sun-bathed. Disinfectants and instructions were left behind, and sail set again for Semporna, which was reached the next morning just as the doctor was about to set out for Danawan.

Of course there was nothing for him to see: no patients upon whom he could form a diagnosis. So, after looking at the eyes and tongues of everyone in the village, he pronounced his verdict. There was no cholera, and no need for the quarantine that had been imposed.

But—there is always a "but"—events proved the doctor wrong, for, shortly after Christmas, reports came in of a similar sickness in another island, and investigations showed beyond doubt that it had been brought by a visitor from Danawan.

From now on reports came in quickly from various quarters of the district, and I had to cope with the disease—that it was cholera I had no doubt—as best I could, while awaiting the advent of the Principal Medical Officer from Sandakan.

He came, he saw and pronounced his verdict—cholera.

On the football ground at Semporna a house was quickly erected as hospital, and as each native became sick he or she was lodged in this. One person only was allowed in attendance on the sufferer. Other inmates of an infected household were removed to the quarantine huts till declared free of infection.

This system was carried out at each village or island for it was obviously impossible, and unnecessarily dangerous, to attempt to bring all the sick people into Semporna. Each house where the disease first broke out was turned into a hospital, and the next house into a quarantine station. Each headman was informed of, and the villagers lectured on, the danger of disregarding orders; of the necessity for cleanliness and care; of the rapidity with which the disease would spread; of the fatality of its grip. Each and all were so to speak "left on their honour," for there was no other way of enforcing or supervising orders, since the police force was hopelessly inadequate to meet the demand of placing guards at each infected island or village, and I steadfastly set my face against the importation of extra police, of the Pathan or Sikh persuasion, from Sandakan for such purpose. That way, I knew, trouble would arise.

But the greatest difficulty of all was the water, for in many cases infected villages would have to draw their daily supply from the same well as an uninfected village. The most I could do was to give them different and definite times for drawing their water, and treat the well with permanganate of potash.

Then the question of supplies arose. How were the quarantined islands to get food? How would the populace live if cut off from their daily fishing and search for sea-produce? This riddle was easy of solution, but not of accomplishment. The solution was "Government must feed the quarantine areas." But would Government do so? To that question I never obtained a definite answer, nor was I ever given definite instructions by the Resident or the P.M.O. till the epidemic was nearly over; and then the amount allowed each week was so small that I found I had, acting on my own responsibility, exceeded it three times over.

Thus, in the "Silam," from January to the end of April, a continuous round of the district had to be made; distributing medicines and food; cheering and supervising.

At Semporna itself, where the epidemic broke out

three times after we were apparently free from infection, the shopkeepers anchored their tongkangs (large boats) at the end of the wharf and sold from these impromptu shops to natives arriving only from uninfected areas.

And I think it says much for the sense of duty, obedience and loyalty of the natives, that, in spite of their ingrained fatalism and their belief that cholera was not " jangkit " (contagious), out of a population of about four thousand only just under one hundred and fifty died during the four months the epidemic ran its course.

I was not alone during all the time for Government sent Dr. Lau Lai to take charge medically under my administrative control. But he proved more of a hindrance than a help. The natives would have nothing to do with him. So, in the end, I dispensed with his assistance, and he gleefully returned to Tawao.

There was nothing much that he could do from a medical point of view, and his failure to understand the natives, to appreciate their outlook, limitations and susceptibilities, and his want of administrative experience, more than counteracted his skill and somewhat limited energy.

As an epidemic I must acknowledge that the cholera, for cholera, was not really severe, and I doubt whether the deaths need have been so numerous had some of the natives taken more care to carry out instructions, and had been more regular in giving their patients the hourly dose of permanganate of potash, for I frequently saw a bottle that should have been sufficient for only two days nearly full at the end of a week ; also the necessity for care of hands after handling the soiled garments of some sufferer was never properly understood.

It is curious to note that though the disease attacked Semporna and the mainland three distinct times yet not once did any of the Chinese suffer. The timber camps, of course, had been rigorously quarantined, so remained immune from attack.

But perhaps the most remarkable episode of the whole epidemic was that of Bungaima, a relation of Panglima Udang. She was married, and, in the early days of the epidemic, had contracted the disease. Under the care and nursing of her husband she recovered. The call of death had been very close to her ; still, though frail and wan and but a shadow of her former self, she lived.

I remember meeting her in one of the shops as she bought some rice and foodstuff, and had cheered her up by saying she was beginning to look fatter and stronger. To give her a rest from domestic duties I promised to take her a four-day trip round the islands on the " Silam." She smiled her thanks and pleasure, and we went our ways, she to her home and husband, I to the Block House and a late dinner.

As the sentry struck nine o'clock on the office gong my orderly came up to me. Bungaima was sick with cholera, he said, and her husband implored me to go and see her at once.

I went immediately. There was no doubt. She was in the grip of the disease. As the pains in the abdomen, and cramp in the calves, seized her she could not repress her groans and cries of agony.

What could be done at that late hour I did. Medicine was left and the husband (I have forgotten his name) took up his lonely vigil and fight for her life. The hour was past ten when I left them.

That night I slept badly ; the strain was beginning to tell on me. I could not help thinking of Bungaima and her fight for life ; of the cruelty of Fate that had attacked her twice ; of this second blow which she was so unfit to receive. At 5 a.m. I was awake, so calling for tea I went on to the verandah. Hardly had I sat down and sipped my tea when the corporal came up.

"Well?" I asked him.

"Bungaima's husband is dead," he answered.

I raised my eyebrows in silent query.

"He died at half-past four," he continued, "and she is alone in the house, save for one small child."

"Alive?" I questioned.

"Tuan," came the reply.

Without a word I followed the corporal downstairs out into the fast breaking dawn.

The corporal's story was true. There on the floor lay the husband, already fast stiffening in death. In a corner a small child was unrestrainedly sobbing. In the middle of the floor lay Bungaima, and she was breathing! Her feet were cold; her fingers and hands ridged and coruscated like a washerwoman's, her eyelids were closed; her forehead damp with sweat. Her breathing hardly moved her breasts; her cheeks were but hollows in her face; her eyes so sunken that they seemed only two empty sockets. Her body was devoid of flesh; only a covering of dry hot skin veiled her bones and seemed to give a semblance of life.

I stood lost in wonder at her amazing vitality! What was the source of this desire to live, while her husband lay dead beside her? From whence did she draw her powers of resistance?

From out of the corner came the answer to my riddle in a child's plaintive cry of "Mamma." Then I remembered her family and the babe who so recently had been at her breast, and I was filled with a great determination to cheat Death of his prey. So, in the end, after a long strenuous fight, I drew her back from the very threshold of Death, and, before I left in May for transfer to North Keppel, I had met her once again in the shops, a little stronger and fitter, a little fatter; with less sunken cheeks and hollow eyes, and hanging round her knees a laughing, chattering, clamouring brood of children.

CHAPTER IV

TUARAN

In March, 1915, I had received intimation that a transfer to Tuaran was imminent. The folly of changing officers, during the cholera epidemic, was, however, realised by Government, and I remained at Semporna until I was able to give the district a clean bill of health.

My successor was to be another A.D.O. who had lived with me for a month in the old days at Tenom. As a matter of fact I did not " hand over " to him but to Pang Eng Guan, as the other man had not arrived by the time my steamer sailed.

This time I sailed by the s.s. " Kinabalu," a new steamer put on the coastal run and especially built for the Sabah Steamship Company. She was making her second voyage to Tawao and the engineer-in-charge suggested my going back to Jesselton with him, instead of travelling by the " Straits " boat sailing two days later.

I caught on to the idea at once, but said nothing of my sudden change of plans, as I hoped by this means to avoid and escape the farewell dance and " general bust-up " that was being organised as a mark of honour and affection at my departure.

My desire may sound mean and selfish, but I was dreading the parting, and knew I should be called upon for a speech. Fate, however, was against me, for, somehow or other, the news leaked out and the "affair," though shorn by its ante-dating of some of its glory, took place.

As I rose to my feet, about four in the morning, to render my thanks and make my farewell speech, and looked upon the crowded faces pressing around me I was deeply touched, for I realised that this was no mere excuse for a dance or a "drunk" as beloved by the Muruts; no mere formal display of good manners or show of wealth, but the very genuine expression of affection of those among whom I had lived and ruled for the last fifteen months.

Some well-known faces were missing, for cholera had taken its toll, but Panglima Udang, Kaludin, Besari and Kayu, Imam Mohamad and Saringayer—my favourite boatman—Pang Eng Guan and Tai Soo, the Chinese shopkeepers and their clerks, the *mandors* and *tandils* (overseers) and coolies of the timber camps were all present. And, though his Malay was insufficient for him to follow all that was said, loudest in leading applause and shouting good wishes was my friend the Plymouth Brother.

There was much that I had to say. I touched on the war and its causes. I mentioned India's loyalty to the Empire, I emphasised the need for thrift and greater efforts at planting, and drew pictures of the joy of ownership of land. I asked for loyalty to, and co-operation with, my successor. I referred to the Prentah's parental care and wisdom.

Had I not, I asked, on behalf of Government, fed them during the cholera? Had not the Government sent doctors and medicine? Were not these doctors wise? Did they not rid the district of the cholera so long as the people obeyed their voice? Was not their Allah and my

God the same ? Did he not send the sun and the rain ? Did he not in the end remove the cholera ? Had they not twice sent forth to sea the " Spirit-boat " blest by the Imam and decked with offerings, heavy with prayers, laden with jimats (charms) that it might take away the dread scourge and lose it in the mighty ocean ? Had it not twice come back, rejected by wind and sea, those agents of Allah the All-powerful, and All-Merciful ? And why ? Because they would not hearken to my voice or the voices of the doctors. Because in their fatalism and pride they thought they knew better than the Prentah. So Allah in his anger sent back the Spirit-boat and the cholera raged again. But in the end when they obeyed me, listened to my voice and took heed of my precautions, then the disease abated, and Allah accepted their prayers. The Spirit-boat was launched again and sailed forth, never to return. And it bore in its hold the germ of the epidemic and lost it in unfathomable depths of the restless ocean.

I sat down. For a full minute there was silence. Then the strains of " Salamun " broke the stillness. In a far away corner of the crowd the young girl of the incest case broke into song :

Dawn is breaking roseate o'er the sky,
In the trees the birds are carolling.
Listen now, my Love, and do not sigh
After bracelet, jewellery or ring,
Love is ours and it can never die.*

Others took up the words and the volume of sound swelled louder and louder, till its haunting notes seemed a very song of acclamation, which went echoing—and re-echoing up into the star-lit sky.

It was their way of saying they would miss me ; of

* Translation

telling me how much I had found my way into their hearts, and, as they finished, I confess I covered my eyes with my hands. I would not have them see the tears that were gathering.

Eventually I went to the Block House, but not to sleep, for there I was to bid farewell individually to those who might be termed my personal friends: the Panglimas and Imams, the Chinese Towkays (shopkeepers), the Timber Camp Mandors, Bungaima, Patima and Saringayer; the corporal, police and clerks.

A few hours later I was aboard the "Kinabalu." As she left the wharf, and turned her nose to Lahad Dato and the West Coast, three long, loud blasts sounded from her syren. They were my final farewell to Semporna. On the wharf handkerchiefs were being waved and gongs beaten. As we drew level with Panglima's house a fusillade of crackers rent the air, to be followed by the boom of old muzzle-loading cannon. Then the town grew smaller and smaller, the colours of the shops lost their hue; we rounded Pulau Larrapan and Semporna was lost to view.

In less than five hours we reached Lahad Dato, where we were to stop for the night. The Resident with whom I "put up," seemed at first a little annoyed at my not having waited as arranged for the "Straits" steamer, but he became less "sticky" when I reminded him of Government Circular No. —— (and their number is legion) which stated that, "officers are instructed whenever travelling on official duties to travel, whenever possible, by the Sabah Steamship Company."

Such meticulous remembrance of, and obedience to, a circular really merited only approval, and that Resident, who above all else was a sportsman, readily appreciated this point.

The trip to Sandakan was uneventful, and daybreak of

the following morning found us gliding slowly into Sandakan harbour.

As usual the first person aboard was the Agent. As he crossed the gangway he saw me, started backwards, slipped, nearly fell into the water, pulled himself together, and dubiously came forward.

" Hullo," I cried, " how are you ? "

" Good Lord ! " he gasped. " You here ? Why—I —we thought you were still in Semporna, in your plague-stricken district. What's it mean ? "

" It's all over," I answered, " and I'm on transfer to Tuaran. It's all right, you can shake me by the hand ; there aren't any germs," and I put out my hand, which he grasped and wrung strenuously.

" But we've had no news," he continued. " As far as we know officially you're still in quarantine."

" Rot," was my answer. " I saw the telegram to the P.M.O. There's not been a case for sixteen days, and, anyhow, I'm here."

Just then the Chief Police Officer, the Customs officer and others came aboard, and I had to explain all over again.

For myself it did not matter, but for my servants and other deck passengers the matter was of some consequence, as, unless satisfied, the Authorities would not let them land. So the P.M.O. was rung up on the telephone at his house, traced to the Civil Gaol, and from there run to earth at the hospital just as he was leaving to visit the leper station on Bahalla Island. His orderly, it appeared, who was in love with a pretty girl in the village, had forgotten to deliver the letter informing the Authorities concerned that Semporna was free of cholera !

During the three days the " Kinabalu " was in Sandakan I stayed with the P.M.O. Dr. Orme was a cousin of the Governor, and a member of the Federated Malay States Civil Service. He had been seconded and lent to Borneo for a term of years in order that the Medical Service might be reorganised and put on a sound administrative basis.

He was a charming host, a delightful raconteur, and of course a good Malay scholar, but he was always puzzled by the peculiar use of certain local idioms and colloquialisms till I explained their inverted meaning.

Malay is the medium of conversation in Borneo, but it is a very different language from the Malay spoken in the F.M.S. This is not to be wondered at when the number of races—Chinese, Dusun, Murut, Bajau, Suluk, Besaya, Tidong, Brunei, Sungei, and Javanese—using it is taken into consideration. Naturally it becomes shorn of much of its purity and individualism, with the result that a comprehensive and expressive though bastard dialect comes into being.

It always seems a pity to me that Europeans—and especially Government officers—do not take a little more trouble to speak the purer and infinitely prettier language. For much insight into, and understanding of, the native mind can be obtained by a close study of their language.

It is difficult, I agree, when using Malay as a medium, one minute to a Chinaman, the next to a Murut and a few minutes later to a Brunei, to remember the niceties of expression, but none the less I am convinced that the effort would be fruitful, as the bastard language in use is more a stringing together of English or European thoughts with Malay words than the interpenetration and translation of these thoughts into those of an oriental.

This may seem a trivial affair and yet in reality is one of some importance, for, to my thinking, the successful administration of native races does not consist only of the enforcing of European ideas and standards, but of the probing of the native mind ; thus establishing a community of thought and understanding on which may gradually be grafted the more civilised and nobler ideals.

But this digression, like my stay in Sandakan, must come to an end and once again I must board the "Kinabalu."

Sixteen hours steaming brought us to Kudat—the old capital of British North Borneo. Only a stay of a few hours here ; a hurried run ashore ; breakfast at the Residency—and we were under weigh again.

As we turned North Point—the most northerly promontory of the Territory—and started our run south for Usukan and Jesselton, the wonderful mass of Mount Kinabalu, rising to a height of 13,545 feet, came into view. From Kaningau I had almost daily gazed at the mountain, but now I looked at it with a closer and more personal interest since its western slopes formed the furthest inland boundary of Tuaran, my new district.

And as I looked a desire grew within me, and a determination, that I would one day climb to its topmost pinnacle and from that height look down on the tropic wonders that lay spread out beneath me.

Usukan possesses one house, the D.O.'s rest house, where, for a night, when he is down for the sole purpose of meeting the steamer, he can, if he so wishes, stay.

A horse-shoe bay, fringed with a sandy beach, and backed by low hills, which, on the left are covered with dense jungle, and on the right show barren and stony, completely hiding from the view of those on the incoming steamer the magnificent plain behind. Usukan is of no importance save as a small port or distributing centre for the outgoing and incoming produce and stores so necessary to daily life.

As we entered the bay an air of somnolence seemed to brood over the spot, but as the steamer drew closer to the wharf—in those days made mostly of nibong (a palm)—a change took place with magical suddenness. In a few moments the place was so humming and teeming with life that I was forcibly reminded of a busy anthill.

Down the wharf strode a steady stream of gaily-decked people, headed by a Chinese clerk with Customs permit books and passes tucked under his arm. From behind small patches of scrub suddenly appeared cattle and buffalo, dragged to and along the wharf by shrilly shrieking Bajaus or Dusuns, who had sold their animals to the Chinese butcher, who supplied Jesselton and Sandakan, and sometimes even the island of Labuan, with meat. From stacks of goods piled up on the T head kajang covers were hastily removed disclosing to view Basongs or Kranjangs of native-grown tobacco, sacks of damar (resin) or guttah (rubber), and the hundred and one other oddities that form the stock in trade of Chinese merchants in tropical dependencies.

In the bows of the steamer stands a klassi (sailor). In his hand is a coil of rope. A sharp command (in Malay) from the serang on the bridge reaches him, and the rope is hurtling through the air to fall on top of some of the tobacco. With a lusty cheer and cries of delight it is pounced upon by half a dozen natives, and in a minute the heavy tie-up rope of the steamer is made fast. The "telegraph" on the bridge rings, the engines are reversed and then in obedience to another ring are silent. From the shore another rope is flung on to the wharf and the "Kinabalu" is safely alongside. A gangway is slowly pushed out but few on the wharf wait for that—with a spring and a jump they are aboard, greeting their friends,

On Topside, Kinabalu.

On Top of Kinabalu. The bottles held the cards and names of all previous explorers. The writer was the 18th.

The Jesselton Hotel.

p. 98

giving and hearing news, laughing uproariously over the latest joke.

Regularly four times a month the steamers call at this tiny port, yet always is there the same sense of expectancy and delight ; a feeling of holiday and change, and a pleasurable break in the monotony and routine of daily life. Even a tropical downpour is unable to damp the natives' exuberant spirits, or lessen the Chinaman's keen business instinct.

There must be something in the very soul of a steamer—of almost any incoming vessel—that subtly calls to the wander-lust and enquiring mind of man.

What news does it bring ? What weather has it met ? Who is on board ? Where are they from and where going ? When will the steamer be back ? What wouldn't one give for just a short trip ? To see the sun rise on a limitless horizon ; to see it set in a blood red sky over a dark grey, turbulent sea ; to feel the infinitude of space around one ; to realise the strength and power of wind and sea ; the fragility, yet wonderful resistance of the tiny craft that bears one safely from port to port ?

All over the world it is the same. Be the port Usukan or Singapore, London or a sea-side place like Margate. Be the incoming vessel a Cunarder or the " Husbands' Boat " from London, the " Kinabalu " or a native sailing boat, the feeling is the same. " Oh, let's go down and meet her ! You never know—you never know ! "

Some such thoughts were doubtless in the mind of a very tall, dark man who slowly strolled down the wharf. His air was preoccupied, yet he was careful to answer the native greetings as he passed by. He was the District Officer—my immediate superior—for Tuaran is one of the districts which, with Tempasuk, or, as it is more often called, Kota Belud, comprises the district of North Keppel.

He came on board and was greeted by the engineer; then he turned to me, and, putting out his hand, enquired,

"You are Mr. Cook, I suppose?"

"Yes," I answered.

"Ever been in Tuaran before?" he asked.

"No," I replied, "but I'm jolly glad to be going there."

"You're lucky. It's one of the best districts in the country, and there's heaps of 'em applying for it. You're a lucky young man. Of course the A.D.O. should really be at Kota Belud. But, for the moment, and since the trouble of a few months back, I'm there, but in a little while, if things keep quiet, I expect we'll change."

All the time he had been speaking I had been slowly puzzling my brain and memory as to where he and I had met before. His name, his face and manner were familiar. I was about to ask him when my attention was claimed by one of my dogs on the wharf, which had slipped his collar and escaped from the custody of my "boy." With a murmured word I ran down the gangway and on to the wharf. At the sound of my voice "Mike" came bounding up to me and I handed him back to my "boy." Then I returned to the "Kinabalu," and joined the D.O. and the engineer.

The former was smiling, and looked rather pleased with himself as he turned to me.

"By the way," he asked, "have you ever lived at Broxbourne?"

"Yes," I answered, and I began to see light. "Have you?"

He nodded. "And you went to St. Catherine's School, and used to be in the choir at Wormley Church?"

" Yes," I answered again ; " and you used to give me dictation and take me in Latin ; and you sang bass solos in the ' Crucifixion.' "

" Good Lord," he said, " you remember that—I'd almost forgotten those days," and we both laughed together.

" I was puzzling," I went on.

" So was I," he interrupted; " your face seemed familiar—your initials I couldn't remember—but when I saw your back view, and you walked along the wharf with that curious uplift on your toes, I knew you in a minute."

My reply was drowned in the shrill blast of the syren, the warning for " all ashore."

The D.O. rose from his long chair and made his leisurely way down the gangway. From the wharf he shouted his good-byes ; then, as an afterthought, he shouted to me as we were casting off and the space between wharf and the steamer grew wider and wider,

" Report to the Resident of the West Coast as soon as you arrive. He'll give you instructions. You won't be able to do much till I visit you as there's no officer there, and I've got the safe keys. Expect me to be with you in about five days. Cheerioh."

His last remarks just reached me as we backed from the wharf and began to head for the open sea.

Next morning when I awoke we had arrived at Jesselton.

In due course I reported to the Resident and received my instructions. I was to start for Tuaran the next morning and " carry on " as best I could till the D.O. came down from Kota Belud and properly " handed over." Then, with a wave of his hand I was dismissed, but, as I turned to go, he added cheerily, " See you at the Club to-night. If it's fine you'd better play tennis."

That remark was typical of him. At this time he was the Senior Resident in the Service, and could rise no higher unless appointed Government Secretary. Yet there was no " side " or stiffness about him. A cheery word, an amusing story, an interest in your ponies and dogs, a piece of advice, an invitation to dinner or a night or two at the Residency, the utmost trust in you, the minimum of official correspondence, the plain home-truth without any sarcasm if you'd made a mistake or been forgetful! Such was his idea of administration. And all his juniors worked for him. All did their best for him, and smiled if sometimes he was a wee bit " short," or his minutes occasionally expressive. Nobody minded or felt hurt; everyone knew of his liver; all recognised his years of splendid service, and envied him his unrivalled knowledge of the natives and the country.

The district of Tuaran though small in area is yet the most densely populated part of British North Borneo. Its southern boundary ran right into the confines of Jesselton itself, with which it was linked up on the telephone. The line also extended from Tuaran to Kota Belud.

My headquarters were situated twenty-one miles from Jesselton, and could be reached either by bridle path or by a combination journey by sea and road. This latter way was the one always adopted by anyone travelling with barang (luggage) as it meant a great saving of porterage.

The next morning then found me setting sail from the Customs with three large pakarangans (boats of a special design of Brunei origin) loaded to their full capacity with my servants, dogs, cats and household effects.

The route was across the bay to the small hill of Gantisan. Here everything had to be unloaded and carried across the hill to where on the other side more boats were waiting to take me as far as Mengkabong, where I was to disembark prior to the three miles' ride into Tuaran.

After leaving Gantisan rain commenced to fall, and on my arrival at Mengkabong was coming down in such torrents that I decided to wait a little in the hopes that it might, if not cease, at least ease off. I had had no lunch save a few sandwiches and some cold tea, so was glad to accept the native clerk's hospitality and indulge in some coffee and biscuits.

Two of the local chiefs who lived in the village came and paid their respects. There was the usual crowd of small children, some dressed, some naked, mooning round, and from out of various doors and windows of the houses, most of which were built over the water, I could see curious heads peeping, the owners of which were anxious to obtain a glance at the new tuan.

I was pleased to notice that both the police in charge of the transport coolies were men I had known and played "footer" with in the old Tenom days.

A new district is fascinating, but at the same time I always felt rather strange and lonely at the idea of a change, and was always glad to find, as generally happened, a "friend" among the constabulary.

For the native (Muruts and Dusun) police in Borneo I have a very real affection. I will not pretend that they are highly intelligent or brilliantly military, but as a force they are sportsmen—keen on hunting and games: loyal and trustworthy. If you once gain their confidence and esteem there is little they will not do or suffer for you; while, on up-country trips in the district, they will delight in "fathering and mothering" you, and attending to all your wants.

Their duties, a combination of military and civil, are

manifold. They serve summonses, warrants and attachments : they provide sentries for the district offices and treasuries ; form escorts for the transfer of money or prisoners ; act as interpreters, and sometimes as clerks and collectors of revenue. If there is a rising or a riot on an estate, or a " bad-hat " to be captured, they go forth to fight with a light heart and with one great idea : that of getting rid of their ammunition as quickly as possible, so that they may get to work with their beloved parangs (swords).

About 1913 an epidemic of murder and crime broke out, principally in connection with Sapong Estate.* In two instances I remember no trace of the perpetrators was ever found, but, in a third case—the murder of a Chinese coolie on a lonely road on the Estate—evidence pointed to two Muruts as the criminals, and, after searching investigations and a preliminary enquiry before the Magistrate, they were committed for trial before the Sessions Court, and finally convicted and hanged.

The Muruts, a very backward, pagan tribe—the aborigines of North Borneo—used in the old days to collect heads as a pastime. But as the influence of Government spread, and the country became opened up, the practice, on a large scale, of necessity died out. But the instinct to kill remained, and since a decapitated body was " prima facie " evidence of Murut handiwork, the criminal covered his tracks and yet satisfied his collecting instinct by acquiring first a finger, and then, when that became too obvious, a snick of the murdered person's ear.

In the case mentioned above it transpired that the motive of the murder was blind revenge. A man of the same village as the murderers, and I think a distant relative, had been admitted to the Estate Hospital and in

* Chronologically, this episode should be recorded in Chapter I., but has been transferred for the better balance of the book.

Dusun Belles.

p. 104

an unsuccessful attempt to save his life the doctor had amputated a limb.

Muruts in those days had an unholy horror of a hospital, and could hardly ever be induced to come in for treatment. The amputation of a limb, therefore, constituted an offence only to be wiped out with blood. But the doctor was beyond their reach—though they went the length of sending threatening letters—so they retaliated on the Estate by attacking and killing a solitary coolie late one night as he was returning to his home from the hospital.

A drizzling rain—a cold day—the time about 4.30 p.m. —a new district—an empty house and the prospect of my luggage being a long way behind me ! Such was the outlook as I mounted a constabulary pony at Menkabong and cantered off along the slippery path to Tuaran. Oh well, I thought, it's no good grousing, the sun will probably shine to-morrow and after all there would be a roof over my head and a bed and a mattress to sleep on.

A loud voice broke in upon my reverie and looking up I found I was near the house, and that on the verandah someone was waving lustily to me.

The population of Tuaran, and I might say of North Keppel, consists of Bajaus on the coast—but a different type from the Bajau of the East Coast—and Coast and Hill Dusuns. Of these it is the latter who provide the nucleus of Free Estate labour in the territory.

The Dusun is by nature an agriculturist ; stolid and leavened with the homing-instinct. On estates where the Management knew how to handle him and were prepared, in reason, to consider and study his few foibles, he quickly became an invaluable asset.

According to his financial state he would sign on for a year's contract, or more, as an ordinary monthly labourer.

His object in signing a contract would be the acquirement of the usual advance of $\$30.^{00}$—given as an inducement—granted to a coolie on signing, and which he would repay by monthly deductions from his pay.

The Bajau would generally—as also would the Javanese and Chinese—spend this money, or most of it, in a night's gambling, caring little whether he won or lost. In the latter event he would frequently make his loss the excuse for desertion, pleading as a palliative against his offence that life was no longer worth living as he had no money, or that he dare not face his wife's wrath (always supposing he was married). A pair of cheap American shoes; a gaudy silk handkerchief or an elaborately pocketed and waisted coat would always prove tempting baits.

Not so the Tuaran Dusun. Money for him spelt an equivalent and solid value; was a means to an end. In his village in the hills—perhaps two or three days away—was a maiden—shy, pretty and fascinating. His desire was to " bertunang " (become engaged) with her. But her father would only countenance a man of stability. In the pawnshop was an ancient and venerated " Langui " (a kind of rose-bowl made of brass) which was " pusaka " (an heirloom) and must be redeemed. In a neighbouring village was a Kerbau (buffalo) with curious twists and curls in its scanty hair. These curls were signs of great strength and vitality, pointed to unusual breeding capacity, or signified good luck for the owner. This animal was worth acquiring even at a stiffish figure.

And so the Dusun would " sign on " on an estate. But he did not spend his money foolishly. Often he left it in the manager's care till his contract was finished. Sometimes he sent it to his home by a friend or relative who was returning. Sometimes he would be granted leave himself for a certain time and always returned punctually.

If prevented by untoward circumstances he would send a substitute—his sister, brother or cousin, or even a friend.

A trusting, unsophisticated race ; an ideal labourer ! Few estates, however, cared to humour them, and, for administrative and economic reasons, Government began to look with a disproving eye on any tendencies that bound or induced them on to estates.

This attitute is sound enough in its way, for British North Borneo only grows half its normal rice supply, and has to import the remaining fifty per cent., whilst the Dusuns are the great agriculturists of the Territory, producing at least half the rice that is cultivated.

Every native away from normal village life meant less rice grown during that year. But this, though serious, was not the worst feature of existing conditions. It was noticed that the younger generation showed a distinct disinclination to return to the old life. Planting failed to attract them ; they lost their sense of individuality and clever craftsmanship ; they became one of a crowd —housed, fed, and cared for. In the end they would succumb to cheap and gaudy clothes ; to gambling and an easy prostitution—for women as well as men formed part of the labour force of an estate.

True, they were given medical attention ; learned the value and necessity of discipline and cleanliness. But these virtues or advantages never became more than skin deep, and a return—if return there was—to village life meant a return to the old bad habits with new bad ones added. The old independence—a blend of communism and individualism—was obliterated, and, in its place, there flourished the lower instincts of modern civilisation.

Thus, there seems little chance that Borneo will be free of the so-called stigma of employing Indentured Labour for many years ; for, apart from the reasons given above, the country is but sparsely populated, while the Dusun alone, of the many races in the Territory, shows any real inclination to drift in any numbers towards estate life.

So the importation of labourers, principally Chinese and Javanese, must continue, and this importation alone means a large capital outlay for each estate, which otherwise could not possibly be expended nor justified, unless there was a reasonable guarantee of a "quid pro quo" in the shape of permanent labour for a certain stipulated period.

I have met many people who lift their eyes and raise their shoulders in holy horror at the idea of Indentured Labour, and who hold that such a state of affairs within the confines of the Empire is a blot on the fair name of Britain. But I can never quite see why, and generally find that their opinions are founded on extreme ignorance of existing conditions.

After all, every contract in the world has within it the germ of slavery. There are conditions which must be fulfilled, and which, if unfulfilled, incur penalties. There are ways and means of determining the contract, but if the ways and means cannot be found or met then the conditions must be abided by. It would, therefore, seem both unfair and fanatical to condemn a system of contract labour merely because one of the parties is an Asiatic. Furthermore, and apart from what may be termed the purely legal aspect of the contract, the state of development of the country, the supply of, and demand for, labour, and the mentality and civilisation of the labourer are to be considered. A tropical country in the throes of development, plus an insufficiency of local or indigenous labour, and the consequent importation of a supply from an outside source; labourers of Asiatic origin, and of a low mentality and natural standard of living, are all part of conditions which, if they do not actually demand indentured labour, at least go far to excuse its employment.

Such at least are the conditions in British North Borneo, but so carefully has the Labour Ordinance been framed, and so strict an eye is kept upon the Employers by the Authorities, that the labourer is indentured really only in name.

Three hundred working days is the period of contract. At the expiration of this time the labourer, if he so wishes, must be repatriated to his country of origin at the expense of the estate. Two holidays a month, for which days he must receive pay, are his by law. No advance over $30.^{00}$ is recognised by the Government as reclaimable, either as an enforcement of contract or a claim to be taken to the Civil Court. The contract is terminable by the labourer giving a month's notice, and repaying all, or any part of his debt, owing up to $30.^{00}$ and such proportion (if he is an imported coolie) of expenses as were incurred in his importation, and as the Protector of Labourers shall think fit and proper.

It is only in this last clause that any suggestion of slavery can be levelled against the indenture. The germ lies in the fact—generally not known to the majority of critics—that the average Chinese or Javanese coolie is never in a position, or likely by his instincts, training and earning capacity, to be in a position to repay his debt or unworked off expenses. The money he gets he spends with but little thought or care for to-morrow. But surely he is not unique in this? Surely this natural human instinct and failing is not sufficient to condemn a system necessary to the progress of the world?

And just as there are conditions on behalf of the

labourer so are there conditions on behalf of the employer. Few people, if any, cavil at the necessity for discipline in an army, a civil service or even a big departmental store. Why then cavil at discipline on an estate?

Many an estate is in an isolated spot; the work is carried on by one or two white men amongst many hundreds of Asiatics. There must be discipline; but this does not necessarily mean ill-treatment and brutality as so many people imagine; and discipline alone is not sufficient unless it is backed up by the full authority and support of Government.

To those who have never been abroad, or seen or met a native, to those who have never lived alone among an Asiatic population, to those whose minds are already biased by the extraordinary theory of "our little brown brother," I suppose it is almost a waste of time and will be considered a brutal statement to say that often the kindest and most sensible punishment to award an offender under the Labour Ordinance is a flogging. Yet it is so. And I say so in all honesty and sincerity, with the experience of ten years to support my statement.

I remember a case, not, by the way, of a contract labourer but a free Chinese—one of a band of settlers or immigrants brought into the country under a special Government scheme. The settlers had been given land, found a house, and provided with money, under a liberal system of repayment, till such time as their gardens reached a state of production. Their settlement was close to Mengatal Estate, about half way between Tuaran and Jesselton, the Manager of which was always complaining of the thefts of his young rubber stumps from the nurseries.

At last he caught a thief in "flagrante delicto" and

sent him up to the District Officer under the charge of an opas (watchman) with instructions to prosecute him before me in the Magistrate's Court.

The accused was a weedy, undersized Chinaman, hollow cheeked, spotty faced, and with receding chin. His eyes were watery and his ears enormously large. Altogether it was a most unprepossessing specimen that stood before me in the office, nervously twisting and untwisting his hands, as I read the Manager's letter. The opas carried a bundle of rubber stumps which every now and then he rustled and tapped in a manner which seemed to say, " Look here, these are stolen and there's the thief. Punish him and punish him well for I caught him—yes, I did." All estate opas seemed to hold the opinion that they should be treated with a sort of " favoured nation " consideration.

For once in a way I was not very busy in the office, and so was able to take the case at once. During my tenure at Semporna I had reached the rank of a Magistrate of 1st class. Apart from increased powers in judicial work, this meant a great saving of time, as in certain cases of a minor nature it obviated the writing down of all evidence. The present case came under this category.

In a few minutes I was on the bench ; the accused, more unprepossessing than ever, stood trembling in the dock. The opas, truculent, swelling with pride, and a sense of " something accomplished, something done," entered the witness box.

" Sergeant," I said, " swear the witness." And the opas mumbled a Mohamedan oath under the Koran.

" Well," I said, " tell me your story, and remember I don't want to hear what you think, or what happened a week ago ; I only want to hear about what you personally know, and saw the accused doing."

The opas, in spite of admonition, launched forth into reminiscences and opinions. But the gist of his story was plain, and there appeared to be no doubt concerning the accused's guilt. The case was one of those that are obvious, but over which a Magistrate must pay the outward observances due to the dignity of the law.

The opas's evidence having been translated to the accused in Chinese—for he knew only a little Malay—he was asked whether he pleaded Guilty or Not Guilty.

"Not Guilty," came the reply, and a long rigmarole followed, which the accused fondly thought was a defence. He admitted taking the rubber stumps, but not stealing them. They were not his, that is to say he had not grown or bought them, and, as far as he knew, the Estate had planted them; still he wanted them for his garden. Other Chinese had frequently taken some, and he was an immigrant—a kind of special protege of the Government—and everything in the country was his just for the asking, or the mere wishing. Oh, no! he was not a thief, but a poor struggling Chinaman, a husband and father, in a strange country, living under strange laws, a public benefactor in so much that at the Government's wish he came and planted a garden, and so, well, of course, he had a right to the stumps, and his acquiring them in the way he did was no offence.

A charming sophistry I admit! But—well, there was the Law to be considered, there was the Estate to be considered, and so I pronounced a verdict of "Guilty."

Then the floodgates of his eloquence were opened in earnest, and a torrent of pleading poured forth.

"Tuan, Tuan," he cried, "you are the Magistrate and the Law and omnipotent, and you can do no wrong, but have pity, have pity on me, on my wife and on my children. They were away from home when the opas caught me and on their return they will not know where I am! They have no money, no food, and they will starve! Oh, my poor wife, my dear, dear children. They will starve, they will die, Ai-ah—ai-ah," and he began to weep copiously.

Though his grief and fear were perhaps genuine he angered me. He was such a worm, such a despicable creature and yet he had the courage to steal. In the witness box the opas openly grinned with delight. There was something in the scene that appealed to the low-caste Pathan's sense of cruelty.

At length the wretch ceased his snivelling and silence reigned in the Court. I was about to give judgment when he started again.

" Tuan, don't send me to gaol, don't lock me up. If you do my wife and children will die. They have no food, no money. Have pity, have pity."

" The quality of mercy is not strained." The words came into my mind as I looked at the accused. They caused me to smile. Administratively I did not want him in gaol. I had plenty of prisoners, and he was a poor specimen of humanity.

Could I punish the accused for his offence, fulfil the letter and the spirit of the Law and yet grant his request? Could I satisfy justice and yet show mercy? Yes.

I called him to me. Pulled down his lower eyelids. There was no sign of anæmia. Looked at his tongue. It was fairly clean. Felt his pulse. Its beat was almost normal. Tested his spleen. It was not unduly large.

He went back to the dock, and for a few moments I wrote, then I put down my pen and addressed the accused.

" I find you guilty of the theft of the rubber stumps and sentence you to six strokes of the rotan (flogging).

If unfit for rotan to a fine of $3.^{00}, or in default to 7 days r.i."

I turned to the Sergeant. "Put up the triangle, Sergeant," I said. "The accused is perfectly fit. Give him six."

In accordance with regulations I witnessed the flogging which was not severe. Of course the prisoner howled and wriggled—nearly all Chinese do—and no doubt the salt and water smarted, still, he had his wish, and half an hour later, after a good feed of rice and salt fish, was on his way home to join his wife and children.

But even so I was not to be left in peace, for a little while later the Resident rang me up.

"That you, Cook?"

"Yes, Sir," I replied.

"What's all this about the Mengatal Immigrants? My office is besieged with them, and there's one woman and her children howling like 'blue murder.' Woon" (the Superintendent of Immigrants) "has brought them round. He's as mad as a hatter—simply furious."

"What's the trouble, Sir?" I asked, as he paused for breath.

"That's what I'm asking you. Woon's tale is you've got the woman's husband languishing in gaol. Some story of petty theft. What's it all about. Better let him out."

"He is out; he's on his way home; he's never been in gaol," I said.

"Good. I'll tell Woon and quieten him. He's touchy you know over his blessed Immigrants. But what happened?"

"One of 'em stole some rubber stumps from Mengatal Estate, was caught red-handed, sent up to me, admitted the theft and has been punished."

" How ? "

" He implored me not to send him to gaol, said his wife and children would starve ; he had no money—none of them has—and he owes Government a lot. He admitted his guilt and—well, so I gave him six rotan. . . ."

" What ! ! Six rotan ! You rotanned one of Woon's lambs ! " (Such was the designation impiously bestowed on the immigrants.) Good Lord ! you'll never hear the end of it. He, he . . . all right, I . . . don't you worry," and as the receiver was being put on I heard sounds unmistakably like chuckles.

And that was all I ever heard of the matter, but for quite a long time the Mengatal Immigrants gave up thieving. No doubt they found honesty the better policy.

This may seem an extreme case, but I think it points the moral of my contention. Besides, it must be remembered that every day a labourer is in gaol means the loss of his labour to the Estate, while he himself must make good such enforced absence.

There were in Tuaran four groups of Chinese Immigrants. One settlement was at Inanam near Jesselton ; another one was at Mengatal, the third was at Telupuk, and the fourth at Tuaran itself. All showed signs of possibilities and self-support with exception of the Tuaran settlement. Here the settlers eventually proved to be not agriculturists but shopkeepers and artisans. But taking them all in all they were always a considerable nuisance. It was not that there was any friction between them and the natives, but that as long as they could squeeze any subsistence money out of Government they saw no reason why they should exert themselves over their gardens. I grant that for the first two years of their existence in Borneo weather conditions were against them, but really there was little excuse for their laziness. As an appeal always lay over my head to the Superintendent who granted their every request I began to detest " Woon's lambs " as cordially as he liked and humoured them.

This sort of dual control is one of the drawbacks of a D.O.'s position. He is administratively in charge of the district, responsible to the Resident for law and order, a sort of advisory committee and channel through whom everything must flow; yet, in actuality, he has direct and ultimate control of no one. Over constabulary matters he deals, if not through the Resident then direct with the Commandant. Judicial affairs are passed to the Sessions judge or judicial Commissioner. Customs matters are referred to the Commissioner of Customs. Land concerns find their way to the Commissioner of Lands.

The system which ultimately makes the Heads of Departments the deciding factor, and fixes on them the final responsibility, is no doubt necessary, but in the satisfying their various claims the D.O. finds his ingenuity taxed to the uttermost. Each department has quantities of returns and reports it requires sent in by a certain date—and the date for the rendering of these always coincides—each department imagines It and It alone is of any importance and that extra special care should be shown to its affairs. Each department in turn always forgets there is a department bigger than itself, bigger than the union of all the departments together—a department which is the sole cause of the appointment of a D.O. and by reason of which the other departments have their existence, a department generally silent and long-suffering yet liable at times to kick over the traces in no uncertain manner—the Public.

Another experience, one of a rather gruesome nature, comes to my mind.* The Resident was away, as also was

* Chronologically, this episode should be recorded in Chapter I., but has been transferred for the better balance of the book.

the Medical Officer, and I was on Sapong Estate sitting as Magistrate. Early one morning the Sectional Engineer informed me by telephone that he had over-night discovered the dead body of a railway coolie on the line. There was no mark on the body, no suggestion of foul play, no theft of his money, and his effects were still intact. He was known to be short-sighted, suffering from a weak heart, and to have started alone for his home down the line, some five miles from Tenom.

To have returned to Tenom would have been inconvenient. To keep the corpse till my return next day would have been unsavoury. I ordered his burial, and on my return held a careful Coroner's enquiry. But the Resident was not satisfied, and five days later ordered the exhumation of the body, and instructed the Medical Officer to examine and state cause of death.

Accompanied by four Murut prisoners from the gaol, under the charge of a Pathan policeman, the Medical Officer and I set forth. On arrival at the grave our prisoners commenced to dig. As they dug lower and lower the air became more and more fetid. At length the Medical Officer put disinfected bandages over our noses and the digging went on. Soon a toe could be seen sticking out of the ground and simultaneously I discovered the Pathan policeman to be missing. Horrid sounds from a neighbouring bush gave us the reason for his hurried departure. Then one by one the Muruts laid down their tools and slipped away just as the corpse was exposed to full view.

The Medical Officer and I looked at one another and then at the grave. The sight was not a pretty one. Then he stooped over the body and laid hold of a band of cloth that was passed round its middle. He gave a pull ; there was a rending sound, the cloth parted and the Medical Officer was precipitated on to the top of the corpse.

Almost quicker than he fell in he scrambled out. " For the Lord's sake, cover it up quickly," he gasped. " It's no good, I could not give any evidence on *that*." Then he also retired behind a bush—and small shame too !

The Muruts did not like the task, but they covered up the grisly sight somehow, the Pathan regained a little of his military precision, and, eventually, we all returned to Tenom. But it was days and days before the smell left our nostrils or our ears lost the buzzing of the flies.

Land settlement, which some years previous had been partially undertaken in the district, was again proceeding apace, for the Dusuns and Bajaus on the plains, unlike the Muruts of the Interior, readily appreciated the benefits of indisputable land ownership. New applications for land, as well as the settlements of old tenure, came in daily, and two demarcators working with prismatic compass and plane-table were kept busy to their utmost capacity.

This meant a very great deal of increased work for me, for, though the actual settlement of most of the lands had previously been determined by a Settlement officer, the plans of the demarcators had all to be checked and passed by me before the Commissioner of Lands would accept them for the issuing of the Native Definitive titles. Incidentally the issuing of some hundreds of titles, the writing them up in the Native Title Registers and the entering them on to the Yearly Rent Rolls meant considerable additional labour for the clerical staff in my office.

As a matter of fact there was sufficient work in connection with the Land Settlement to occupy my individual attention for many months. But such was impossible. The three Estates required regularly visiting and reporting on. They also provided a quantity of work for me in a judicial capacity. Bridle-paths required cleaning and the coolies work checking and supervising, bridges were in need of mending and being rebuilt ; the district, especially up-country, had to be visited. So it can easily be seen that the great big department known as the Public made large inroads on my energy and my time, and that the official hours of 9.30 a.m. to 1 p.m. and 2 p.m. to 4 p.m. were hopelessly insufficient in which to accomplish the average day's work.

A very great deal of my time would be occupied in Court listening to the intricacies of buffalo theft cases. Buffalo stealing in North Keppel reached an epidemic stage, and became to certain natives as much an obsession or craze as Bridge or Poker is to some Europeans. I am quite certain the thieves stole in many cases for the sheer delight of stealing, or for the excitement incurred owing to the risks they ran. Certainly neither hunger nor poverty inspired the thefts. But whatever the reasons, Government quite rightly looked upon buffalo theft as a very serious offence, and by an unwritten law the minimum sentence for a first offence was always one year's r.i.

It was not so much the actual cash value of the animal that made the offence serious as the potential wealth—quite apart from a breeding capacity—that was invested in it. For ploughing and transport it would be in almost daily use ; as a contribution to " brien " (marriage dowry) it possessed its value ; wealth would be counted by the number of head of cattle ; as security for debt or for raising a loan it was eminently acceptable.

To the European the average buffalo is similar to his fellow, but the natives show a remarkable degree of cleverness in distinguishing and recognising animals, and after a most cursory glance will be able to retail any distinguishing features.

It is this very ability which gives so much trouble to the Magistrate in Court, for the animal in dispute will have either been impounded or tied up near the Court House during the trial and in consequence has been open more or less to inspection, with the result that minute and correct evidence from both parties as to peculiarities and distinguishing marks become practically valueless.

As a check to buffalo theft, and also cattle stealing in general, Government instituted a system of district branding and registration for births, deaths, sales and slaughter, but up to the present the ideal system has yet to be found. The special difficulty in regard to buffaloes is that an average brand becomes obliterated in about two years. The practice of cutting out snicks of the ears, as indulged in by the natives, has obvious limits of differentiation.

One of the charms of a change of districts lay in the fact that, generally, each district possessed some distinct feature of its own, which, to a great extent, dominated daily life. Thus it was that in North Keppel, and at Tuaran in particular, I made my first acquaintance with a Tamu (a Native Market).

These tamus were held at stated places in the district at regular and fixed dates. Some, such as Tamu Office at Tuaran and Tamu Darat at Kota Belud, were large affairs; others would be quite small and very local; but all were picturesque, and a source of prosperity to the people.

Tamu Office gained its name from the fact that it was held every Sunday morning on a small elevation behind the District Office, and, owing to the proximity of Tuaran Estate, was always exceedingly well attended.

All paths and tracks across the padi (rice) -land seemed to lead to the Tamu, and from an early hour could be seen steady streams of gaily-dressed people converging upon

TAMU.

A FLEET OF SULUK "DAPANGS" IN SEMPORNA.

p. 120

the spot where stood a small flag-post, at the top of which hung a furled flag, the " breaking " of which was a signal that the Tamu was opened.

From the break of dawn they come. Riding on a buffalo come three Dusuns, garbed in their tight-fitting black coats and trousers edged with small brass buttons. On their heads are folded wonderfully coloured hand-woven " dustars " (kind of turban) ; round their waists are similar scarves, into which are tucked their " parangs." These latter, ere they enter the Tamu, they give up to a policeman on special duty ; for no one may attend a Tamu armed. In their hands they each carry a bundle of fowls.

On a half-breed sapi (ox) jogs a Chinaman, a local trader. He is almost hidden by the bundles of goods, sarongs, combs, mouth-organs, cigarettes, buttons, lace, cloth, perfumery, powder, kerosene oil, candles, cakes and what not that somehow or other are fastened behind, in front and around him on his sturdy little beast.

With long swinging strides, in single file, and with an alluring sway from the hips, come four Bajau girls. On their ankles, just visible beneath their blue, red and golden sarongs, jangle silver and brass anklets. On their heads are balanced wicker baskets full to the brim with fresh gathered padi.

In the distance a long black trail is noticed, winding and wriggling like a serpent. Closer and closer it comes, and resolves itself into a company of Dusun women of the Plain. In single file they stalk, in perfect step, their short black skirts, reaching only to the knees, swish in regular time ; from right to left over the shoulder is slung a black garment (really a sarong) like an enlarged sling. No other covering do they wear, yet their breasts never escape its folds. In its lower folds are stowed their commodities of barter: home-made salt, betel-nut, sirih-leaves, and even eggs. And as they walk they swing their arms in a curious sideways motion that clears the goods they bring to market.

From the west comes a string of Dusuns, male and female, with " basongs " piled high on their backs. The women's legs and arms are encased in coil upon coil of bright brass wire, while coil upon coil is around their waists. They come from Tambunan or Ranau, four and five days' journey; and their basongs are full of home-grown tobacco.

To the tune of a concertina, from across the river comes a noisy, happy batch of Javanese coolies from Tuaran Estate. The men are resplendent in new khaki coats, well pressed white duck trousers and shiny cheap American black shoes. Some even wear bright hued socks. The women's hair, oiled and combed, is adorned with golden " chuckok-sangol " (hairpins). On their fingers are rings with gems of fabulous size—cheap stones from Ceylon or coloured glass from a factory. Their sarongs vie with the rainbow, and their coats put Joseph's to shame.

In a whirl of dust, and to the jingle of bells, come four Bajaus racing their ponies over the plain. As they draw nearer their excitement grows. Their cries split the air; they raise their " pasuts " (rotan whips), wave them over their ponies' heads, and settle down to the last and final effort. No fancy seat almost on the ponies' withers here; no short American stirrup: but a seat well down in the middle of their mount; no stirrups at all, only their legs swinging to the ponies' stride, and the thud, thud, thud of their heels which they dig like spurs into the heaving sides.

The Tamu itself is a babel and buzz of excitement. In little groups the natives sit and spread their wares out on the ground before them ; bananas, langsats, pines and bread-fruit ; and, in season, that much beloved but foul-smelling fruit the Durian. Mats and straw-hats and ropes ; fowls, ducks, goats and buffaloes ; pepper, gambia, sirih and vegetables ; rice (padi), sweet potatoes, ubi kayu and indian-corn ; dustars and handkerchiefs, silver and brass-ware.

In little booths, made of wood, with open sides and floors of split bamboos and roofs of attap (sago palm leaf), squat the Chinese traders along one side of the Tamu. For cash or barter they will sell ; and many a wrangle, haggle and bargain is driven and fought ere the goods change hands, or money is parted with.

Every now and then an eye is lifted to the flag, still furled at the top of the post ; every now and then a policeman warns some over-anxious purchaser that the Tamu is not yet open. Round chosen and much-desired goods a prospective buyer hovers, torn with doubt and conflicting desires. He wants beyond all else that double-sized " tikar " (mat), woven in zig-zag pattern in blue and red and green ; and there, on the far side of the Tamu, is just the very pair of silver anklets his wife has commissioned him to buy ! A shout breaks in on his meditations. " Selim ! Selim ! " reaches his ears. With a start and a curse he looks up to discover his kerbau has broken loose and is engaged in combat with another. Gone are the thoughts of tikar and anklets as he rushes away to capture his beast, and put an end to a fight that may well prove fatal to one of the combatants, and cause a stampede among the other animals.

With a resounding clash, just as he reaches them, the two great pairs of horns come together, then, for a time, remain immovable as each beast with lowered head strives its utmost to push the other back. Not an inch of ground is given way. Two tails angrily flick their great dark sides. Two pairs of eyes glare fiercely into each other. Two pairs of long black ears flap backwards and forwards. Then sideways, upwards and downwards the huge heads sway, still pressed tightly together. A sudden movement, a little quicker and shorter than the one before, a harsh, cruel, grating sound as the horns rasp each other, a tossing of heads and the animals are apart and backing, backing slowly from each other.

In a flash Selim has flung a rope over the horns of his animal and slowly draws it to him. In a trice the nose-ring is threaded and the great beast is being led away. But when Selim gets back to the Tamu both the mat and the anklets are gone beyond recall.

Disgusted with life Selim makes the round of the Tamu. Everything he wants has been bought by someone just before him. All that is left is not worth having. His foot is sore and swelling, for the kerbau trampled on it. His temper—and Bajaus are quick of temper—is rising, as he arrives in front of a chinaman's booth.

" How much is that Songko ? " (Malay cap), he asks.

" Dollar fifty," comes the reply, and it angers Selim all the more for he is only possessed of a dollar. His reply is an insult—a pantoon (verse of four lines) :

> "Hujan datang
> Kambing lari.
> Orang china
> Makan babi."*

" Lu makan babi juga," shrieks the Chinaman in

---

* Translation :

> "The rain comes
> And goats take shelter
> But the Chinaman always eats pig."

reply, "for my cakes are cooked in pig's fat. Lu orang Bajau miemang sombong."*

But he gets no further, for the double insult, the use of the despicable word "Lu," and the accusation of eating pig, is more than Selim can stand. Forgetful that it was he who picked the quarrel, and gave the first insult, he hurls himself upon the Chinaman, scattering his stores in all directions.

A shriek rises above the babel of voices; a police whistle is blown; two policemen make a dash for the booth. There is a scuffle, and from the debris are dragged the struggling breakers of the peace. Dishevelled, they glare at one another; the Chinaman's forehead is bleeding and his lip is cut; Selim's coat is torn from shoulder to waist. Slowly, through the crowd that has collected around them, the Sergeant forces his way. Both culprits start to speak and explain at once. For a minute or two the Sergeant listens, then he silences them, waves his hand towards the gaol, and they are led away. To-morrow—Monday—the case can be heard. To-day is Sunday and Tamu day to boot!

As a matter of policy the culprits are detained till the Tamu is over. Then they are released on bail till the case is heard in the Magistrate's Court.

It was at a Tamu that I learnt, from some up-country Dusuns, that an American Army Chaplain and his wife, who had climbed Kinabalu to make a collection of orchids, were returning to Jesselton via Tuaran, and might be expected any day towards the end of the week.

I did not envy them their journey, for the weather was wet, and I knew from experience the route they must

---

* "You also eat pig,
You Bajaus are always stuck up."

follow. In the last two days travelling they must cross and recross the Tuaran river twenty-five times, or, as an alternative, if the river was in flood, come through a belt of land that was practically one large kerbau wallow.

This latter, as matters turned out, was the route they took.

Never shall I forget their arrival, or their stay in my house! I was having tea on my verandah about half-past four. The rain was coming down in torrents; the padi-fields were one large sheet of water; the river, which I could see from the verandah, was a turgid, racing torrent. Suddenly there were sounds of footsteps on my stairs. Then came others lighter and quicker. I looked up and for a second gasped. On the topmost step stood two drowned rats, dripping water and oozing mud from every article of clothing they wore.

"Good Lord! Padre!" I cried. "Come in, come in. You must have had a hell—I mean the devil—I mean an absolutely rotten journey. Come in and sit down both of you, at once."

They entered and squelched all over the verandah. It wasn't their fault but my misfortune.

"Now, Padre," I said, "you'd both better have a strong 'stengah,' and then a bath and change."

But at first they were adamant. No, they would have nothing, absolutely nothing; but if I would let wifey (the Padre always referred to his wife as wifey) have a glass of cold water that would be all they required.

Under protest I supplied the desired beverage. My soul revolted against the idea. If they wouldn't have a "stengah" at least they'd have tea? And in the end I won. Gingerly, first hubby then wifey sipped a cup of tea. Its warmth thawed them and gradually they realised their hunger and fell to the temptation of hot toast, sandwiches and cake. And they fell in no uncertain manner, for, when I rang for the tea-things to be removed, the tea-pot was dry and the plates were empty.

But as yet the coolies had not arrived with their luggage, and to get them a change of clothes seemed a matter of paramount importance. Mrs. " Padre " was looking at some pictures hung in a corner of the room. I seized the opportunity.

" Padre," I said, " now what about a change and bath for you ? I can fit you up with a sarong and a kabaiah (sleeping coat) till your own things arrive. But your Mem . . . I can't run to things like camisoles and such like, but if she'll get into a sarong also I can manage a kimono as well. Just to carry on with, you know."

At that moment Mrs. Padre turned from the pictures. She had evidently heard our conversation.

" My dear," she said, addressing her husband, " we're quite all right as we are," and continued her tour of inspection.

" But——" I commenced.

" My dear young friend," broke in the Padre, " we thank you very much, very much indeed, but wifey would rather wait, and, if she does, I will too."

I mumbled something about asking to be excused and made my way to the kitchen to order lots of hot water to be ready. On my return I saw the first of their coolies entering the garden gate.

He was the first of many who came slowly limping in with curious square-shaped wicker cases on their backs. If the Padre's clothes were in those weird things, I thought, they must be wet, and saw my sarongs being utilised after all.

As the first coolie reached the front door Mr. and Mrs. Padre made a combined rush at him, squelching more than ever, and leaving a trail of mud and water behind them. The coolie squatted down on his haunches and slipped the green-bark straps from off his shoulders, whilst they hovered and fussed around him like old hens over their chickens.

"Case No. 9," said the Padre as he lovingly turned the basket-like thing over. "These," he continued, looking at me, "are some of the orchids."

"Oh yes," I answered, "how topping, and have you many?"

"Nine cases," he replied, "and I think two hundred different varieties."

"Splendid," I murmured; but really was wondering when their clothes were coming.

Mrs. Padre looked up from the package with a smile and remarked, "Isn't it?"

"And you've really collected all these?" I began, but broke off as cases Nos. 2 and 5 came staggering in, to be followed by a sodden Willesden-canvas suit-case, a collection of pots and pans, and a much overfilled and bulging "hold-all."

"Put them here, put them down gently. Oh, the dears!" cooed Mrs. Padre, and fussed around the incoming cases.

I pounced upon the suit-case and "hold-all," called my boy, and had them taken to the spare-room. Then I braced myself, for I had an idea a struggle lay before me.

"Padre," I cried in rather a stern and magisterial voice, "your suit-case has arrived, it's in your room, and your bath water's ready. I see other luggage coming—a wicker basket and small hand-bag—and I think, I really do, that you and your Mem ought to change."

A look, a blend of sorrow and surprise, came into the Chaplain's face.

"My dear young friend, my dear young friend," he said, "our orchids—they are precious, very precious; on them wifey and I have lavished much care—they are the 'raison d'être' of our trip. We must not spoil them now. There are some still that require pressing and drying. If we may spread them out——"

"But——" I tried again, but Mrs. Padre attacked me on the flank.

"It won't take long, Mr. Cock."

"Cook, my dear, Mr. Cook," corrected the Padre.

"I'm sorry," said wifey, humbly, "it won't take long, dear Mr. Cook, and Urag, our head coolie, is so quick and clever. We'll help him and it won't take long."

What could I do but give way gracefully? So the wide passage from my dining-room to the kitchen, the verandahs outside all the bedrooms, and even the rooms themselves became a drying ground and museum of orchids. Behind each case squatted a native. In front of him arose a pile of straggly, weedy flowers, and all around there grew a litter of dirt.

In the midst of it all the Sergeant came up to make his nightly report. The hour was 8 p.m.! I began to get desperate. Would my guests never change and bathe? Well if they wouldn't I would, so I left them, stealing quietly and unobtrusively away to my bedroom. Over my bath I lingered. Lingered still longer over my dressing; tied and retied my bow. But still no sounds of splashing came from their bath-room. At last I could linger no longer. I went out. They were as I had left them, just as they had arrived some four hours earlier.

"Padre," I cried cheerily, "you must excuse me, I simply had to have a bath and change. Come and have a 'Gin-Pahit' (gin and bitters)."

He seemed horrified, and wifey looked pained, so,

with a muttered apology, I had to drink alone. I felt "one" was necessary. The night was damp and cheerless, and my guests were not exactly lively. I would have liked to have quoted St. Paul to them both, but felt such an action would have infringed good taste.

And the orchid pressing continued. I walked about —looking here, looking there, making a remark or two, attempting a joke and all the time feeling hungrier and hungrier, and more and more fatuous. In the kitchen Cookie was becoming restive as he saw the efforts of his labour getting spoilt; my boys were looking glummer and glummer as the minutes ticked on.

At length action became imperative.

"Boy," I called out, "bawah makan." (Bring in dinner; literally, bring food.)

He did so with alacrity. But, even then, with the soup getting colder and colder every minute, I had to drag my guests away from their orchids.

I sat down and was about to gulp my third spoonful of soup when I realised that matters were not as usual. Of course I had put my foot in it. As the saying goes, "I was up to the fetlocks in the consommé." There was a pained silence, a sort of "Oh, how could you!" atmosphere. I looked up quickly and the soup spilt itself out of that third spoon. Mrs. Padre was sitting with folded hands on her breast, and her eyes upraised to the ceiling. The Padre was standing. His hands too were folded on his chest; his eyes too sought the ceiling.

"Sorry, Padre," I mumbled, and my hands became clasped over my soup plate, and my eyes looked steadily down on the soup growing colder and colder.

For what seemed an age there was silence, then the Chaplain found his voice and said grace.

Then he sat down and the meal ran its course. But

there was no lingering over coffee, for the orchids called insistently.

Just as they were finished the Padre came across to me.

" About to-morrow," he said: " wifey and I must get on to Jesselton. Can you assist with coolies ? "

I replied I had already arranged matters with the Sergeant. Coolies would carry their barang (luggage) to Mengkabong ; boats would be waiting to take them the rest of the journey.

" There's no climbing, or walking, or mud," I added, " so you'll be all right as regards clothes ; you can arrive spotless."

" And payment ? " the Padre asked. " How much is it ? I'd like to pay you."

" Oh, the clerk at Mengkabong attends to the transport, he'll pay the coolies, if you'll settle with him on th way down."

" I'd rather pay now," he insisted, " to-morrow is Sunday and I never pay money on Sunday if I can help it."

There was no arguing with such a man, or against such a cast-iron creed, so I roughly calculated the charges at 50 cts. a coolie—there would be three sets of them—and took the money.

" Heavens, Padre ! " I cried a moment later. " It's after eleven o'clock and you've a long journey in front of you to-morrow. How about a little bed ? "

He acquiesced after appealing to wifey, and we went to our different rooms.

Just as I was falling off to sleep and beginning to dream that I was being crushed to death by the long tentacles of an enormous orchid a strange and unusual sound penetrated my room. Was I dreaming or awake ?

Was I really being crushed to death and was the blood singing and surging in my ears as the last breath left my body ? Down, down, down my soul seemed to be sinking ; tighter, tighter, tighter the tentacles coiled around me ; louder and louder grew that strange and distant sound. In despair I made a frantic effort. I would not die. I found myself sitting up in bed. My knees were almost in my chin ; my hands were locked together ; my whole body rigid with emotion as I listened. And the sound came from the spare-room—stealing across the passage and pervading my room. I listened. The tension relaxed and I sank back on my pillow. I closed my eyes and understood. They—the Padre and his Mem—were singing, and the burden of their song took me back for a fleeting moment to my childhood's days of Sunday-school, for they sang " There is a green hill far away." I smiled perhaps a little wanly, wearily and cynically—then, fell asleep.

Morning broke radiantly fine ; a morning of hope, promise and glorious sunshine. How blue and sparkling would be the sea in Gantisan bay ! How the sand would glitter and wink and twinkle in the sunlight ! How gently would the waves caress the sloping beach !

Such were my thoughts as I " tubbed " and dressed. Then they fled with the suddenness of the fairies at the approach of man. And in their place there rang in my ears two tuneless voices, with pronounced American accents, singing " New every morning is the love."

But as host I must smile and hide my feelings, so, at breakfast, I greeted my guests cheerily. I had schooled myself for anything, and it was a wise precaution for they emerged, both of them, just as they had retired on the previous night. The same clothing, and the same mud !

Later, from the garden gate, I waved them on their

way, and as I re-entered my " boy " met me. On his arm he carried two stained and filthy sheets, stained with the dye of " Kayu asap " (a grey colour) cloth ; filthy with the mud of jungle and kerbau wallows.

" Tuan . . ." he began haltingly.

I looked at the sheets, then at him, and speech failed.

" They didn't even change, Tuan," he murmured.

" So it seems, Uto, so it seems. Burn them both at once." I flung myself down into a long chair and closed my eyes in an attempt to capture once again the vision of the golden sun, the sparkling deep blue sea and glittering sand at Gantisan Bay.

Tuaran and the Estate were so close to, and accessible from Jesselton that the " jaded city workers " were fond of making an excuse for week-end visits, and there would generally be someone staying with me, and on such occasions as a football match—North Keppel versus Jesselton—the house would be filled to overflowing.

To the Jesselton folk the Tamu always proved a certain lure. It always struck me as a curious fact to find so many people who had lived longer in the country than I so ignorant of native customs and handiwork. Yet I suppose such ignorance is not really strange, for, even in a small town like Jesselton, life for the white people runs along more or less accepted European lines, and English is more often spoken than Malay. There are always tennis, bridge and poker ; there is the Club to be visited daily ; there is the routine of " calling " and tea-parties ; there are the ordinary social amenities to be considered and to occupy one's mind. Whereas in a district the D.O. is generally alone. His daily and hourly life brings him in constant contact with natives. Sometimes, in some districts, for several months on end he may not meet another white man, and excepting for conversations over the telephone he may not even hear English spoken. Books and papers have been read and re-read. Ultimately the district and the natives creep into his being. Unconsciously he learns and listens to their superstitions; thinks and feels from their point of view. Somehow or other he gets to know the cleverest cloth-weavers, the soundest planters; a certain old woman, and she only typifies for him a certain kind of pottery; so-and-so above all others has the greatest knowledge of local folk-lore. A certain village is noted for its mats; another for its "basongs"; in another are two "Gusi"—the sacred jars peculiar to North Keppel—and the festival known as "Mandikan Gusi" (the Bathing of the Gusi) will shortly take place.

I do not think many people in the territory have witnessed the ceremony of "Mandikan Gusi." I have never seen the full ceremony myself, but was privileged on one occasion to attend part of the festival.

I knew the festival was about to be celebrated, as for days preparations had been made. From my garden I had contributed the leaves of a certain Croton (plant) much beloved on such occasions for decorative purposes.

The Commissioner of Lands, and a keen student of natives and their customs, was staying with me. It was, therefore, with pleasurable anticipation that we set out one night for a house across the Tuaran river at Kampong Buayer, made famous in St. John's book on Borneo as the scene of a "Mandikan Gusi," and the richest house in the district.

The house according to custom was built well off the ground and was about thirty yards in length. Under it were tethered kerbaus and goats. We climbed the steps, hewn out of a solid log of wood, and entered. The house was as many others. Down the entire centre ran a passage of about four feet in width. On the left, and raised a little above the passage, was a platform running the full length of the house. On the right were six or eight rooms, each the apartment of some family comprising the inmates of the house. From out of each of these rooms smoke arose and curled up into the attap roof. The smell of cooking smote the air. The house was teeming with people and the doors of the rooms kept opening and shutting as the inmates passed in and out.

Down the full length of the platform squatted, in alternate numbers, young men and women. In the hands of the men, which rested in those of the women, were eggs. All were dressed in gala clothes. Just below them, on the left hand side of the passage, were the Gusi which once, according to legend, were human beings, but now expatiating their sinful desires and broken pledges as lifeless jars, and round which native superstition has woven a romantic sacredness. It was in honour of these the festival was being held.

There is nothing actually in the colour, size or shape of these jars to account for their excessive value, which may be as much as \$6,000.^{00}, yet, to the Dusuns of Tuaran, they are nearly priceless. So valuable are they that no one individual, often not even one family, is the sole possessor of a jar. They are heirlooms that have been handed down for countless generations, and are the possessors of spirits good and bad that must be placated.

Though the spirit of evil is powerful it is interesting to note that even a pagan race like the Dusuns ultimately gives supremacy to the Spirit of Good.

There is a priesthood of the Gusi, and the priests are old women. Young girls are admitted into the priesthood as Novitiates, and only become priestesses as vacancies arise owing to natural causes.

The Commissioner and I were courteously received by the owner of the house, and provided with chairs. Around us stood and squatted a crowd of natives. Then, to the accompaniment of gongs and gandang, various natives danced in turn in a cleared space of the passage. This went on for several hours. Every now and then an old woman would wipe the mouth of a Gusi ; every now and then a young woman from the platform would retire, but the men sat on in stony, stolid silence, with their eyes mostly fixed on the eggs in their hands. Every now and then one of the resin-torches would peter out and be replaced ; every now and then someone would stagger in under a fresh supply of Tapai.

It was not exceedingly interesting to watch, so, as the air became more and more fetid with the mixture of smells so distinctive of a mass of natives congregated in the limited space of a native house ; as the room grew smokier and smokier with clouds of Dusun and Javanese tobacco smoke from cigarettes and pipes ; as the Tapai fumes became stronger and stronger and the beating of the gongs grew less and less regular, and the dancers' steps more uncertain, we thought it time to return to home, especially as the next day the Commissioner had a long journey to Kota Belud in front of him. So we left, not much wiser, but a good deal sleepier, than we arrived.

As we descended the rough-hewn steps how we opened our mouths and lungs and drank in the cool, pure air ! It was like plunging into a deep jungle-hidden pool after hours and hours upon a dusty road under the scorching, blinding, tropical sun.

But even more attractive to the Jesseltonites than the Tamu was the promise of a Deer Drive. It mattered nothing to many of them that they knew little of a rifle, were atrociously bad shots and were even less accustomed to horses. To ride and shoot and hunt was the thing! And think what "copy" it would give them to write home to their adoring people at Wimbledon or Clapham, at Tooting, Brixton or Finsbury Park! One visitor, I remember, was offended because I especially procured for him a pony from a Chinese shopkeeper, and paid for the hire myself rather than lend him one of mine. He failed to understand that I strongly resented seeing my pony's mouth sawed about in a manner well calculated to file its teeth. He saw no reason either to my objection to his bumping up and down in the saddle till the pony's back was one raw wound. He scoffed when I told him that any animal he rode would be out of action for a month, and muttered something about "soft-hearted fool, and animals were meant for the use of man."

Just such people as these see no beauty in a doe bounding along in the tall, thick "lalang" followed by its young. They see no poetry in the stately stride of a stag as it threads its way through the jungle to reach a limpid stream that it may quench its thirst. They see no majesty in a herd of Temadu, as, at the approach of the hunter, all heads are raised with ears alert and nostrils wide distended.

Excitement and novelty are all they want. But there must be no danger and they must be comfortable. They must ride to the spot chosen for the "drive." They must sit under the shade of a tree. Their Thermos flasks must be full; their beer must be cold. They must have time to adjust their sights and take a long steady aim, or—well—the deer drive is a failure; the wretched animal broke in the wrong direction; those damned natives were so slack—they didn't even know their job—they didn't yell nearly enough, and their dogs were no use at all. Miss the animal? Didn't even get a shot, the infernal rifle—a .303 borrowed from the constabulary—misfired—the usual rotten ammunition supplied by Government! Heat?—the beastly district was like an oven, the bridle paths were in a disgusting state, and the bridges were rotten. The whole bally show from beginning to end was bungled, absolutely bungled; no system, no order, no control. Now, if only the speaker had been in charge!

Such is the story they tell their friends on their return; such is their gratitude for efforts at hospitality!

Personally I never was very partial to deer drives; they always seemed too set, and frequently, I admit, the deer did break in the wrong direction. As an outing or picnic they were fun, but from a hunting point of view they were not so successful.

A quiet evening stroll with a gun and a bearer was more to my liking, and many is the evening I have wandered round the boundary fences of Tuaran Estate with the manager and rarely have we returned home empty-handed, for pig and deer abound in Tuaran if only hunted at the right time.

One evening in particular is indelibly branded on my memory. The manager and I were out together. He was carrying an old snider, I was using a double barrelled shot-gun loaded with buck shot. We had been threading our way through some dense undergrowth, and suddenly emerged into a tiny open glade. Down its centre gently trickled a small stream of clear, sparkling water, babbling over its stony bed. The grass was short, sweet and wonderfully green, the turf soft and springy. From somewhere in the jungle the stream came, and to somewhere in the jungle it went. But just in this spot, its waters were kissed by the sun and the moon and the stars. The clear, green banks embraced it; and withered blossoms of blood-red hybiscus, and yellow oleander, their short life of beauty and perfume over, fell into its waters to be borne away into the unknown through jungle and plain.

The shadows of the mighty trees that stood like sentinels over the glade were lengthening on the grass. The sparkle of the water was dying out as the setting sun slid slowly, almost reluctantly, behind the western jungle. The rising moon had not yet topped and cleared the eastern wall of tropic growth.

Involuntarily we paused and gazed around us. Beauty held us spell-bound—not with an overmastering emotion of tenseness or passionate vitality, but with a sense of fragrant purity and peace, a feeling so exquisite and gossamer, so light and yet so poignant that it seemed as if, for a moment, we ceased to live and breathe on earth ; as if some fairy-wand had been waved over us and transported us to Paradise.

As we gazed the branches at the far end of the glade parted, and a stag stepped out. For a second he stood still, his beautiful head held erect ; and the moon just topping the jungle, as the dying rays of the sun cast their last long shadows, kissed the tips of his splendid antlers.

Slowly, proudly, trustingly, he stepped towards the stream. As I watched I found myself trembling, so exquisite was the enchantment of the scene.

We had come to hunt. Here was our quarry, delivered into our hands. It was the manager's shot, and he could not miss. Would he shoot ? I watched. The manager stood immovable, and the stag came nearer and nearer, till, at length, he reached the water's edge. His fore-feet were in the stream, and slowly he lowered his head. I could not see, yet I could sense his mouth and nostrils lightly bathing and battling with the gentle stream, the little waves breaking themselves against the soft dark nose and sending small showers of spray over the broad deep forehead. The arched neck, the splendid shoulders, the long sleek back and sides, the magnificent quarters—all were exposed to view. Then as his playful mood passed I could see the water, as he drank, going gulp by gulp down the slender throat and his sides gently heaving in response.

Over the top of the trees came the half crescent moon, a pale band of silver in a sky still radiating the light of a buried sun. From the jungle came the cry of a night-jar; the hoot of an owl disturbed the peace; at our feet rose the voice of the crickets. Then, for a second—one fleeting moment—silence. Then the bark of a deer close at hand. Was it the call of the stag's mate? Was she too coming to drink or did she feel a presage of coming evil? Did her quickened senses tell her of our presence? Did she seek to warn her mate? I do not know to this day, but I watched.

At the bark the stag raised his head, and the water dropped like diamonds from his lips. His ears alert, he listened. Slowly the manager raised his rifle. Into his shoulder he nestled the butt. His finger caressed and curved round the trigger.

I watched the slow and steady pressure—no pull, but the relentless pressure of the experienced hunter—and waited, trembling, as though I were gun-shy. But no report came. There was a click—the cartridge had misfired.

But faint as the click had been the stag had heard the sound. He half wheeled round, winded and saw us, and, with a bound, sprang straight for the jungle.

The spell was broken. The manager had missed. He was fumbling for another cartridge; fumbling wildly in his haste, and the deer had nearly reached the jungle.

I raised my rifle and my finger pressed the trigger. Suddenly I collapsed in a heap on the grass—a cold sweat breaking out all over me. In my hands I limply held the rifle, and I was trembling in every limb. Thank God I had not fired. Thank God! For I was loaded with buck-shot and the manager, a few feet away, was in the line of fire. The shot would not have had time to spread. Thank God I had not fired!

Then there came a report that broke the stillness of the glade; a cry of " Kena " (hit) from the native bearer, and, on the edge of the jungle, with eyes fast glazing in death, lay the stag.

Stillness—a brooding heavy peace—the silver crescent of the moon veiled by a fleecy cloud. The bark of a deer—was it the dead stag's mate?—sounded near; then, from a distance, it came again. And the manager, oblivious of his narrow escape, crossed over to gaze upon his trophy.

CHAPTER V

KOTA BELUD

A FEW weeks later found me in Kota Belud—the smaller district, which, with Tuaran, forms the district known as North Keppel.

The District Officer had gained well-merited promotion, had been transferred to Kudat as Resident, and his place was taken by another, who, for his sins—chiefly, I am afraid, an unconquerable laziness—had been reduced in rank to a D.O. With him was his wife, one of the most loyal and charming women I had met in B.N.B. Kota Belud was considered too wild and too far from headquarters and civilisation for a white woman, so the new D.O. and his Mem were stationed at Tuaran, and the old régime of stationing the junior officer at Kota Belud once again took place.

The change this time was not so complete an upheaval as from the Interior to Semporna, or Semporna to Tuaran, for the natives were similar, and the country, save for being more open, very much the same. Yet there is a distinct difference, and a different appeal in Kota Belud. From whence it is born I know not, unless it is cradled in the stony lap of the topmost peak of Kinabalu.

Law and order, peace and contentment, prosperity and agriculture, were the dominant notes of Tuaran. The plains were well tilled ; the hills rose gradually around

KOTA BELUD, LOOKING NORTH. THE DISTANT HILLS RUN DOWN TO THE SEA.

p. 142

Kinabalu ; Jesselton was close ; the paternal eye of Government seemed ever watching the district ; watching, not with a vague apprehensiveness, but with the gaze of proud achievement. An English Eastern county, with scattered villages ; with one or two large industrial centres (the three Estates) ; with a few embryonic garden villages (the Chinese settlement) : such was the atmosphere of Tuaran.

But Kota Belud breathed a more virile and turbulent spirit. As I climbed the dividing range of hills, and halted my pony for a rest at the last upward bend, I saw before me the new district spreading out. On my left the sea at the edge of a plain ; in front more plain, then rolling hills, and in the distance the great plain of Tempasuk, with the Krah swamp in its centre. On my right high hills, and yet more hills that covered and hid the small and smiling valleys in between. High up in the sky a dense grey cloud that I felt rather than knew must be enfolding Kinabalu. A district turbulent, restless and lawless yet tractable and affectionate, so I had been told. A district to be ruled but not driven ; to be inspired but not cajoled. A district to be won and well worth the winning—Kota Belud—the Hill Fort.

I looked back. Tuaran was out of sight. But the village and Estate of Tengilan were winking in the sunlight. Another chapter of my life was closed, and I was about to begin a new one.

Was I sorry ? Had I any regrets ? Perhaps, and perhaps not. Tuaran was so very close to Jesselton, and the red-tape tentacles and the telephone were always stretching out, and during the last few months I had, in one way and another, fallen foul of some of the Authorities' pet ideas and notions.

I gathered the reins in my hand, dug my heels into

my pony's side, and left Tuaran behind. In front lay Kota Belud, a new and unknown district. It breathed a spirit of adventure and a freer, less trammelled life. So I went forward to a new romance—to live under the very shadow of the Solitary Father, Mount Kinabalu.

And as the months sped I came to understand and realise how the spell of the mountain gripped the natives. For just as it dominates the lives of the natives, and especially the hill Dusuns, who live on and around its lower slopes, so to me, in spite of possible faults in etymology, its name will always mean the Solitary Father.*

Unconsciously the mountain wove itself into my life and thoughts; unconsciously, when difficulties or perplexities beset me, I sought its might and solidity. Each morning, on waking, my first thought would be, "I must look at Kinabalu"; each night, ere getting into bed, my last action would be a long and earnest gaze at the mountain. Almost I took my prayers, hopes and fears to it. It breathed majesty, strength, and beauty. Towering above its fellows of three thousand feet it reared its head another ten thousand feet. The same and yet not the same, for the sunshine and the moonlight would clothe it in different garments of various hues, now shining black or dull dark green, now deepest, glinting purple, or pale slate blue; now shining silver or burnished gold. And at times lost; wrapped up and blotted out in blanket upon blanket of dark, black-grey clouds and torrents of rain.

---

* Major Owen Rutter was, I think, the first to propound the theory as to the origin of the name—Kinabalu. The A of Aki, he suggests, has been dropped for the sake of euphony, while "na" is the favourite prefix used by Dusuns for a similar purpose. Personally I prefer his suggestions to any others that are current.—O. C.

Ak=iFather in Dusun.

Balu=Solitary. Na is merely a euphonism.

The river may be a swollen, raging, mud-thick torrent that has burst its banks, and is flooding the padi-fields and "lalang" plains. The trees may be bending and snapping under a hurricane of wind. Then follows a stillness, save for the roar of the river and splash of the rain; then, sheet upon sheet of vivid, purple lightning and the crash and boom, echoing and re-echoing among the hills, of thunder claps as they burst hard upon each other ere the noise of one has died to silence. And Kinabalu stands alone; its mighty head the first to meet this tempest of storm and rain.

"Aki! Aki!" The words are torn from me and I cover my eyes from the blackness and fury that are raging round that mighty, solitary form.

As I look the lightning ceases and the thunder rolls no more. Slower and less fiercely the rain falls down; the clouds begin to break; over the heavens spreads a bow of many colours, its ends just resting on the earth. The song of a bird once more reaches my ear; the lowing of cattle and the bleating of goats is borne upon the air. Lighter and lighter grows the sky; paler and paler the darkness, till all the heavens are once more blue. Only the river is still in spate; muddy, dark and turbulent. Only one huge great cloud is hanging in the heavens, locked in its death struggle with the Solitary Presence.

How strange it is that with this mountain at their very doors so few people living in Borneo have ever climbed it. Two only that I know of—Messrs. W. H. L. Bunbury and D. R. Maxwell—have scaled its peaks, and even their ascents were under Government orders, for the former was attached to a Naval Survey Party, and the latter upon a botanical expedition.

But this neglect was soon to be remedied, and due homage paid to the mighty, towering sentinel that stands, as it were, guardian over the territory, blessing it with copious rains, enduing it with fragrant, cool, wind-swept nights, for out of a laughing suggestion of mine to a padre and his wife that they should spend their Easter vacation with me, at Kota Belud, and climb the mountain, the idea grew till it became a fixed determination, and, in the end, an accomplished fact.

May 13th, 1916, was the date we three started on our trip. By 7 a.m. all our luggage, transported on three pack-bullocks and twelve coolies, was under way, accompanied by two boys, the cook and a private of the constabulary. We three, mounted on my ponies, followed an hour later.

The first seven miles of the road were flat as the path follows the course of the Kadamaian river, so we made good time to Tamu Darat. Here a halt was called for tiffin, and a lie-off during the heat of the day. By 2 p.m. the luggage was again under way on the eleven miles' journey to Kabaiau, a small village situated on the left bank of the river, where there was a small Government rest-house—a building constructed chiefly of bamboo, and roofed with attaps, as are many others at convenient distances along bridle paths, or native tracks—for the use of district officers when on rounds in their districts.

In spite of having travelled during the cool of the declining day we were hot and dusty, for the last six miles of the path had followed the crests of the hills, and frequently reached an altitude of 1,000 feet. So, though the sun had set and the moon was shining when we reached Kabaiau, our first and common thought was a bathe in the river; to lie at the foot of some boulder over which the moon-kissed water was breaking in silver cascades.

Then a camp dinner; a final cigarette over a desultory, happy conversation—and bed. Is there any bed in the world to equal a camp-bed, stretched on the bamboo floor of a tiny rest-house, in the heart of a tropical country? Is there any peace to equal that of such nights as we spent in Kabaiau? The music of the rushing, falling river; the sigh and rustle of the encircling jungle; the whisper of the wind in the mighty trees; the cry of the night-jar; the hoot of an owl; the bark of a deer; the chirping of crickets; an occasional laugh from our coolies; the snoring of our sleeping policeman; the stealthy movements of our tethered ponies; the scrunch, scrunch of the bullocks as they slowly, methodically chewed the cud! Never utter silence. Yet a sense of solitude and peace; a sense of having shed the garments of civilisation, of wars, rancours, bickerings and strife; a sense of being enfolded in the arms and resting deep in the lap of Mother Nature.

But Nature is an exacting mother and six o'clock found the first rays of dawn streaming through the lattice-work windows of our tiny house. From the back quarters came a babel of voices and the smell of cooking as our coolies prepared their early morning meal.

Hardly had I finished stretching when Uto, my "boy," came and announced that tea was ready. I plunged my head into a canvas camp basin. Then, luxuriously inhaling the first cigarette of the day, I went out on to the tiny verandah that overlooked the river. From an adjoining room came a ripple of laughter, the patter of feet and "Peter," as I christened and was allowed henceforth to call her, in an adorable kimono and boudoir cap, joined me, to be followed almost at once by the Padre.

There was no need for us to hurry as Kaung, our next halting place, was only eleven miles away. So we lingered over our tea and bathed at leisure, waiting for the sun to top the jungle that we might feel its rays benignly shining down upon us as we clambered over rocks and boulders in search of undiscovered pools and tiny waterfalls.

In a way I was loath to move on for Kabaiau was very beautiful. I always seem loath to leave one place for another. Yet I knew Kaung was even more delightful and the Padre and Peter were longing to start the real ascent of the mountain, which would not be till after we left Kiau, the last village on its lower slopes. So reluctantly, as is my way, I gave orders for the luggage to move on, and half an hour later we three followed.

Though riding, our pace was but little quicker than the coolies, for travelling on the hill roads is limited to about three miles an hour, since the everlasting twisting and turning of the narrow stony path, intercepted and cut with gullies and culverts, gradually rising, as it frequently does, to an altitude of 2,000 feet, makes cantering almost impossible.

The sun was at its zenith when we reached Kaung. For some time, as our path wound round the contour of the hills, we had seen the tiny spot below us in the distance. For Kaung, like Kabaiau nestles on the banks of the river, whereas our path was ever leading us upward to the slopes of Kinabalu.

As we slowly descended the zig-zag path we felt the difference in temperature ; we lost the cool breeze that fanned our faces, gaining in its place a gentle and persuasive warmth.

"Look," cried Peter in astonishment, "there's our luggage ! How quick the coolies have been."

"Yes," I answered ; "they took short cuts up and down the sides of the hills, crossing and re-crossing the river—no contour paths for the Dusuns !"

Just then we emerged upon the level ground that stretched from the foot of the hill to the river bank.

" Come on," I cried, " I'll race you for the odd sausage in the Crosse and Blackwell's tin, which we are going to have for lunch."

With a laugh Peter, not even waiting to accept the challenge, darted ahead of me ; but I was not dismayed at the start she gained, for she was mounted on " Hitchyban "—my favourite hack, a beautiful glossy black of 13 hands—whereas I was riding " Shooting Star," a racing pony of some promise. But I had overlooked the shortness of the distance and the lightness of Peter's weight, and so forfeited the sausage, for " Hitchyban " passed the door of the rest-house a winner by a short head to the accompaniment of shrieks of delight as our coolies scattered in all directions.

Laughingly Peter descended and handed the reins to my No. 1 syce, who was as proud as a peacock over his favourite's win. He loved " Hitchy " almost as much as I did, and for a Bajau was wonderfully tender with the ponies. He was one of the few native syces I have met, whom I felt I could absolutely trust to place mine and the ponies' interests before his own.

Lunch followed as a matter of course, though as a matter of fact the Padre and I shared the odd sausage since Peter's appetite proved unequal to the task. To be strictly truthful, I fancy she was reserving herself for the savoury that was to follow. Savoury in the jungle! Why not? There is little a good Chinese cook cannot turn out when he wants to and mine was on his mettle, for I rarely took him on up-country trips, generally preferring to leave him in charge of the house, asserting that in the jungle a Chinaman was more bother than he was worth. " Cookie " therefore was out to prove his salt. Incidentally, I think Peter had found the soft spot in his heart, while I know that he was rather fond of me.

We were not granted a very lengthy siesta for soon after lunch Lumanden, the headman of Kaung, came to pay his respects. He talked a great deal in a desultory fashion, making many remarks to Peter, who actually understood but little Malay. She was the second white woman he had ever seen, and certainly the prettiest. I was interested in watching the impression she made on him, and indeed on all the natives throughout the trip. They were amazed at the idea of any woman attempting to climb Kinabalu; but that a white woman, and one so fragile as Peter—who was the living image of Pauline Chase as Peter Pan—should contemplate such a feat completely passed their comprehension.

At long last Lumanden came to the real and vital point of his visit: "Has the Tuan brought any 'obat'?"* As it happened the Tuan had, so Lumanden's heart was filled with joy at the prospect of dynamiting for fish.

To fishermen this must sound a most heinous offence, but to the natives it is a Godsend, and with luck means a good feed for the village for two or three meals. Incidentally a good deal of sport and fun is provided in the diving for and catching the fish, as comparatively few are killed outright, the majority, being only stunned, quickly regain consciousness though not their full agility.

Unfortunately for the village I threw the first charge in before the fuse was properly alight; while the second, though well alight, for some unaccountable reason failed to explode.

The Dusuns, however, are a cheery people and though there was no feed of fish a dance in our honour was arranged that night in Lumanden's house. The inevitable Tapai was produced and great was Lumanden's sorrow at

* By "obat" he meant dynamite.

"Hitchyban" and "Shooting Star," the Author's Favourite Ponies.

p. 150

Peter's failure to sample his choicest vintage. She appealed to me, but honestly I could not recommend her to drink a drop of Tapai ; I knew Lumanden of old ; he had a head as strong as any man I knew or have ever known, and a palate so coarse and deadened that nothing but the most potent and fiery of liquids would tickle at all. So Peter, and the Padre also, compromised and drank coconut water direct out of the nut, with the result to their clothes that can well be imagined. There is nothing much more difficult, till the trick is learned, than to drink out of a coconut without spilling the water all down one's chest.

The hour was late when we left the village and crossed the river to return to the rest-house, but it was of little consequence. There was no need for an early start on the morrow since Kiau, our next resting place and furthermost base, was but two hours' walk distant.

At Kaung we were to leave the ponies and pack-bullocks till our return and here also we were to make our first change of coolies. As a rule I always rather dreaded changing coolies, for there was always the possibility of the required number failing to turn up, which meant a delay in getting off " on the road " while the recalcitrant coolie was being found or a substitute provided. But no such friction ever occurred at Kaung, for Lumanden was a very sound headman and possessed of authority. But a greater factor than Lumanden's authority was the alacrity always shown by the inhabitants themselves.

I always made it a rule to order the coolies to be in readiness an hour before the time of starting. Such precautions, however, were never necessary at Kaung. Dawn found the rest-house surrounded and besieged by a laughing, chattering crowd of Dusun women, waiting, and struggling with the keenness of bargain-hunters, to carry our loads.

I knew what to expect, so I was not surprised at the noise that greeted us on waking; but the Padre's and Peter's astonishment at seeing female porters was amusing to witness. Some of the women, indeed, seemed too frail to carry our heavy loads, yet they made no fuss about the weight and carried their burdens as easily and quickly as men.

"Loading up" at Kaung always fascinated me. There was nearly always the same crowd of women and I got to know their names and peculiarities. Some of them were coy and some very shy, some were as bold as brass, others frankly uninterested in me. After a time, when I had made several journeys through Kaung, the fixing up my loads became almost a matter of habit; the same loads always being carried by the same women. Once or twice I missed a familiar face and enquiries would elicit the fact that the absent one had married and left the village, or that another had just presented her lord and master with a baby, but that the Tuan had promised on his next visit to give her both an empty sausage and empty cigarette tin—items much prized and of inestimable value —and she hoped I hadn't forgotten.

So she had the large Crosse and Blackwell tin and the Padre emptied out his tin of "Capstans" and we were about to start, when nothing would satisfy Peter but that she must go and see the new-born babe and proud mother.

But at last we got under way and in due time reached Kiau, after a walk of just over two hours along an easily graded path that ultimately reached a height of 2,900 feet.

The Padre and Peter, agog to commence the real ascent, were all for an immediate start. Such, however, was quite impossible for now the really serious business of the trip had to be considered. New coolies—Kiauites—had to be engaged ; the headman of the village had to be interviewed ; terms for our transportation and guidance had to be settled ; the coolies had to prepare food for a five days' trip, while finally the " Fates "—in the shape of Kinaringan the Dusun deity who presides over Kinabalu —had to be propitiated.

There is no denying that, if necessary, all these arrangements could have been made in one day, but the powers that reigned in Kiau had no wish to start the ascent until the second day after our arrival, so I urged and counselled my friends to patience and they wisely forbore to press their point.

Time, to the extent of a day or so, was no object to us. What was to be gained then by pressing our point of view in contradiction to that of the natives ? Why run counter to their wishes over a matter so momentous to them as an ascent of their almost sacred mountain ? Nothing was to be gained by so doing. And to add weight to the villagers' desires for the full observance of all ritual, Umpoh—who was spokesman and guide—told how six months previous an American and his wife (they were my friends the orchid fiends) had gone up the mountain without regard to the natives' advice and desires for full preparations, with the result that their Chinese " boy " had died on the journey !

We passed the enforced day's idleness in walking from Kiau to Singarun and back, treating the trip as a preliminary canter to the real hard work of climbing the mountain. Singarun, at an altitude of 3,100 feet, lies on the opposite side of the river from Kiau and to reach it we had to descend to the valley, follow the stream for some distance and then climb again. From the Singarun rest-house is obtained a magnificent view of Kinabalu—when free from clouds—and the smaller hill of Mt. Nunuk, which the Dusuns poetically call Kinabalu's child, and the whole stretch of the Kadamaian valley as far as the sea.

On the way down from Kiau Peter was delighted to find quantities of wild raspberries, and it must be confessed ate rather too lavishly, with the result that on the upward climb the berries had their revenge, and Peter suffered considerable distress. Of water there was none to be obtained nearer than Singarun, so a coolie was sent on to fetch some while we three waited. But the coolie was long in returning, so the Padre went ahead to see what had become of him. Like the coolie he did not return either, so finally Peter and I climbed on slowly, reaching the rest-house just as a very cowed coolie and an indignant Padre turned up, each bearing a couple of bamboos filled with water.

Just then rain began to fall ; the clouds rolling up the valley like the onset of a London fog, blotting out the landscape and enveloping us in their thick folds. Then the rain came down in torrents and in this tropical downpour we had eventually to make our return journey. But in spite of the wet our spirits would not be damped, for to-morrow was to witness the commencement of our ascent.

The morning broke fine and seven o'clock found us all ready to start. Those to essay the trip were Peter, the Padre, myself, our two boys, the cook, Umpoh the guide, Lumanden, Baiaiai—one versed in prayers acceptable to Kinaringan—Tambaga the son of Sumpot, headman of Kiau, who was himself too old to accompany us, my dog Bob and thirteen coolies under the charge of the private of the constabulary.

By 7.15 a.m. we were under way, descending the mountain side from Kiau to the valley beneath—whence the route for the first day lay—following up the course of the Kadamaian river practically to its source. On the lower slopes of the hills stretched the Dusun plantations, basking in the sun and well stocked with Kladi—a species of potato—with ubi kaya (tapioca), bananas, papyres and native tobacco. It is interesting to note that the reports of those who first ascended Kinabalu make no mention of papyres growing at Kiau, so it is reasonable to suppose that the seeds were planted from fruit brought by these early travellers.

After a time we left the plantations behind us and proceeded along the bed of the river, climbing from boulder to boulder ; crossing and re-crossing the stream as it twisted and turned. One minute the right bank would rise sheer to a height of several hundred feet, the next minute the left. Then, at a bend of the river, we came to a standstill with a gasp of amazement, for the gorge had suddenly narrowed to a width of little more than ten yards, and on each side cliffs rose up to a height of about one hundred and fifty feet, forming in very truth a gateway to Kinabalu, a door to the Halls of Kinaringan, the Home of all dead Dusuns. Rumour has it that in days long gone by, the tops of those two cliffs overhung and so nearly met that a man might jump from one to the other. If such were the case then the effect must have been even more wonderful than it is to-day.

Up this gorge we continued for some time, then eventually left the river bed and started to climb up the side of the cliff. In places the ascent was so steep that footholds had to be found in twisted roots and creepers that grew out of the rock ; in other places the track crept sideways along the slopes over a path hardly nine inches wide ; but always and ever upwards till we reached the first day's halting ground—Lobung—at an altitude of about 4,500 feet.

No friendly rest-house was expected or found here, only, as the name Lobung curiously implies in Malay, a cave. And cave is really a misnomer, for Lobung is nothing more than a huge mass of overhanging rock, under which there is shelter from the wind and rain from all quarters save the west.

Here at noon we pitched our camp: the coolies at one end; the "boys" and cookie in the middle; we three at the other end. Just below us was a small mountain stream. All around was jungle. Every now and then could be heard the bark of a deer, and occasionally the call and answer of Kijang, but we never actually saw any game, though the jungle was quite thin owing to the altitude and possibly to the fact that it has been systematically worked over by the Dusuns in search of jungle produce.

That night we began to taste our first experience of cold, and at 5 a.m. next morning I think we would have promised cookie and the boys anything they liked to ask of us when they brought us our early morning tea. Just our noses peeped out over the blankets, and having quickly gulped our tea we snuggled back into our beds again, curled up like kittens, while waiting for a second cup. I could hear the two "P's" having a whispered conversation. I saw the Padre nod his head in an authoritative manner and Peter's answering shake. Then they both caught my gaze and our eyes travelled to the little stream—and then we shuddered. I confess I did not exactly jump at the idea of cold water or rather perhaps the combination of cold air and cold water and yet—well it had to be, for if we funked this stream whatever would we do higher up the mountain.

I seized hold of my blankets; the Padre did likewise,

and Peter snuggled the closer among hers. How we envied her, but her turn was to come and she must bathe alone !

" Are you ready, Padre ? " I cried.

" Yes," came his answer, but it wasn't a very ready reply.

" Then, one, two, three," I sang out, and flung off those blankets, seized my towel and raced for the stream. The Padre won—he was a long, loose-limbed built fellow —but he was also the first back to camp, over which I unmercifully chaffed him as we put the finishing touches to our toilets.

Thus we braved the stream and had our reward in a steaming hot breakfast of porridge and sausages and coffee.

After breakfast, amid the bustle of striking camp, the first of the three misfortunes of the trip happened. The Padre lost his pipe, the only one he had brought with him ! In fairness to him I must say he bore his loss most stoically, and when it is remembered what a pipe is to an inveterate pipe smoker I really think that his subsequent good nature throughout the trip was little short of marvellous.

If in parts the previous day's climb had been arduous to-day's was much more so, and after four hours' hard slogging I was horrified to find, in answer to my plaintive query, that half-way had by no means been reached. Such a blow had to be met with some sort of solace, so I shouted to my boy to bring some cold tea. But there was no cold tea—mishap number two—for cookie had forgotten to make any. I was almost forgetting the presence of the Padre, not to mention Peter, when she threw oil upon the troubled waters by a reminder that " Tommy's cooker " was in one of the boy's haversacks. It was, but a cooker however useful at other times proves only an insult to injury when no water is procurable. So after half an hour's rest and an " attack " upon tinned tongue " washed down " with raisins the ascent was continued

By now we were surrounded by a dark thick mist while the route—it could not even be designated a native track—wound up and up among curious bent and overhanging trees, the branches of which were covered with long, hanging moss ever dripping with moisture. It was an eerie and fantastic walk and one to breed wild flights of fancy and dreams—almost I might say nightmares—of a man-eating orchid, whose long, clinging tentacles would reach out and clasp us and draw us into its capacious maw to be sucked down into the very depths of its voracious stomach.

But still no water, only the galling memory of Tommy's cooker and the silent jeer of the Pitcher plants, growing in profusion, as they lifted their heads as much as to say, " There is water in us, but you'd best not drink."

Still we plugged on, though we were all beginning to feel the effects of having had nothing to drink since morning. Silently, doggedly we climbed—gone were our jests and quips—only an occasional question to Umpoh as to how much further passed our lips. And now it commenced to rain, not a gentle shower, but a steady downpour that chilled us all to the bone. I looked at Peter ; she was beginning to show signs of fatigue but gamely walked on. If only the rain would cease matters would not have been so bad, but that steady chilling rain sapped our strength and so greatly added to our discomforts. For the hundredth time we turned a sharp bend and there in front of us appeared a bare rock. " Umpoh," I cried, " how much further ? Is that, that ? . . ."

"Pakha-Pakha," he replied, and I knew we had reached our destination. I looked at my watch: the hands pointed to 3.15. We had been on the road since quarter-past seven.

Fortunately the coolies were not far behind us and ten minutes later our luggage, much of it wet, was being unpacked. But though we had arrived, our troubles were not over, for the wood around was so damp and sodden that it would not properly kindle. Thus Tommy's cooker came into its own.

Curiously enough not one of us three had brought an aneroid, but a rough estimate would put the altitude of Pakha-Pakha at not less than 10,000 feet. At this height the cold was—or seemed—terrific and was intensified by the dampness of the mists which perpetually rolled around the higher points of the mountain. Everything was always more or less wet and clammy, while the fitful flickering fire gave out but little warmth and was frequently doused by the spray from a big waterfall that came roaring down past the mouth of the cave, the volume of its water varying most rapidly according to the rainfall round the top of the mountain.

However, in spite of the hard climb, the rain and the discomforts of the cave, the Padre and Peter were in good fettle and thirsting for the morrow's final ascent. But it cannot be said that I was equally lively, for I was beginning to show signs of mountain sickness, while I was extremely tired and suffered a good deal of pain in my injured left leg.

Early to bed was the order of the day as a start on the morrow had to be made by 6 o'clock in order that we might reach the summit before the mists began to rise from the valleys below and so blot out all prospects of the promised view.

Five-thirty a.m. found us doing our best to do justice to as near a steaming breakfast as cookie could manage, and a few minutes before 6 o'clock found us ready for the start. Umpoh was the last to be ready, but enquiry showed that he was making a final inspection to see that none of their offerings to Kinaringan had been forgotten. Baiaiai carried the fowl, destined first for sacrifice and ultimately for the cooking pot. Tambaga looked after the rice and tobacco. Lumanden carried my gun from which at different times salutes must be fired. Even Peter absorbed some of the spirit of ritual, and carried a few cents as offerings to the mystic deity, of whom the Dusuns seem to know so little yet revere so deeply, and whose abode of many mansions for their departed spirits is the summit of the mountain.

That Kinaringan is a very real deity to the Dusuns is a matter beyond dispute, and I noticed that the further we ascended the quieter became our guides and coolies—while when after an hour and a quarter's climb we emerged from out of the moss-laden jungle on to the bare rock the transition to awed respect was almost completed. A little later at a sign from Baiaiai all chattering ceased as he prepared for the first and minor sacrificial offering and composed himself to raise his voice in prayer. I am afraid that for just a moment the Padre's and Peter's faces showed more signs of amused interest than awe, since Umpoh felt it incumbent to whisper that now we must be prepared to witness the appearance of many spirits.

Plucking two feathers from the tail of the doomed fowl Baiaiai stuck them in the ground. As the second feather was so planted he called in a low voice once, "Aki" (Father). Silence was intense ; expectancy was written on the natives' faces. Then from the hand of Tambaga, Baiaiai took a little rice and while sprinkling it on the ground once again intoned his incantation. As the last grain of rice fell from his hand, once again he raised the cry

Mount Kinabalu, Sandakan, B.N.B.

River Padas.

p. 160

of " Aki." Then for a few moments the silence was unbroken, till Lumanden came over to me and handed me my rifle with the request that two shots should be fired. As the echo of the shots reverberated and re-echoed round the many peaks of the mountain, the sense of mystery seemed to deepen in the minds of the natives.

The ceremony over, the Padre, Peter and I changed from our leather-soled to rubber-soled tennis shoes, in order to get a better footing on the granite slopes, moist and slippery from the mists and dew. The wisdom of this change was amply proved, especially during the descent.

Though we had halted in all for about ten minutes everyone was glad to begin climbing again, for the air at this early hour of the morning was most chilly and the newly-risen sun gave out but little warmth. For nearly three-quarters of an hour we toiled up the slippery slopes —scattering a little as each individual chose his own path. The Padre and Peter were well to the fore ; I, in spite of Umpoh's help, was some way behind. In the end, as we emerged upon an open piece of level rock, I decided to give up all hopes of reaching the summit for I was suffering too much from mountain-sickness and lameness for my continued presence to be anything more than a drag on the party. I wanted my friends to reach the top and gain their heart's desire, and I realised that if they kept to my pace there was small chance of their seeing any view even if we reached the top. So I communicated to them my intention of resting where I was for a little while and then slowly returning to camp. At first they would not hear of my decision but at length I prevailed upon them to see the wisdom of my view. And so for a while we parted. They to ascend—I to limp slowly and painfully back to Pakha-Pakha, where on arrival I went straight to bed.

I was keenly disappointed at my failure, but consoled myself with the thoughts of the nearness of my achievement, and fell asleep in my camp bed dreaming that my name was among those of the immortals who have climbed the mountain and left their names to posterity inside the collection of various bottles that are hidden in a hollow on the topmost peak. And the dream came true for on the Padre's and Peter's return about 12 midday they told me they had inscribed my name along with theirs and placed the glorious record in the care of an Eno's Fruit Salt bottle. If not quite worthy of this highest honour perhaps I may be forgiven the award, since failure meant so much to me !

The ascent was over. The summit reached by two of the party, and now all that was left us was the return journey. But we could not leave that afternoon and hope to reach Lobung before dark, so we rolled ourselves up into as many blankets as possible and yawned and slept the intervening hours away. How the coolies survived the cold and damp we never could make out for not one of them had a blanket, and wood fires, as I have said, gave out but little heat.

Seven-thirty the next morning saw us bid good-bye to Pakha-Pakha, not I am afraid with many regrets. For some time we three kept together and frequently stopped to take in the beauties of some view, but eventually, as the strain of descending began to tell on me, I begged the others to go on alone and let me crawl along at my own snail's pace.

And once again I was justified of my wisdom for I reached Lobung two hours behind the others. And here befell our third mishap, for on my limping into camp I was greeted with cries of " Where's Cookie ? "

Camp and no cookie ! Could anything be more tragic ?

But as the minutes sped on and he came not I began to get anxious, for it appeared that, distressed over my slow progress, the faithful soul had told the Padre he would wait for me. But I had never seen him on my way down, and so as the minutes dragged on and still there was no Cookie I sent out search-parties, one of which eventually brought him in. He was completely done up and shaking like a leaf, and full of a wonderful story of how he had sat down and waited for me, and then suddenly become faint and sleepy and was just falling off to sleep when he was seized upon by a spirit and whisked away to the bottom of a ravine, where the search-party found him. I was sorry for the old thing for in his loyalty to me he had fallen asleep and tumbled down a small precipice and suffered a nasty shaking.

That night my boy turned chef, but we didn't grumble over our food for, after Pakha-Pakha, Lobung seemed a veritable Paradise of warmth. The next day's journey to Kiau seemed mere child's play after the rigours of the one we had so recently undergone.

Yet one more curious incident was to occur before we left the mountain, for we found Sumpot, who was so ill when we left, completely restored to health. We were glad of this, but worried to find a bottle of undiluted Jeyes' Fluid, which with other unnecessary stores had been left behind, missing. To connect Sumpot's recovery with the missing Jeyes' Fluid bottle seemed rather an absurd flight of fancy. Yet it proved a correct conjecture, as Sumpot gleefully informed us he had used the " obat " (medicine) as an external embrocation !

How homelike and civilised the rest-house seemed after the wilds of the mountain ! How perfectly splendid it was to get into dry, clean clothes ! Kinabalu —it is true—presents no great difficulties as a test of mountaineering; yet as a test of endurance and good-fellowship under tropical conditions it may well claim a pre-eminent place.

I think the Padre and Peter would have liked to have spent a few days at Kiau resting after our labours, but the duty of Sunday Church called them back to Jesselton, so we left Kiau the next morning and reached Kaung before breakfast. Here we said good-bye to Lumanden, picked up the ponies and pack-bullocks, and after lunch rode to Kabaiau, where once again we stayed the night. This time the tropic peace was not so pronounced; the sense of solitude was absent, for Kabaiau was a-hum with life. Inside the fence enclosing the rest-house and for a hundred yards up and down the bridle-path flickered some forty or fifty camp fires, round each of which squatted numbers of natives, cooking their evening meal. They were returning to their villages after having attended Tamu Darat. But they were not really disturbing, for soon they rolled themselves up into their sarongs and with any old bundle for a pillow, or with no bundle at all, fell asleep with the stars and sky their only canopy. And by the first faint streaks of dawn next morning not a trace of them was to be seen save the smouldering remains of their fires, for no one appreciates the wisdom of an early start more thoroughly than the Dusun. By 7.15 the rest-house was entirely deserted as we began our last day's journey into Kota Belud.

Here, after a day's rest, I bade good-bye to my guests. For me, most of the travelling was in the nature of my daily work as District Officer, but for the Padre and Peter it was an unusual experience, and I still frequently wonder at the gameness and cheeriness of both, under conditions that were frequently trying and never the acme of comfort; and, like the Dusuns, I marvel at the temerity and stamina of that fragile, golden-haired Peter Pan. I can picture her to this day as she strode gallantly up the mountain slope, in a pair of my khaki shorts—her own riding breeches having proved too cumbersome and heavy at the knees—her golden hair, escaping from her topi (sun-helmet), blown hither and thither about her head by the strong upland breeze ; a smile on her lips and a leaping light in her eyes ; or in a rest-house of a night, when, bathed and clothed in a skirt after the labours of the day, she played Russian Dominoes with us ; or at Lobung or Pakha-Pakha nestling among her blankets, with just her face above the piles of clothes, looking for all the world the very embodiment of the boy who will never grow up. And the Padre too, setting, of his Alpine experiences, a pace that would not unduly tire ; helping Peter and myself over difficult places, his teeth biting a good-sized twig instead of the stem of his much-loved pipe, but never a word of complaint. Goodly and cheery companions both. Friends to have made and keep !

During my eleven days absence work in Kota Belud had accumulated. Two mails had come in and required attention, while several cases of buffalo theft awaited trial. But even so I could not spend long in the station for I was bound, with Orang Kaya Kaya Haji Arsat, to visit Mantanani Island, where there was a large village of Obians—a rather undesirable and treacherous race who had migrated from the outlying islands of the Phillipines and settled at various places along the Northern and Eastern coasts of the Territory. Their land, though they were poor agriculturists, had been demarcated and I wished to check the demarcators' plans.

Haji Arsat, who held the newly-appointed rank of Deputy Assistant District Officer, was by birth a Brunei, but long residence in the Tempasuk, from his early trading days, had given him an unrivalled knowledge of the district and an authority among the natives that was almost unique. Like Panglima Udang at Semporna he was invaluable to Government and, as he could read and write Malay, of inestimable assistance to the D.O. The turbulent Obians at Mantanani held him in very great respect, and to them he was a kindly Providence, for he held practically full proprietory rights in the famous birds' nests caves on the island and so as the collecting seasons fell due could give them considerable employment.

Our visits synchronised: Arsat to make arrangements for the collection of his nests; I to check the demarcator's plans, and at the same time use Arsat's services as an interpreter.

It was about 4 o'clock in the afternoon when we left Arsat's house, situated some way down the river from Kota Belud, in dapangs—a long shallow craft, very like the Katamarangs of Ceylon, with big bamboo outriggers on each side and carrying, for their size, an enormous sail area. At the mouth of the river we stopped to take dinner and await the favourable night breeze. At last it sprang up and we set sail with an eight knot breeze blowing on our beam.

And once again the wonders of a tropic night made their full appeal to me; once again the fascination of space and infinitude bred by the ocean and the sky stole over me. A frail wooden craft—the restless waters—the limitless sky and myriad stars—9,000 miles between me and Europe and so-called civilisation—a crew of natives—our destination an island peopled by a truculent race with piratical and murderous instincts—and I, a solitary white man, a youngster of 27.

Head-hunting and murders; cattle and even wife stealing; love charms and poisons and blow pipes! What are they after all but relics of the basic law of Nature—the Survival of the Fittest ? They are not im-moralitics—but only non-moralitics. They represent, not a different life, nor a different species of humanity, but a different and backward outlook of life by sections of one common humanity. And to change that outlook, to graft a saner, purer, healthier conception of citizenship and yet retain essential individualism is the great task of colonial administration.

It is not an easy task and the moments of black depression and disappointment are many. No one feels these dark moments more than the lonely District Officer in the frequent solitude of his far-away district. To him frequently comes the thought that he is forgotten by the Authorities or curtly treated as but a small and insignificant cog in the wheel of Administration. His pet schemes so often get turned down ; money which to him and his district seems essential is not forthcoming ; official communications are so soulless and disheartening ; his latest protégé and chief is not fulfilling his early promise ; the mail has brought no letters from home and his papers and magazines have gone astray ; the rice crop has been attacked by a plague of rats or sparrows ; an epidemic has broken out.

Such are the almost daily disappointments of a D.O. and yet he persists ; yet carries on and in some marvellous way is nearly always cheerful. For there is a fascination and appeal in the work, and its very variety breeds an unconquerable optimism that nothing can quench.

Suddenly I awoke with a start and a shudder as a wave of salt water broke over me, drenching me from head to foot. The wakening was complete, the transition from dreams to facts immediate. For a moment I did not move but my eyes sought the sky. The stars were no longer visible ; the night was pitchy dark. The dapang trembled under me, then rose and rose to fall quickly and wallow in the trough of a mighty roller. The ropes strained and groaned in tension and the sail had been hurriedly furled. Cautiously I raised myself and looked around. I could just see either end of the boat. I peered and peered. Surely, we started with a crew of three—but now I could only see one—the helmsman sitting rigid and tense in the stern, straining to steer a safe course. Then something seemed to be bobbing by our bows, bobbing and bobbing in unison with the boat. As I intently looked I saw it was a human head, and then I saw a hand upon the gunwale. And I looked astern to see another head bobbing and another hand clinging to the gunwale. I rubbed my eyes and wondered if I was still dreaming, but another drenching wave dispelled such belief. There was nothing of the dream in its force or coldness. Then a cheery voice came out of the deep.

" Don't be alarmed, Tuan—it's not a ghost—but only me."

" But——" I began.

Then the helmsman spoke. " The storm came up suddenly, Tuan. We were heavily loaded and we had to lighten the boat and so—— "

" Trimah Kasih, Amat " (Many thanks, Amat), I broke in and there was a break in my voice, " trimah Kasih."

" Tipada, Tuan " (It's nothing, Tuan), " when the storm's over they clamber in. I was frightened we'd founder or the Tuan's barang get wet and so—— "

" You suggested they should swim ? "

" Tuan," was the laconic reply.

There was silence for I could not speak, but my lips trembled and a curious tremor ran through my body.

Was it the cold or did it voice a stirring of emotion, a sense of gratitude too acute for speech, or was it a thrill of shame at the memory of the rather unkind thoughts of these people—these murderous, treacherous Obians—that had previously been mine ?

I had seen little of them up till now and knew them chiefly by repute ; had only met a few of them at Tamus ; given them some medicines and seeds to plant and one of their number was in gaol and on remand for his trial for murder. And then they did this for me !

I was still pondering the riddle when the storm passed and the sea calmed down and the two swimmers clambered into the boat. I had not found my answer as the sail was un-reefed, nor when a little later a light shone out faintly on the horizon and Amat broke the thread of my thoughts with a laconic " Mantanani, Tuan."

Thus I reached Mantanani. I had left Tempasuk in glorious sunshine, passed through a night of storm and darkness but arrived amidst the promise of a glorious dawn.

I spent two days on the island, but unfortunately was too busy over land matters to explore the caves, which were in the side of a hill at one end of the island. None theless I was glad to hear from Haji Arsat that the crop promised to be an unusually good one. I was glad not only for his sake and for the Obians, but also for my own, for Government claimed a royalty on the sales of these edible nests, built by swallows, and which are such a delicacy to the rich Chinese of Hongkong and China, and the bigger the royalty the greater would be my month's revenue.

With the greatest pleasure in the world I could have spent a week on the island. There were the caves to explore ; shooting and bathing were good, while close by were two small islands, the haunts of turtle and jungle fowl. But there were other parts of the district that I must visit.

So under a cloudless sky and with the sun a shining ball of brass I left, on the third morning, for the most northerly point of the district. For some distance a fleet of dapangs accompanied us. Then as the island began to grow smaller and the houses became almost undistinguishable it turned back and I and my consort were alone. Slowly the white sails grew to small specks ; slowly the opposite coast grew more defined. Gradually the wind grew less and the sun's rays hotter. The glare became unbearable ; the heat under the Kajang awning insufferable ; the very water itself felt hot. A heavy stillness came creeping over the waters—the wind died down—we became becalmed on a motionless glassy sea—only the drift of the tide bore us slowly away from our destination, for there was something fatalistic in the air that ridiculed the very idea of the use of paddles.

Then from the north and west, from furthest horizon, insidiously began to creep a haze. Slowly at first, then quicker and quicker it crept, catching us in its folds and pressing on till it blotted out the coast in front of us, and obliterated the sun. And still not a breath of wind—not a ripple on the water—only the thick and darkening walls of the haze. Silence, utter and complete ; a silence such as I had never experienced ; such as I shall probably never experience again.

Then somewhere—North or South, East or West, we knew not—came a distant sound : a blend of muffled roar and rumble. Nearer and nearer it came ; louder and louder it grew.

I looked at Amat in silent query. He shook his head in reply. The roar grew louder and closer and still the haze enveloped us ; still the sea was as a pane of glass. Both boatmen fingered the jimats (charms) which hung round their necks. And unconsciously I too toyed with a bracelet of camel's hair, said to have come from Mecca—the gift of a travelling hawker I once befriended in Tuaran and which I wore—why I really knew not—on my left wrist. He had begged me to wear it, promising me, if I would, immunity from all accidents and ills, and in a weak moment and as a result of his importunity I had put it on and it had stayed on my wrist ever since.

Once again my eyes met Amat's and this time I spoke. " Rain ? " I asked.

He shook his head, then added, " Wind first ; perhaps rain afterwards."

As he spoke a cold breeze lightly struck my cheek ; a ripple spread over the face of the sea ; the boat slowly rocked and trembled as the ripples grew with suddenness to waves and rollers ; the haze passed away, pressed and squeezed out as it were between the sea and dark lowering clouds that seemed falling from the sky. And through this narrow space, this neck of air, where clouds and sea just failed to meet, the wind roared and rushed in hurricane fury.

Like a wisp of straw in a gale or a cork upon turbulent waters our boat was blown and tossed about with almost maddening speed. There came a snap and the mast broke in two ; the halyards blowing out in the wind like streamers. The heavy Kajang cover, half rolled up and taken down, was wrenched from its remaining fastenings, and went careering madly over the sea, twisting and turning for all the world like a great eagle that had been shot and was falling in its death agony. One minute a mountainous wave came rising up behind till it seemed that it must swamp and break all over us ; then just as we held our breath and waited our stern rose up and up till it seemed we poised upon our very bows ; then came a shudder, a sickening jerk, a slipping, falling backwards ; the wave had passed and we were wallowing in its trough, seeming to sink and sink and then lie still. Yet all the time we were being borne onwards and Amat strained every nerve to keep us head on to the rollers.

But for an hour the rain did not fall ; then suddenly the heavens opened and the deluge came. And once again the coast was blotted out, only this time by the sheets of rain. As the rain descended the hurricane died down, and gradually the sea grew calmer, till at length we were able to set and rig up a temporary mast. Just as the task was finished the heavy clouds rolled away and the sun smiled out from the bluest of skies upon a grey-green sea and, in the distance, the glistening green plain and rolling hills.

The boatmen kissed their jimats and Amat muttered something about Allah, and I—well I fingered my camel's hair bracelet and thought of the hawker who gave it to me, and then, remembering I was hungry and thirsty, set to upon some cold tea and cabin biscuits and handed cigarettes round to the crew.

It was late that night when we reached the village and the headman's surprise on hearing we had weathered the storm was immense.

" Allah," he said, " is merciful to all true Believers and—— " he broke off, but I saw he was looking at my bracelet. Then he continued, " Did not the Tuan give twenty dollars towards the building of our new Mosque ? The Tuan is not a Kapir (Pagan) but an orang Kitabi (a believer in the Bible) and Allah knows."

Life seemed at this time bent upon giving me either shocks or surprises, for two days later, on my return to

Kota Belud, as I climbed the hill to my house, I began to question the veracity of my senses. For there, stretched upon a line fastened in a part of the garden where no line was ever fixed before, hung washing ! And chief among the garments, easily distinguishable by their colour and pattern, hung two kimonos. Thunderstruck I stood and looked at them ! What could they mean ? Had Cookie and my tukang ayer (water carrier) suddenly acquired wealth and blossomed forth into an orgy of new garments ? Had either of them suddenly taken leave of his senses and imported a wife—and a Japanese to boot—into my establishment ?

I cried aloud, "What does it mean ? " And approached the house red hot with curiosity.

My return home had been from across the river, consequently I entered the house by the back way. As I neared the kitchen I could hear the everlasting chop, chop, chop of cookie's chopper ; he was obviously preparing the ubiquitous mince of sorts, made to disguise the ever present Borneo chicken. For whom was he cooking, I wondered ! Not for me, for the date and time of my return had been quite problematical. Then for whom ? Not for himself for he'd never trouble to make a mince. For the Japanese ? . . . But I didn't stop to consider any longer.

" Cookie ! " I yelled. " Cookie, come here ; what the devil does it all mean ? Whose are those clothes and for whom are you making that disgusting mince ? "

The chopping ceased ; a sizzling noise escaped the confines of the kitchen ; a smell of frying onions came wafted across to me and cookie came out.

" There's a tuan——" he began.

" What ? " I cried.

" An American tuan," he answered.

But I did not care what nationality the visitor was so

long as he was not Japanese. The relief I felt must have shown in my face for cookie went on: "Bukan Japun, Tuan. Orang American betul" (Not Japanese but a real American). I did not stay to hear any more, but entered the house to meet my unexpected and I hoped pleasant guest.

Fortunately my hopes were fulfilled to the uttermost, for Greville Haslam proved one of the most charming fellows I have ever met, and it is to his generosity that I owe many of the photographs that help to illustrate this record.

He had come to Borneo with letters of introduction from the Governor and Bishop of the Phillippines to our Governor, and was visiting the country for the dual purpose of collecting moths and butterflies and ascending Mt. Kinabalu. Of course, I should have been warned of his intended visit, but the Authorities in Jesselton or at Tuaran had overlooked the matter, and, when it was remembered, I was away at Mantanani. So after staying a day or two at Tuaran, and a night at Tengilan, Haslam had pushed on and with official consent taken charge of my house in my absence.

He was full of apologies for what he termed his cheek, but I think after a little while he really understood that I was only too pleased to find him, so to speak, in residence on my return and only sorry I had been unable to welcome his arrival.

Two days in the station, and I set forth again. This time to accompany Haslam, but only as far as Kiau. I could not grumble now at the want of homage paid to the Solitary Father, for Haslam's made the third ascent within a year. My desire to make another effort to reach the topmost peak was very strong, but I could not really spare the time, and the memory of my mountain-sickness was very vivid. So after handing Haslam over to the care of Sumpot and Umpoh I left him, crossed to Singarun and went down the Tuaran side of the hills into Tuaran to consult over matters of state.

On my return to Kota Belud life began once again to pursue the more even tenor of its way. But in Kota Belud this way is always just a little more strenuous than in many districts: the buffalo theft cases would be so frequent and the thefts so daring; and every now and then a wave of cattle maiming would pass over the district, which generally coincided with the harvest—a time, as I have said, dedicated to the cult of Tapai consumption and practised so religiously by the Dusuns; feeling among the Bajaus and Dusuns in almost adjoining villages would sometimes reach beyond the mere limits of insults; or a Chinese trader would break the law and, in search of gain, go travelling alone up-country and in the end pay for his temerity with robbery and sometimes violence; or the factory at Tengilan Estate, which though actually in Tuaran had been temporarily placed under my jurisdiction, would get burnt down and necessitate my paying a hurried visit to inspect the smouldering ruins to enable me to swear to complete destruction for the purposes of insurance and make endless enquiries for fear the fire was caused by arson; or a Chinese shopkeeper, suspecting his wife and cashier of being too familiar, would charge the latter with criminal misappropriation and on failing to prove his case would employ some desperate and well-known characters to attack the erring and amorous one at night.

One case I recall in particular. A Chinese shopkeeper who lived in Kudat made a trip round various islands accompanied only by two Suluks. During his journey he collected from his scattered shops and trading just over \$700.[oo]. Then, pleased with life, he started the return journey. But he never saw Kudat again, for the boat returned with a broken mast and torn sail and only the two Suluks in it. And the story they told was that a storm had sprung up with suddenness and the boat had turned turtle, and everything in it, including the anchor—one borrowed by the Chinaman from a friend—had sunk to the bottom, and the towkay (shopkeeper) too; that he had sunk like a log—as Chinamen often do—and never risen at all.

A very good story and very well told! And it rang true, for there had been storms and the boat was known to be well and heavily loaded; also the Chinaman, as a matter of fact, could not swim. Yet the Authorities together with many Chinese were suspicious. Watch was kept on the Suluks, but nothing suspicious occurred, they shewed no signs of new accession to wealth and went quietly about their daily life. Still suspicion, born of an intuitive knowledge, lingered, till on the fourteenth day it was justified. And Nemesis dealt the cards with ironic justice for it was four Dusuns from Tempasuk—despised as Kapirs by the Suluks—who played the final hand in the gruesome drama.

The quiet sleepiness of 3 p.m. was brooding over Kudat; even the sentry outside the Resident's office was languid and his footsteps dragged as he walked up and down his beat. The Sergeant, in the police room, was frankly resting. In the Court House the Court clerk had not even opened his papers, and a bottle of Ice-Cream Soda was only half hidden underneath his desk. Wearily the notes of a typewriter came intermittently from the chief clerk's office. The Resident's desk was empty.

Into this scene of tropic languor strode the four Dusuns carrying a sack. The sentry turning upon his beat met them, then noticed a rather objectionable smell. He was a Dusun—so they spoke together. A few words, a gasp of surprise and the sleeping Sergeant was being roughly shaken by the shoulder. Into his astonished ears the policeman poured his story. A second later and the telephone bell was ringing in the Residency. A few minutes more and the Resident was on his way to the office —the Court clerk forgot his ice-cream soda and the chief clerk's typewriter became silent.

A little knot of clerks, police and boatmen were gathered round the office. And though the sack gave out its pungent odour excitement ruled the day. Into this little crowd of people an Irish terrier wriggled his way. He heralded the Resident's approach on whose arrival the group opened.

With pursed-up lips and wrinkled nose he looked at the sack—then at the Dusuns—then once again at the sack. Then made a sign to the Sergeant, who in response stepped forward and, holding the sack at one end, proceeded slowly to rip it open, exposing to view the almost miraculously preserved remains of a drowned Chinaman.

Swollen and distorted as the corpse was it was yet distinctly recognisable. There was no doubt as to identity.

Then a tremor ran through most of the group as the chief clerk, with pointing, trembling finger gasped out, " Look—look—there's the anchor—and it's tied to it."

It was as the chief clerk said, for tied tightly to the corpse was the borrowed and missing anchor. Yet not quite all the anchor ; for the long heavy flat piece of stone that is frequently fastened, for weighting purposes, to the native-made wooden anchors, was missing.

" Poor devil ! The damned swines ! " The words were muttered by the Resident and they voiced the opinion of all present, for the fate of the wretched Chinaman was beyond doubt. He had, as the Suluks said, been drowned. In that they spoke the truth, but they had omitted the one word "deliberately."

There was no doubt in anyone's mind as to the murderers; their guilt was too self-evident. Yet one small link was wanted to complete the evidence—the absolute identification of the anchor—and this was easy to obtain, for in ten minutes the owner of the anchor had been sent for, arrived and indisputably claimed his property.

Then the Dusuns retold more fully how when walking along the beach they had come across the grisly object, high and dry upon the sand, rolled up by the sea after the stone had become loosened and slipped from its binding.

As they spoke the picture of the drama must have flashed before the eyes of their audience with almost unbelievable clarity. And as I heard the story—though second-hand—I could see the poor wretch in his last moments, being tied to the anchor. Vainly appealing for mercy, vainly offering his wealth for his life, praying, pleading, impotent to the last and . . . then being thrown overboard. A splash, a body slowly sinking in deep clear water, the rush of fishes, a nibble here, a bite there; a widening, lessening ripple of water, a few air bubbles and all trace of the crime was obliterated. At least so thought the murderers. But . . .

What were their thoughts I wonder, that warm sleepy afternoon, when they were told that the Resident wanted to see them—of what were they thinking as they accompanied the Dusun policeman to the office? Did they feel any premonition as they neared the little knot of people? Did their pulses quicken or their hearts tremble as they entered that small circle and looked down upon a heap of—what?—covered with a sack? In the death-like silence that followed their arrival what were their thoughts? Who knows? For their faces were masks of blankness. And as the sack was slowly dragged from off its gruesome heap exposing first the feet, then legs and body till finally the whole poor corpse lay stiffly in the sun, what were their thoughts? I only know that one of them without a word fell down and fainted, while the other, with a shudder, covered his face with his hands.

There came a click and the handcuffs were on his wrists. As he was being led away he looked at his still swooning companion and said, "He made me do it. Tidapa (never mind), it's Fate."

Of course they were both hanged. And in their house was found nearly $700.^{00}.

CHAPTER VI

NORTH KEPPEL

No one seemed more securely settled in his district than I in Kota Belud but a transfer happened with startling suddenness.

The telephone bell rang and I recognised the D.O.'s voice. As he spoke I realised that his news would not be ordinary for there was a quality of sombreness in his tone that was unmistakable.

" That you, Cook ? "

" Yes. What is it ? "

" The Commissioner's dead."

" Good God ! How ? "

" Drowned. He was out sculling before breakfast. Never came back. They found his boat and later his body. It's rotten, damnably rotten."

" But, what was it ? The weather's fine. Was it one of his fits ? "

" They think so. He must have had one while sculling."

" Poor old thing. It was never really safe for him to be alone. He never knew when they were coming on. God ! I'm sorry. I was awfully fond of him and he used to teach me Latin. It's rotten, damnably rotten. I'm—I'm—oh well, it's just rotten."

And I put the receiver on.

The Sergeant came to me and spoke but I heeded not. Then suddenly my mind awoke.

"Sergeant," I said. "The Tuan Commissioner is dead. Lower the flag to half-mast. You all loved him here and this is his old district. Put off the buffalo case till to-morrow—I don't feel like it to-day. Send news to Tuan Haji Arsat for they were great friends."

Then I went to my house, but the telephone pursued me. It was the D.O. again.

"That you?"

"Yes."

"News just through from the G.S. I'm to go back to Kudat. You're to come down here as Acting D.O. You'll have no A.D.O. at Kota Belud but Haji Arsat must do all he can. It's a bit steep I know, but it can't be helped."

Thus I went back to Tuaran, and though the appointment, though probably only temporary, was promotion there was no elation in my heart.

Two districts and no A.D.O.! Two sets of monthly Accounts! Three demarcators engaged on land settlement; three estates and the four Chinese settlements! If Tuaran alone in former days had kept me busy what was my day's work going to be now? And to crown everything it was the end of the year and two Annual District Reports loomed ahead of me!

But work never killed anybody and I don't think I was ever fitter than during the next two months when I had so much to do that I had to plan my days out to a rigid time-table and yet found time to spend a very cheery Christmas on Tuaran Estate. And on my way to Kota Belud, to close the monthly cash accounts and reports, I spent the New Year (1917) at Tengilan.

Many houses, perhaps nearly all the European houses

in Borneo are said by the natives to be " berhantu " (haunted), but this one at Tengilan is the only one I know of in which the Europeans put much faith.

My host's predecessor had seen the ghost; had even shot at it, and he was the most matter-of-fact, phlegmatic man I have met. There wasn't an ounce of romance or mystery in him. My host had seen it and was often disturbed, and he was a long-headed, shrewd planter, a man of business, of facts and figures and a scoffer of the mystic. And then I, knowing nothing of it, was disturbed too.

I hope if the man does walk that house of a night his spirit has at last found peace; that the thirst which was always tormenting him has at last been quenched.

I was staying there for the night on my way back from Kota Belud, and after dinner we yarned till about half-past ten. Most of the time, I remember, we were talking " shop "; certainly we touched upon nothing psychological; our " good nights " were quite ordinary and in no way tinged with an element of the supernatural.

I could hear him moving about in his room. I could see him dim his lamp, and could catch the faint light of his night-light. I lowered my lamp and climbed into bed.

" Nighty night, old thing," I cried out.

" Good night," came back his sleepy reply.

Then all was quiet. I heard the opas at the Estate office strike eleven o'clock. Then I fell asleep.

Suddenly I was awake—wide awake—but I had not awakened with a start. I was not strung up nor excited. Nothing, no sound nor presence, as far as I knew, had aroused me. I was simply awake. I turned on to my left side, looked at my watch, saw it was after 1 a.m., closed my eyes and was about to fall asleep when I heard footsteps coming up the steps that led from the garden to the front door.

I listened. Slowly the footsteps mounted the stairs. Then I heard the catch of the low wooden gate pulled back and the creak of the doors being opened. Down the full length of the verandah came the footsteps and passed into the dining-room. Whoever was walking kept straight on, for I heard the noise of the doors, that shut off this room from the passage leading to the kitchen, being opened and the footsteps went along this passage. Then they halted.

" Boy." The call was clear and decisive, but I failed to recognise the voice. There came no answer.

" Boy ! " This time the call was sharper, and impatience was in its tone.

Still no reply. For a while silence. Then the footsteps descended the stairs that led from the passage to the kitchen. They halted on the bottom step.

" Boy ! " the call was long, loud and angry ; yet no answer came.

Again silence. Then up the stairs came the footsteps. They passed back along the passage. The dividing doors were closed. Along the dining-room, out into the verandah they went. The creak of the gates reached me and I heard the closing of the latch. Down the steps the footsteps clumped ; out into the garden and then silence !

" What's the matter ? " I wondered, and fell asleep.

When I entered the verandah next morning my host was already there. He paused with a cup half-way to his mouth.

" Morning, R.M.O.," he growled—he was never very talkative first thing on getting up—and then on with his tea.

I answered and busied myself with the tea-pot. Then,

under cover of meticulously choosing a piece of toast, I studied him. He showed no signs of having spent a disturbed night. Suddenly he looked up and caught my eye.

"Well?" he asked. "What is it?"

"Nothing," I answered curtly.

"Then why look at me like that?"

"Sorry, old thing, didn't know I was looking at you. I was only wondering——"

"Yes?"

"What you were up to last night—walking all over the house, and shouting for your boy?"

"Then you heard it too?" He asked the question with relief.

"'It'! What's 'it'? I heard *you* come up the steps, open the gates and then walk to the back. You called 'boy' three times. There was no answer. Then you walked back through the house and down the steps. What was wrong?"

"Nothing! Nothing was wrong, and I never moved from my room till this morning. It was G——."

"G——! What on earth do you mean? Who's G——?"

"You know," he answered. "The man here before my predecessor. He died in your room—on your bed. The doctor visited him one day, hearing he was ill. He gave him five minutes to live. Tough luck I know, but old G—— just managed to sit up in bed, smiled and asked for a cigarette. He smoked a while and chatted—and then . . . the half-smoked 'gasper' dropped from his lips—and he was dead. He's buried in the garden just on the slope of the hill below your window. Awful pity—but—drink and a native woman. . . . Nice chap, but . . ."

Then I remembered the story—and G—— too. I

had met him once in 1912 at a race meeting in Jesselton. He had kept and was frightfully keen on a native woman, a rather beautiful and fascinating girl who became the most notorious woman in Borneo. She had been lured away from him by the manager of a certain Estate, and G—— felt her loss greatly.

I looked at my host for a second or two, trying to decide whether he was " pulling my leg." He was perfectly serious.

" And that—that was he last night ? "

" Yes."

" But good Lord, man ! " I exclaimed. " You don't mean—you can't—it's preposterous ! "

" I know," he spoke slowly and carefully, " it sounds absurd—doesn't it ? But the last man went through it, saw him and spoke and one night even shot him."

" Shot him ? "

" Yes—and there isn't much mysticism about him—he's as much imagination as a turnip."

" But—— "

" All the ' buts ' in the world won't alter matters—he's seen him, I've seen him, and you've heard him. It's there—and it happens—and it's always the same. Get on with your tea. Then we'll go and look at his grave. I always inspect it twice a month and put a coolie on cleaning up and tending it. To-day's the day."

What was his spirit wanting as it wandered through the house ? What was the message, conscious or unconscious, that was conveyed in that call for " Boy " ? All three of us have each read the riddle according to our needs, and if my thoughts and answer have given him some little peace, I am content.

Such thoughts could not stay long with me, for after breakfast I said good-bye and rode to Tuaran and there was much on the journey to occupy my attention. The section of the bridle-path over which I was riding was being cleaned and some new wooden bridges were being erected. Two of the demarcators were working on lands just off the path and their plans wanted checking and passing. Evening was approaching as I entered the grounds that surrounded my house.

But, though I was tired from a long day's work and ride, the comfort of a long chair was not for me ; for scarcely had I entered my house than the Sergeant reported a suspicious sickness in the Barracks. I did not stop even to change my clothes, but at once accompanied him. There I found two or three children and a few women covered with spots.

Small-pox, chicken-pox or measles ? I doubted the former and prayed that it wasn't. I suspected the last and proved to be wrong, for Jackson, for whom I had immediately telephoned, declared the illness to be chicken-pox. Not serious, thank heaven, yet annoying, for it meant the building of huts and the instituting quarantine regulations. But I knew my natives. A severe illness they will take seriously, but a mild complaint only irks them for they fail to realise the possibilities of subsequent complications if precautions are not taken. They loathe getting hot or having a temperature and only know the crudest methods of keeping cool—to lie with as few clothes on as possible in the biggest draught they can procure.

It is this difficulty of controlling and combating these instincts that makes an epidemic such hard work, and often so fatal, in a country like North Borneo. Luckily the present sickness was of a mild order and the only real trouble was the preventing the spread.

One crowning piece of bad luck, however, befell me.

My chief clerk's child developed the complaint, and the doctor ordered the clerk to quarantine! A fortnight without him and the annual District report still unwritten!

Then came another epidemic! This time among the buffaloes. First from Kota Belud, then from parts of Tuaran itself came reports of an unknown sickness. The animals broke out in good sized spots, which burst and discharged a fluid. At the same time their throats and necks swelled enormously, till ultimately the animals died—apparently from suffocation.

I at once realised the seriousness of the situation for much of the native wealth in North Keppel consists of buffaloes. And Government had no Veterinary Surgeon! There had been one in the Service but he had quarrelled with the Authorities and joined Tuaran Estate as an Assistant. However, luckily I was able to obtain his help.

So once again I was on the road to Kota Belud, where the disease had first broken out and was most virulent.

As usual we stopped the night at Tengilan Estate, and I decided the next morning before continuing the journey to attend to a few matters on the Estate. In particular, some trees had been badly damaged by a dissatisfied coolie and it was necessary for me personally to see them so as to assess the damage accurately. This entailed a long walk to almost the far end of the Estate, and we did not return to the house till nearly 11 o'clock. All three of us, without changing, flopped into long chairs and in the cool of the verandah dozed off into that light sleep which is akin to semi-consciousness.

Without warning, our peace was suddenly disturbed. Loud voices, excited and angry, came up the hill and approached the house. Shuffling footsteps drew near; then stopped.

Awake, I waited ; waited purposely, hoping nothing would happen, but I hoped in vain.

" Tuan ! Tuan ! " came the cry in a strident Chinese voice.

Still I pretended slumber. The footsteps climbed up two steps, then stopped.

" Tuan ! Tuan ! ! " came the strident cry again. " Tuan—ada orang kena luka ! Banyak darah " (Here's a wounded man and he's bleeding profusely).

In an instant I was out of my chair and leaning over the verandah railing. A second later the others were alongside me. On the path stood three Chinamen—two of whom were supporting the third, whose face and clothes were literally covered in blood.

I had hardly begun to question them as to what had happened when a horrid feeling crept over me. I strove to shake it off but it persisted. I was going to faint ! There was just one chance I might prevent it. Spluttering something about getting a smoke I went to the table, picked up a cigarette, deliberately dropped it on the floor and stooped to pick it up. My fingers and thumb were just touching it—when, flop—I knew nothing more till what seemed ages and ages later I dimly heard someone saying, " He's the devil of a time coming round. Do you think ? . . ."

And I thought so too, for a second or so, for the struggle to regain consciousness seemed almost beyond me. I seemed to be hovering on a brink, to be struggling to come back and terribly afraid that I could not. Then—I opened my eyes and saw them both looking at me.

" Sit quiet," said the vet. as I struggled to sit up, " you've flopped pretty badly, so take it quietly."

" But what's the matter ; what's happened to that nasty looking Chinaman ? " I asked.

" Gone to wash his face. He's got a gash or two. His pals will come back when they've left him at the hospital."

I lay back in my chair and closed my eyes for I felt absurdly weak. Then I opened them as footsteps approached from outside. The two were returning.

Out of consideration to me, so as I need not get up but could easily hear their story from the depths of my long chair, they were allowed in the verandah.

" Well ? " I questioned.

And then they burst forth. Both tried to speak at once ; both were so excited that they could hardly splutter out a coherent word, and an excited Chinaman talking Malay is about the most incoherent thing on earth. But by dint of questioning and cross-questioning and repeated stoppings we managed to elucidate their story.

A village about two miles away was holding a small " drunk." Our coolies had looked in " en passant," so to speak, and the Murut policeman in charge of them had a decided leaning towards Bahr—the local drink of fermented coconut water. The coolies, who upkept the telephone line from Tengilan to Kota Belud, " dropped in" too. The three Chinese, who were plank cutters of the Estate, were working close by and had been attracted by the sounds of revelry. Most of those present were drunk ; some were very drunk ; the policeman and the telephone mandor (overseer) were the drunkest of all. The inevitable quarrel arose, and the policeman and mandor set upon the unfortunate Chinaman as the cause of it all.

Before he realised he was being attacked the policeman had picked up his rifle and swung at him. He only partially dodged the blow and in doing so bumped the mandor so hard that the latter fell down. In an instant though he had gained his feet, and picking up a heavy stick that was lying on the floor rushed at the Chinaman and caught him a glancing blow on the head.

Then the policeman had an inspiration ! He would shoot the Chinaman like the dog he was. With trembling fingers he fumbled in his pouch, found and extracted a bullet, which he rammed into the breach of his rifle. But the inmates of the house waited no longer. They fled and the Chinamen with them. As they ran in all directions they heard shot after shot being fired—at least four or five shots.

I knew that policeman and mandor well. A certain amount of drink in either and there was always hell to pay.

I rose from my chair. " Lend me a revolver," I said. " We must see into this ; there may not be much doing, but on the other hand we may have some fun."

" But you're not going."

" I am," I interrupted, " I'm D.O. here and those two swine are playing the fool in the Kampong " (village).

" You're not fit. He isn't fit, is he ? " and my host appealed to the vet.'s medical knowledge. But I disregarded the latter's shake of the head and overruled their objections and ten minutes later we were running at a jog trot to the scene of action.

As we approached the house we could see no signs of life, but two raucous voices yelling from within told us our quarry was there. There was little danger unless the policeman had retained a cartridge or two—an unlikely proceeding I thought in his present condition—but there were the usual two doors to the house and one window, all of which we covered.

We waited till there came a lull in the drunken yelling, of which I took immediate advantage.

" Bensaian " (such was the policeman's name). " Bensaian ! " I called out, " what are you doing here ? And where are the coolies with my barang ? "

A loud and hurried whispering took place in the house and just reached our ears. Then in a husky, shaky voice, one word of surprise.

" Tuan ! " There was fright in the tone, too.

" Apa ? " (What ?) was my sharp reply.

" Apa Tuan man " (What do you want ?), hiccupped Bensaian, who was too drunk to realise that his mode of address was rude. I gratified his curiosity, however, and told him all I wanted was that he and the mandor should come to me as I had some orders to give them.

Without a murmur they both came out, for the fumes of the liquor were wearing off and my unexpected presence in the midst of their carousal had startled them into a realisation of their actions and the probable nasty consequences that must follow. So thoroughly frightened were they that Bensaian even left his rifle and belt and parang on the floor of the house.

Thus the affair fizzled out, and we had had no fun, but only a hot two-mile walk back under the rays of the midday sun.

But in spite of this unexpected interlude it was necessary for us to reach Kota Belud that evening, so after lunch and a short rest we left Tengilan to arrive at Kota Belud in time for a late tea.

Here for the next two days the vet. was busy, rounding up the buffaloes, examining them, holding a post-mortem on one that had recently died, quarantining, issuing regulations and instructions and finally arriving at his diagnosis.

The disease according to him was due to damp and sour pasture and the best preventative was a change of grazing grounds and the liming of the old ones. For animals actually suffering from the sickness he made up a disinfectant wash for external use and lanced the swollen throats of those affected.

Then having done all we could and left instructions with Haji Arsat we returned to Tuaran, where by now the disease was spreading, till eventually it reached Papar and Putatan in South Keppel on the other side of Jesselton. Thanks, however, to the prompt measures taken in the early days of the epidemic and the efficacy of the treatment, the mortality list throughout both North and South Keppel was not a high one.

A few days after my return to Tuaran I learnt officially that a successor to the D.O. had been appointed and that my temporary promotion would soon cease, when I should revert to my substantive rank of A.D.O. Tempasuk and return to Kota Belud.

In due course the new D.O. arrived and I once again packed up my household goods and returned to Kota Belud.

If there is a fascination in going to a new district there is certainly a charm in the return to an old one, for it is extraordinary how soon one's temporary quarters assume the rôle of "Home." It is, I suppose, the constant travelling round one's district, the constant living on camp furniture and among one's suit-cases or "basongs," as the case may be, that engenders the feeling of having settled down, of having arrived back that one experiences as soon as one returns to Headquarters. And a return to a former district is much the same, only I think the feeling is intensified. The favourite long chair in the particular corner; the favourite flower or shrub that grows better here than anywhere else! The scoundrelly, one-eyed vagrant who always haunts you and cadges a

Kota Belud, showing the Office, Court House, Gaol, Shops, Sergeant of Police, and R M.O.C.

A D.O.'s House, Tenom.

p. 192

cigarette, yet gives you "quid pro quo" in a piece of useful news; the young wife who is always running away from her husband and is as often running back. The familiar sights, sounds and smells, each in their way prove a re-union and claim you—speaking as it were in familiar tones that are irresistible and make you say, "Good Lord, this is Home."

So it was at Kota Belud, and though I was no longer Acting District Officer, still I was tremendously happy for I had come "Home"; had returned to the watching care of my beloved Solitary Father.

But as it turned out I was not to stay long in Kota Belud, for in June I was ordered to transfer once again—this time to the Labuk and Sugut as Acting District Officer.

Personally I never sighed for the fear of any man because I was the representative of the Law and the Executive of Government, but I did, and do, value the affection of the humblest native. And so I was touched when I learnt that on the news of my pending transfer becoming public two appeals were organised by the natives and Chinese, in which they begged His Excellency to leave me in the Tempasuk. Had I known that these appeals were in the course of preparation I would have saved the applicants their trouble, and spared their hopes, for there was no more certain way of achieving the end they wished to avoid than the presenting of an appeal; for Government seem to hold the dictum I once heard expressed, "That a popular D.O. must be a bad officer."

Thus once again I had to attend a farewell dance in my honour, and far into the night I sat watching Dusuns and Bajaus vying with each other. And in no way does the North Keppel Bajau differ more from the Bajau of the East coast than in his dancing.

Here there is no individual performance, no snake-like movement, nor preposterous capers, but a concerted dance called " Berumgsai."

Into a semi-circle the dancers—mostly men—form and then join hands, while he at the end of the line holds in his disengaged hand a silken dustar or handkerchief. Then slowly the nearly completed circle begins to gyrate to a measured step in unison—two steps to the side, then one to the front and one to the back, repeated again and again as the line swings slowly round.

From the head of the column a voice breaks into song —a pantoon—a love-call to some maiden. Gently at first the singer woos his sweetheart with words of timid, hesitating devotion ; but as the movement quickens, as the steps grow faster and warm blood races in his veins so does he throw all hesitation to the winds and words of impassioned beauty and throbbing longing fall from his lips. Just for a moment he ceases, but in that short time his comrades have caught the spirit of his emotion and in one loud unison, that will not be denied and that breaks through all restraint, they lend their aid and a mighty chorus rings round the rafters of the roof. Then for a second silence, save for the noise and beat of the ever-restless moving feet. Slower and slower the circle swings, and for a few paces reverses ; then once again the forward movement, once again the singer calls to his love and the note has altered ; under the words of protestation and pleading lurks an undisguised passion, a scorn for her fears and hesitation. Faster the circle flies, stronger and more insistent becomes the beating of the feet, till every movement of the swaying singers is vibrant with intense abandonment, with a subtle and alluring call.

In a corner of the room, watching, hesitating, longing,

are three maidens. Their eyes are downcast and they look demure, yet their hands are nervously twisting and untwisting, their bare feet unconsciously beating time.

Fascinated I watch, for the whole human drama since life began is being unfolded before my eyes. Hunter and hunted. Man and Maid. Primitive longing and forced restraint.

Faster and faster the circle is turning; louder and louder the insistent call. Then he at the end flicks the handkerchief; lightly it brushes a maiden's hair—she gasps, trembles and shudders—her fingers unconsciously clutch its folds. She has answered the call and made her surrender. And as the circle closes about her and the singers, triumphant, pause to take breath, her high plaintive voice is heard gently calling, pleading for honour, for love and respect.

It is a wild dance of almost pure, primitive passion and but few married women are allowed by their husbands to participate, for passion, once roused among the Bajaus, is hard of control.

Yet like the East Coast Bajaus they are a clean living people, and so strong is their sense of decency that a local law sprang up in the Native Court, with the full consent of Government, enabling a woman to obtain her divorce if her husband should be guilty of cattle-stealing and be convicted a second time and sentenced to more than one year's gaol. This law, which at first from a religious point of view may sound immoral, is really but the realisation of their elemental nature, and faces the hard fact that legalised chastity is better than religious immorality. For it gives a woman a definite position and recognises her status and sex desires, and if her husband through his insensate folly and obsessions forfeits his freedom, he has only himself to blame if his wife seeks release from an intolerable position thrust upon her by no fault of her own.

CHAPTER VII

LABUK AND SUGUT

KLAGAN, the headquarters of the Labuk and Sugut district, was an hour's steam up the Labuk river and eight hours distant from Sandakan in which Residency the district is situated. There was no telephone or telegraph and communication was entirely by sea. A launch visited Labuk Tobacco Estate, which was a few miles up-stream from Klagan, twice a month. Apart from this launch there were four Chinese Tongkongs (large sailing boats) which, according to trade and weather conditions, plied between Sandakan and Klagan. Almost an ideal district from the point of view of isolation !

The district was large, devoid of roads and possessed only few paths. Transport was entirely, with one short exception, by river and sea, for the Labuk and Sugut rivers dissected the district in almost parallel courses and each possessed, in the Tungud and Lingkabao, tributaries of considerable size and importance.

Bakau and Nipah ; swamps and jungle, hills and river, a heavy rainfall and frequent floods ; a scattered migratory population that lived practically upon the river banks or on the higher ridges of the hills ; a mixture of races, chiefly primitive, backward and superstitious ; a tobacco estate and three timber camps widely scattered ; a long open coast line, dotted with islands, that stretched from Sandakan to the easternmost point of Marudu Bay. Such was my new district.

No two districts could so widely differ as North Keppel and the Labuk and Sugut. One would hardly believe, unless one had experience, that, in a country so relatively small as North Borneo, such a variety of conditions could exist. Yet as I steamed out of Sandakan on the s.s. "Petrel" the launch that was to take me to Klagan and then go on to Labuk Estate, and remembered my conversation with the Resident the previous night at dinner, I realised that very new and strange conditions awaited me at the end of my journey.

But I was not destined to obtain a glimpse of my new "Home" that day, for we were towing two empty lighters to the timber camps and this so delayed us that as night fell we had only arrived at the mouth of the Labuk. Another hour's steaming and I should have been at Klagan, yet it would have been dangerous in the extreme to attempt to take the launch up the river in the dark.

But the next morning, while as yet the mist had not fully cleared away, we were creeping forward slowly on an ever-winding muddy stream that wended its way through dense vegetation. Every now and then out of the mist I could descry a small clearing and a few native houses, then once again only the enveloping jungle.

At the water's edge, Bakau and Nipah palms; inland, nothing but mighty trees. Such was my first impression of the Labuk—such is the lasting impression to-day. A district of rivers and jungles, vast and almost impenetrable; of swamps and somewhere, somewhere if only one could reach them, hills. But of human beings hardly any linger in my memory as personalities; for in the Labuk the souls of men become dwarfed till they seem but midgets and incidentals to the mighty tropical growths.

Over the whole district there broods an air of sombreness ; there is a feeling of pending calamity. It is as if, though the sun shone, its rays possessed no warmth and so the hearts of men and beasts lack that sense of joy and gaiety which is the very essence of life. Over all there seems a seriousness, a sense of struggle and stern reality.

Gradually the mist began to clear and the view to lengthen and as we steamed up-stream I could notice more signs of life and habitations. Then with suddenness, upon the morning air, burst the shrill scream of our syren.

I turned to the Serang, who, anticipating my question, answered : " Dua tanjong lagi ! Tuan." (Two more reaches, Tuan.) For on the rivers the natives measure distances by the number of reaches, be they long or short, with a complete disregard of their length that at times is almost maddening.

Hardly had the echoes of our syren died away than we swung round a bend and there in full view lay the island of Klagan. A small coconut plantation, five shops and two Chinese houses, the District office, my house, the clerks' quarters, the Barracks, the boatmen's houses and a cattle pound ! In an instant I had seen Klagan—all that there was to it—and yet I was not disillusioned as many had said I would be. For there was something unique in this island, hemmed in though it was by the river, from whose banks stretched swamp and jungle, that made appeal, that created the feeling of a beleaguered garrison holding out against an encircling foe. This much I felt in that first early view of my new " Home," and throughout my two years in the district the feeling never left me.

I cannot help wondering to-day whether there is in some districts an indefinable atmosphere or presence that is beyond our comprehension, which sets its seal upon the white men who have lived longest within their borders and claims for them a toll which must be paid. Strange and fanciful idea ! Yet I remember the Labuk and my mind goes over the names of three who were at one time or another my predecessors and who served the district longest and best. Where are they now ? Dead. And with the death of each is buried a tragedy ! While I—well I am no longer in the Service which claimed ten years of my life and will always hold its place in my affections.

But such thoughts as these were not in my mind as the " Petrel " drew alongside the floating wharf which lay in front of the largest Kedei (shop). To me there is always a compelling fascination in a Chinese store. It matters nothing that I know exactly what I shall find in it ; that the stock of each is always practically the same ; that there is nothing in it that I can really want or buy except cigarettes. The charm and expectancy are always the same ! for there is the one great possibility, that hidden away in some forgotten cupboard or unused corner there lies, unbeknown to and overlooked by the towkays, that which to me is almost more priceless than gold—an ancient and perhaps battered piece of brass—a " langui " or " gador " or " bintang-bintang," a relic of the past and some poor family's misfortune, an heirloom with which its owner would not have parted save under the direst need or destitution.

And as I looked from the bridge of the "Petrel" through the open fronts of the shops that flanked the river I could see many pieces of brass on the shelves that lined the walls, and the shapes of many were new to me and their colour spoke of age. Then a hail came across the water and coming out of my dreams I saw the D.O.—whom I was relieving—standing on the wharf and waving frantically.

In the months that followed my " taking over " I found myself up against a curious habit of suspicion he had possessed, every day of my life. Not a soul in the district had done anything, or would do anything on his own. At the seven out-stations, the native clerks and Government Chiefs were like so many stuffed figureheads. They had not been, so to speak, his colleagues in the administration of the district, but only the interpreters of his wishes. And such a policy in a large and scattered district like the Labuk and Sugut, where means of transport were the very worst imaginable, and where there was no telephone communication, bred complete stagnation, which was made so much more deplorable by the fact that for months past he had been ill and so unable to travel round the district.

But all this I did not know as we walked from the wharf to his house, though I soon realised that he was most nervy, and filled with but the one idea of putting as many miles as possible between himself and Klagan in the shortest space of time.

As we passed the office he made a movement as if he wished to turn in there and then, looked at me in a half-frightened kind of way.

I took no notice, but as I walked slowly on I could see him struggling between hospitality and desire. And desire won. His hand was shaking as he put it on my own to detain me. I waited but gave him no encouragement. Then words came.

" That's the office ! "

I nodded. It was a self-evident fact.

" There's a lot to tell you about, and many papers to explain. When would you like to ' take over ' ? " The last words came out with a rush.

I looked at him. Poor old thing ! He simply could not hide his dread and loathing of the district. His joy at departure was almost more than he could bear. To be done with it all was his dominant idea ! But I was adamant ; I was hungry and disliked haste.

" Later," I said, answering his query as gently as I could ; " later—a little later if it's all the same to you, for just at the moment there's only one thing that really interests me and it's not connected with work."

He looked surprised, then said, " You mean—breakfast ? "

I nodded assent and we continued our way to the house.

Surely one of the most dismal things in the world is an unfurnished house ! But if there is one thing more dismal it is a house stripped only of the personal effects of the owner.

There scattered about are the few articles of Government-provided furniture : a table or two, a chair, a sideboard, a rickety book-case, an ancient what-not, and a couple of broken lamps that are left for the incoming tenant. The walls, stained and parti-coloured, studded thick with nails that have held the pictures, parangs and curios of the departing D.O. Piled around on the floor are his household goods : mats and rugs ; spears and walking sticks, rifles and sporting gear ; " basongs " and baskets ; his baths and camp furniture and an ill-assorted collection of boxes, out of every crack and joint of which pokes the straw-packings, that contain his crockery and glass. On the sideboard a couple of glasses, a few bottles, mostly empty, a plate or two, some knives and forks, a salt cellar and a very old and stained bottle of Worcester Sauce.

The whole scene deplorable and sad. An empty house can somehow breathe a future and express a hope. But, dismantled, half empty and partially inhabited it only speaks of departure, seems redolent only of dead and bygone days.

There is no need to enter the bedroom to look upon the sheetless bed and empty towel-horse, or to pass on to the bath-room to gaze upon the serried ranks of empty and half-used medicine bottles that somehow are always collected in each house. These things will be found as surely as day follows night.

And so it was at Klagan ; only just a bit worse than usual, for in his haste to depart my predecessor had forgotten there would be two of us and had packed and emptied his larder to the utmost limit.

So in the end he had his way, and after an infinitesimal breakfast of one poached egg, that seemed so pathetically lonely without its couch of toast, we went to the office. But on the way I told my " boys " to be quick in unpacking my stores and gave cookie instructions to take charge of the commissariat for lunch and henceforth.

A strange bed or an unfamiliar room is the excuse given by many for a sleepless night. But it always seems to me that too much weight is attributed to these details. For if the excuse is genuine then the average D.O. in Borneo would not sleep for more than half the nights of a year. And if such were the case—well, I only know that nerves and irritability would be much more frequent than they are.

But my first night in Klagan was undisturbed ; no premonitions of the happenings of the next two years came to haunt me and it seemed I had hardly closed my eyes when I heard 6 a.m. striking.

I went to the window and looked out. As I gazed, I felt that something was missing ; I seemed waiting for a greeting that did not come. And then I knew—there was no Solitary Father. In his place were jungle and swamp and river which circled and pressed around me. And in three hours' time I should be alone.

. . . . .

For the next few days I was busy, setting my house in order, digesting facts and minute papers, interviewing local celebrities and becoming as generally conversant as is possible at headquarters, with my new district. Then before making an extended trip to all the outstations I found it necessary to visit Labuk Estate. Here for the first time I met the manager, a Dutchman. And once again I found myself in antipathy with the management of an Estate.

The manager was an extraordinary fellow and apart from his work possessed but one hobby—Gramophones. The science of tobacco planting he knew, I believe, from A to Z ; but he lacked the one great quality of understanding. To him coolies were just coolies. They worked and were paid. He had no understanding of or sympathy for that complaint so aptly named " Sakit Panat " (tiredness). I asked him once if he were ever tired or felt a little " off-colour." His answer was, as I expected, " Why, of course, yes, but I don't see—— "

" No ! I don't expect you to," I broke in, " it's beyond your ken ; I quite understand. But if you do feel a little bit lazy, a wee bit hipped or ' fed-up ' what happens ? "

For a moment he looked at me, puzzled as to what I was getting at, then answered,

" Why, I take a longer rest, or perhaps even a day off and the next morning I'm as fit as a fiddle."

" Exactly. That's just my point, but your coolies—— "

I did not finish, for his eyes were bulging out of his head.

" God verdomp ! " he gasped, " you're mad, mad as a hatter ! They have their work and their pay. Their pulse is normal, their tongue clean, they have no temperature—and you say they are tired ! My God ! where would I be if I listened to you ? I'd be out of a job and looking for another, pretty damn quick if I worked on those lines. No, no ! it may work all right in Government Service, but on an Estate—— No—no—we must show a profit and there's my commission to be thought of ! "

So we left it at that and I knew that his opinion of me as a District Officer was a bad one, and one who, as he would put it, was likely to cause trouble on his Estate. Yet he meant well, for I have frequently seen him thinking out improvements for the health and recreation of his labour force and then ruining the results by some petty regulation or riding the " high-horse " over some quite fancied disrespect.

On this first visit he quickly gave me an insight into his character, which was absolutely typical. I had spent the night on the Estate and had arranged to return to Klagan the following morning, but before leaving had promised to walk to a distant division and harangue some Javanese coolies who were inclined to be troublesome. There was no question of a prosecution ; I was only to remind them of the obligations of their contracts and the possible consequences if they were forgetful.

During the night rain had fallen—not a shower, but a

steady two inches—and though the morning was fine, experience warned me of the state of the roads. Also it was hot—oppressively so—with a muggy steamy heat.

Without so much as looking at my ducks I donned—as I generally did in an outstation—a shirt and shorts. Then I went to meet the manager. He seemed distrait and worried as we drank our coffee prior to setting forth. At last he could contain himself no longer.

" Are you going like that ? " he asked.

" Like what ? " I answered, though I knew full well what he meant.

" In those clothes ? "

" Why not ? They're decent, aren't they ? "

" Yes—but . . . " and he hesitated.

" But what ? " I questioned, determined to make him speak his mind.

" Don't you think you ought to wear a tunic and trousers ? The coolies, you know—they're not accustomed to your ' get up '—it's never been done before, and in Java—— "

" Damn Java," I broke in, " I don't care a continental what they do in Java or in Sumatra either as far as that goes. We're in British North Borneo and I'll wear what I like in my own district ; and as for your coolies—for two pins I won't go near them if you make such a fuss. I'm sick of your rotten Dutch ' adats ' (customs) on tobacco estates and I won't dress up in a tunic and trousers for you or anyone else. It's shorts or nothing, my dear fellow, so you can make your choice," and pushing back my chair I picked up a paper, only to throw it down in disgust as I found it to be a trade journal on gramophones.

There followed, for a few minutes, an awkward silence, which was eventually broken by the entry of a rather dilapidated Chinese " boy " with a thermos flask of hot tea. Then, as quickly as I had flared up, I relented of my temper and spoke :

" But seriously," I questioned, " what's wrong with my clothes ? Half the planters and D.O.'s in the country wear shorts. What's the matter with them ? "

" It's the coolies," was all he could answer. " They're not used to them and—and do you think—of course it's up to you—but do you think they will respect you in—in that ' get up ' ? "

I looked at him and then burst out laughing, but my merriment only puzzled him the more, so I ceased and rose from my chair.

" Let's be going," I suggested, " it's getting late, and if your coolies think they need not respect me because I wear shorts– then I'm afraid some of them will suffer a rude awakening," and I descended the steps of the house.

I knew enough of the cast-iron customs and rigid rules of Dutch tobacco estates to know what a shock I must have given him, but not for the world would I have given way or allowed my life to be ruled by such fads as wearing a tunic and trousers in order to gain the respect of a few coolies. If I could not gain it myself I certainly fail to see how my clothes would.

Throughout the walk I certainly had the better of the manager as regards ease and coolness, for he was fat and over forty, and stiff white ducks, cut with military tightness and with a high collar to boot, are not the acme of comfort for a four mile walk.

As I stood talking to the coolies, I could not help comparing our appearances. One of us hot and perspiring, the collar of his tunic wrinkled and grubby, a widening stain of perspiration spreading under his arms, his trousers crinkled and splashed, his white boots encased in mud, and his topi pushed well off his forehead which he incessantly mopped ! The other cool and comfortable and only shoes of brown canvas and leather a trifle muddy.

A little incident, this, but, like a straw, it showed which way the wind blew ; and I knew that sooner or later there would be friction between us.

A few weeks later, I am afraid, I added fuel to the fire of the dislike of me by my conduct over a certain Javanese coolie named Kromo. This man, according to the manager, was a most desperate character, a rotter, a bad hat, an absolute " Stink-bug " and was charged by him with the serious offence of " Criminal Intimidation." But boiled down I could only make the offence one of a very minor assault and sentenced him accordingly to a month's gaol.

Curiously enough at this time most of my wicker and cane-bottomed chairs required mending and I discovered that Kromo was an expert craftsman. So in prison clothes and keeping prison hours he sat under my house and worked—entirely to my satisfaction. Then one day the manager took it into his head to visit me and the fat was promptly in the fire with a vengeance !

His tirade was long and lengthy and nothing I could say would appease him. " Government was a farce ! the whole system of gaols was a farce, and my behaviour was simply scandalous. Here was the biggest rogue unhung in the district, who ought to have been doing six months at least, sitting under my house and mending chairs ! I was simply the limit, and if that was the way I punished his coolies he wouldn't waste any more time prosecuting them."

This last, unless the cases were serious, was exactly what I wanted. I could not very well tell him so, however, and contented myself with asking him what he would have done had he been in my place and found so simple and obvious a way of getting his chairs mended.

I often wondered whether it was the East or the effect of a little authority that made so many men in Borneo one-sided, for I rarely met one who could honestly see, and would as equally honestly admit, that there were two sides to every question. And the worst offenders were generally that hospitable crowd of men—the Planters. They were as little gods or kings upon their estates and, though most of them tried hard to hide their feelings, I could always feel their resentment at losing a case in the Magistrate's Court. They seemed to think that their word was enough ; that if they accused a coolie of an offence he must be convicted ; they carried about with them an air of "I have spoken," and were perfectly indifferent to the value of evidence; while their ideas as to the fitness of punishments for crimes astounded me.

On my return from Labuk Estate I found Orang Kaya Kaya Pangiran Aji Pati waiting to see me. He was the head chief of the District and a member of the Advisory Native Council, a recently instituted body, brought into being with the idea of keeping the Governor in close touch with native thought. Aji Pati was an old man, and as I looked at him I had a premonition that his days were numbered.

In a way he was the most unique figure among the Chiefs for though he had served the Government loyally and well for many years he would never take a cent of pay, preferring, as he maintained, to keep his independence. His assistance was great and his advice generally sound and worthy of acceptance, though occasionally tinged with self-interest. His sway extended over the whole district, but more particularly was it effective along the Labuk and Tungud rivers.

Like Haji Arsat he was originally an immigrant bent on trading, and his knowledge and authority were founded on close personal contact with the many conflicting tribes and customs that abounded in the large area under my charge.

For no district possessed such a polyglot population as the Labuk and Sugut. There were Dusuns and Sungeis ; Dumpas and Tidongs ; Bajaus and Suluks ; Chinese and Javanese. And all respected and acknowledged the Pangiran.

He himself was a Tidong, a race that originally dwelt in Dutch Borneo and seem to be akin to the Muruts, with the difference that it has become Mohammedan in religion. To this fact I attribute its advance in the scale of civilisation. From Dutch Borneo many Tidongs settled around Tawao and then split up till with the permission of Government Aji Pati founded a colony in the Labuk on the banks of the river opposite Klagan.

Here he lived in patriarchal style, the Father of his people. Into his hands he gathered such trading as he desired, for among the Tidongs he was the only really wealthy man and anyone who fell on evil days would come to him for assistance. And the appeal would not be in vain, but a return—in jungle produce—rotan, damar, guttah—or padi or indian corn—would be exacted.

I had met him first in Semporna, while he was on a visit to friends, and learnt a great deal about him from the Resident who had a great respect and affection for the old man.

It was well that I had learnt something of him and his value and loyalty before my transfer to the Labuk for he was, I think, the most trying of all the chiefs I have worked with. He was old and ailing ; extremely conservative, and his refusal to draw pay made him absolutely independent. Yet his services to Government were very real and I realised that his death would bring

THREE TYPES OF DUSUN WOMEN.

p. 210

many matters to a head which were at present quiescent under his personality, and though I should deplore his loss I foresaw that while he lived fulfilment could not be expected of many new policies inaugurated by the Government.

He had come to see me about the vexed question of the natives' debts to the Chinese shopkeepers, who, he claimed, were exacting exorbitant interest. An old trouble in all districts and one that will last till the end of Time! But in those days I did not quite realise its magnitude and many ramifications, so gaily tried my prentice hand at finding a solution.

Stern economic facts, however, will not be gainsaid, and there was and never can be any legislation to compel shopkeepers to keep and sell any specified commodity.

The natives had no money, yet they required clothes, oil, and tobacco; the harvest was not yet due and their rice supply had given out and they wanted rice for their daily food. So they went to the shopkeeper and obtained these goods on credit and their payment was to be in kind—in jungle produce and padi.

So far all was well, for barter is the essence and basic fact of life and trade. But between the incurring of a debt and the time due for its repayment much may happen, and the contingency when it arises is generally unforeseen and one which operates hardly on the debtor.

Such was the case in the Labuk and so I was honoured by a visit from Aji Pati. For the exchanges on the world's bourses had undergone a change and the prices and demand for commodities in the world's markets had altered. Damar and rotan and guttah were not sought and the price for such had dropped, while the price of rice, the staple food of the East, was rising. So when the natives brought in their produce, the result of weeks in the jungle, they found their debts still unliquidated though their supplies of oil and tobacco and rice had been consumed.

How then were they to live ? Their dilemma became the shopkeeper's opportunity. Another loan would be grudgingly conceded and the terms of repayment raised. And now there was part of the old debt and the new one to be repaid and jungle produce had no sale ! But rice ! That was a different matter ! Rice and padi would fetch a good price in Sandakan and the profit to be made would be worth the risk of a bad harvest. So argued the Towkay. And in his straits so agreed the native, thus literally selling his birthright for a mess of pottage.

But when it came to repayment, the harvest was bad and the rice crop poor and to liquidate his debt the native must part with most of his crop. But if he did so how was he to live, how feed his wife and children ? And if he did not pay his debt there was the fear of a civil summons hanging over him and the costs of an action automatically piled up against him.

So Aji Pati came to me. But what could I do ? This system of double profit—profit on the goods the Chinese sold to the natives, profit on the produce brought in by them and sold in Hongkong or Singapore—always angered me. But what could I do ? It was legal trade and merely the outcome of the Chinaman's foresight and willingness to take risks ; merely the outcome of the natives' intense conservatism and want of looking ahead ; merely the outcome of perfectly logical economic conditions—and yet it rankled.

For a long time after Aji Pati had finished speaking I was silent. Then I became conscious of him looking at me as he said, " Apa Tuan pikir ? " (What do you make of it, Tuan ?—literally, What does the Tuan think ?)

" There's only one thing to do, Pangiran," I answered,

" and I'm going to do it. I'm going to take the law into my own hands. There may be trouble and I may fail, but I'm going to try."

His old eyes lit up for a moment with a gleam of delight for he was by nature and by habit an autocrat and always rather scornful of the constitutional side of Government, but his only comment was the one word " Tuan " spoken with a wealth of meaning.

" Listen, Pangiran," I continued, " you can tell all your people and everyone in the district that they are forbidden to barter or sell rice or padi, except in cases of need and in small quantities, to anyone except to me, that is, except to Government. I will pay them a fixed and fair price in cash per gantang and with this money they can purchase daily necessities or pay off their debts as they choose. On no account need they be frightened of the Chinese nor should they part with more than fifty per cent. of their crop."

For some time the Pangiran remained silent while he digested my remarks. Then he arose from his chair, extended his hand, and with the conventional " Tabek Tuan " (good-bye) departed. His silence was a sure sign of his approval.

As I watched him walk to the river, which he must cross to reach his house, I must admit that I felt rather pleased with myself, for it seemed to me that I had struck a good blow for the natives and driven a nail into the profiteering Chinaman's coffin. So with a light heart I set out on my first big tour round the district, which I reckoned would take me about sixteen days.

Luckily for my peace of mind throughout the trip I had no idea of the storm that I had created. In blissful ignorance I visited first Tetabuan, an island not far from the mouth of the Labuk ; then sailed along the coast, calling at every Chinese shop of which there were several dotted about till I reached Trusan, an outstation placed two miles up-stream from the mouth of the Sugut river. From here I went on to Jambongan, where there is supposed to be smokeless coal, then up the Paitan river to the Paitan station. Here I spent two days, as, besides the clerk and chief, Haji Abubakar, there was a section of police. Then across the rentis (native path) through the jungle to Sungei on the Sugut, up the Sugut to Lingkabao, where later I built a police station, and thence further up-stream for two days to Meridi. Then back to Lingkabao, across another rentis to Besai, down the Tungud river to its confluence with the Labuk and so back to Klagan.

And here on my return " home " I met the full blast of the storm. The Chinese shopkeepers were furious over my conduct and in my absence had complained of my high-handed action to the Resident in Sandakan, who had promised to visit Klagan on my return and go into matters. I had rather expected this to happen, so I was not surprised, but I *did* receive a shock when I discovered there was not a grain of rice to be purchased in the shops. In vain I went myself to buy some, for I was politely told " there was none or only just enough for the consumption of the shopkeepers and their coolies."

This was a counter-attack indeed and checkmate with a vengeance. Without any rice how would the natives live ? How could I compel the shopkeepers to sell a commodity they did not wish to stock, even though I realised their action was premeditated trade bluff ? In the end I had to give way and allow the old vicious circle to continue, but I gathered some small crumbs of comfort from the fact that the Resident approved my exercising control over the export of rice and padi from the district.

Of course I bore the Chinese no ill-will, but a few months later, when their " amour propre " received a nasty jar owing to the conduct of a certain shopkeeper's daughter, I could not help feeling a small twinge of satisfaction, though this was quickly denied me when the incident eventually ended in tragedy.

Ah Sin was young—about eighteen—and very pretty, and many were the young men attracted by her wealth and beauty. But of them all, Sabtu, one of her father's coolies, seemed the most favoured. He was a Bugis and a Mahommedan, but his position was menial in the extreme —a hired hand who earned little pay. But there was a charm and fascination about him for he was strong and good-looking. Altogether he was a pleasing rascal, were it not that he suffered from " Kurap " (a skin disease akin to ring-worm).

I think they flirted occasionally, and Sabtu being a Mahommedan considered he condescended in looking at the daughter of a Chinaman. I fancy Ah Sin encouraged him, and that there had been stolen moments of sweetness in the moonlight and that lovers' whispers had mingled on the night breeze with rustle of the coconut palms. I imagine Ah Sin knew why Sabtu's debt to her father never grew less and frequently most months grew bigger.

This, though probably true, is only conjecture, but what is certain is that, to Sabtu's utter amazement, Ah Sin eventually discarded him ; not lightly, gently nor sorrowfully, but wilfully, cruelly, with a biting scorn. And, in a loud voice that soon attracted a crowd, she called him all the names she could think of ; scorned him for his menial position ; ridiculed him because of his " kurap," while he was too dazed to realise what was happening.

So Sabtu's romance came tumbling about his head like a child's house of cards, and, worse than this, he found himself without employment, for his pride would not let him work any longer for Ah Sin's father.

I had always wanted to get Sabtu into my employ, and, though I would not have deliberately enticed him away from the towkay, now was my opportunity, and I offered him the post of Serang on my sailing boat, which was fitted with a motor attachment.

From coolie to a Chinaman to Government Serang! Sabtu's luck was in, and as the weeks sped by and as he was always cheery and bright and full of fun I thought he had got over his love affair and that his wounded pride was healed. Then just as I was congratulating myself he entered my office, saluted and spoke quietly:

"Tuan," he said, "Ah Sin is my quarters and will not go away."

I looked at him sharply, but his gaze met mine.

"Why?" I asked curtly.

"I don't know, Tuan," he replied, "she was there on my return from bathing in the river. She refuses to leave. I have told her to go but she will not. She says she wants to live with me and that she loves me."

"Is she alone?" I questioned.

"Yes!" he answered.

For a second or two we looked at one another and I could almost swear I saw a twinkle—or was it a gleam of satisfaction?—in his eyes. Then pandemonium broke out in the boatmen's quarters. Hurriedly I rushed out to see what was happening, and as I neared the house the noise and screaming increased. And there I saw Ah Sin, struggling in the hands of her female relatives, her clothes nearly torn off her back, her hair falling all over her shoulders, being dragged inch by inch to her home, the while she cried out to Sabtu for help and proclaimed her love for him for all to hear.

It was a family business, an affair for women, and so I did not interfere and as yet no actual irrevocable harm—at least so I thought—had been done. Yet curiosity mastered me and that night I sent for Sabtu. He came and I went straight to the point.

" Sabtu," I said, " what is the meaning of Ah Sin's extraordinary conduct ? "

For a moment he was silent, then looking me full in the face answered " Pugai " ; just one word, but it told me much and confirmed my suspicions. For " Pugai " meant a love potion.

" You really mean—— ? " I began, but he interrupted me.

" She scorned me and shamed me, Tuan, in the presence of others. It was more than I could bear. I could have killed her but I remembered my mother just in time—she is dependent on my earnings—and so, I had to be revenged and could not rest until I had wiped out the stain. Then I thought of shaming her as she had shamed me, of making her a laughing-stock as she had made me. So I confided in my mother and sought her help. And yesterday she gave me some oil—just a few drops for it is very precious—and taught me a charm. And last night I sprinkled the steps of Ah Sin's house with the oil, incanting as I did so the charm my mother had taught me, and waved my handkerchief three times over the fallen oil."

" Then ? " I couldn't help the question, I was so intensely interested.

" Then I went home and waited, for I was quite confident. I knew the Pugai would not fail."

" And now—do you want to marry her ? " I asked.

For answer Sabtu shook his head. " Not if she came

to me with all the wealth of Borneo ! A harlot and a hussy ! No, Tuan. I am content ; in the sea are many other fish ; in the jungle are many deer. What is one that I should fret myself ! "

He saluted and left me.

But I could not dismiss the matter from my mind as easily as Sabtu, for I feared complications, and I knew enough of Chinese customs to realise the enormity of Ah Sin's offence. What if she had a betrothed in Hongkong ? What would he think of this smirch to his honour ? For on points like this the Chinese are most particular. But though I might think a lot there was nothing I could do. Ah Sin's father would never consent to her marriage with Sabtu, and even if he did Sabtu, I knew, would now have nothing to do with her.

So I gave up pondering over the matter, but on my return from a trip to Telupid, a station five days' journey up the Labuk, I noticed the house in which Ah Sin had lived was empty, and my curiosity awakened.

That night I had a talk with the principal shopkeeper, who told me of the tragedy about to be enacted.

Poor little Ah Sin ! What a fate awaited her ! And I wondered if Sabtu's heart would soften when he learnt the news concerning his erstwhile sweetheart. For her father and mother had taken her to Hongkong. There they would tell her fiancé—for she had been betrothed since infancy—the whole story. It was for him—and him alone—to decide. Marriage with Ah Sin or . . .

" Or what ? " I asked the towkay.

" The choice for her of two evils," he answered, and then was silent.

The Pikongs were alight on the mantelpiece. Smoke and incense arose from numerous joss-sticks. On the walls were pictures and plates. On the floor rolled two chubby children. Busy over a pot of tea and basins of birds' nest soup was the towkay's wife. In a comfortable lounge chair reclined the towkay, contentedly smoking his opium pipe. Comfort and ease and contentment! A homely, happy atmosphere. I looked around me and appreciated the scene. Then I saw Ah Sin—a frail piece of womanhood—disgraced and dishonoured in the eyes of her people—alone, making her choice between two evils.

"You are thinking of Ah Sin, Tuan?" the towkay broke the silence.

I merely nodded. Then lit a cigarette.

"Tell me," I said suddenly, "will her fiancé marry her?"

The towkay shook his head, and his very deliberateness was final.

My vision had been true. Ah Sin must make her choice.

"You spoke of evils, Towkay," I said gently, "what will they be?"

"Death or prostitution," he answered slowly. As he spoke his wife turned round and shuddered. Then passionately kissed both her children.

As I walked home that evening under a canopy of myriad stars and heard the gentle swishing of the river, from out of the boatmen's quarters came stealing across the night the song of "Salamun"—"Love is ours and it can never die." And I thought of Sabtu and Ah Sin and her fiancé and the havoc that had been wrought by a love potion.

But the matter had passed beyond my control and all I could do was to wait and expect one day to hear the end of the story, and hope against hope that it would be a happy one.

Then one night about a month later the towkay sent

me a message and I went to see him. And once again his wife was present and there were tears in her eyes.

As I smoked and drank tea we talked of various topics, but never of the one that I knew was uppermost in our minds. The towkay's eldest daughter—a girl about Ah Sin's age—taught me a new game of cards, then bidding us good night entered an inner room.

Slowly the towkay looked up from the contemplation of his pipe. He saw the silent question in my eyes.

" Ah Sin," he said gently.

" Yes ? " I whispered.

" She made her choice," and I could hear naught but the sobbing of his wife.

" Yes ! and—— "

" There was no choice really ! How could there be ? Her fiancé would not marry her. She was young and beautiful and loved life. Death must have seemed so strange and cold and terrifying and—so—there was no choice."

And once again I walked home under the myriad stars and listened to the swish of the river. Only this time the night breeze brought no song of " Salamun " to my ears. But my eyes pictured a frail slip of girlhood, entering the bedroom of a Chinese brothel, followed by a drunken half-caste from the slums of an Eastern city.

For some time Sabtu seemed very depressed. It was as if the realisation of all that his vengeance had brought about lay heavy upon his mind. He joked and smiled less frequently than in former days and his spare time was given up to reading the Koran. The district was setting its seal upon him, changing him from a happy-go-lucky lover into a serious-minded celibate, till he, who had openly scoffed at the myriad superstitions of his race, became a firm believer in them.

As I saw much of him during the days I was travelling round the district, and our conversation would range chiefly around matters of native interest, I learnt and heard of many superstitions, till I too began to believe in them and it seemed that our daily life was made up of them; that they wove themselves into our waking moments and brooded over us while we slept. And always I noticed the strange, uncanny concurrence between an incident and a superstition.

Was the district setting its seal on me? I wondered and determined to try and break the spell. The opportunity came sooner than I expected.

We were sailing along the coast, visiting some of the islands with which the sea is dotted. Through an oversight we had forgotten to lay in a stock of firewood.

"Sabtu," I said, "we'll call in at the next island we sight and collect wood." Half an hour later a smudge appeared upon the horizon. Rapidly it came into clear view, and disclosed an island, fringed with tall trees. But no shout of joy came from Sabtu or the crew as was usual in such circumstances. I looked at them. Their faces wore a troubled expression. The silence of distress lay upon them. Then I looked closely at the trees, now plainly discernible, and the riddle of their silence was explained to me.

The trees were Kayu Aru (Casuarina trees) around which hung a superstition, believed by all the sea-faring populace of North Borneo. In Semporna and Tawao, in Sandakan and Kota Belud, the belief held good; and no native would ever bring a piece of this wood into his boat, for to do so meant the rising of a storm or the incurring of a head wind.

And here were we heading straight for the island and I had given orders for the collecting of wood! No wonder the crew were troubled! No wonder Sabtu sat like a carved image, grasping the tiller so tightly that the veins stood out purple on his hands.

I looked at the sky. It was cloudless and palest blue. The sun was a ball of molten brass. A steady breeze of six knots was blowing on our beam. The sea was a cradle of dark-blue-green.

A few minutes later we grounded and our bows rested in the shell-strewn sand that glittered red and white and purple. But no movement came from the boat—not a man of the crew jumped ashore. They were waiting—waiting for Sabtu to speak, to voice their fears and express their hopes. And I waited too; for my opportunity had come. Yet I was loath to run counter to their wishes.

"Tuan!" Sabtu's voice was low and very suppliant. "Surely the Tuan knows the superstition! How that if we bring this wood into the boat a storm will arise or the wind will change and blow in our faces. Is it worth it, Tuan, just for some firewood? We will eat cold rice and there is enough wood to cook the Tuan's food. Does the Tuan insist? If so we will obey—but——"

I could not hold out against such pleading, and evident distress, so in the end gave way and laughingly suggested a bathe and a search for turtles' eggs instead. And yet—what harm could come from a piece of wood? Was I a weak fool to submit or did I, too, in my heart of hearts, share this belief? I did not know nor choose to decide for the water called me and I plunged from the deck of the boat deep down into its cool green depths.

And as we searched for eggs and afterwards ate our lunch the boatmen's spirits rose and for the first time for weeks I heard Sabtu's voice raised in song—

" Jikalau Tuan pergi,
Pergi berprang
Jangan Kerim Surat
Choba Kerim Wang." *

But the spirit of hard worldliness that underlay the song, which was of Javanese origin and purported to be a message from a woman to her man at the wars, touched me and gave me a glimpse of Sabtu's heart and told me that he was still brooding over Ah Sin's faithlessness ; was still sorrowful for the effect of his vengeance. And a wild idea sprang into my mind ! What if I could disprove the superstition of the Kayu Aru, break down his belief in its supernatural power ? If I could accomplish this, might not other beliefs lose their strength ? Might he not come to disbelieve the potency of Pugai and so might not his sorrow in the end be less ?

Lunch was over. The sky was still cloudless. The sun still rode in an azure heaven. The steady breeze still blew on our beam. As we " hauled off " from the island no conditions could have been more perfect. There seemed no possibility of a storm ; no reason for the wind to change.

Yet soon I noticed Sabtu gazing skywards and shortly afterwards the sail failed to fill, flapped and then jibed. The wind had changed. It had veered from starboard to port ; blew fitfully from this direction, then veered again —only this time it blew right in our teeth. Sabtu looked at me. I said nothing.

The wind continued to blow " dead on," its velocity gradually increasing. Dark clouds began to appear on the horizon, scudding at first across the sky then finally

* " If the Tuan goes to the wars
Don't send home letters,
Money is more acceptable."

banking up one on the top of another. A storm was undoubtedly brewing.

Once again I looked at Sabtu and our eyes met. In his I saw a mute appeal. It was as if they stated a fact, asked a question, then gave the answer and ended with a supplication.

I put my hand into one of my pockets, and pulled out a small twig which I placed on Sabtu's knee.

For a long moment he gazed at it. Then, oblivious of my presence, he threw it overboard with what sounded like a Malay curse.

Gradually the wind veered round and the sky cleared. Soon we were again sailing merrily towards our destination with a steady breeze on our beam.

Sabtu looked at me.

"Does the Tuan believe now?" he asked.

I merely smiled in answer, but the twig had been a piece of Kayu Aru!

"Coincidence!" I kept saying the word over and over to myself and yet was it? The riddle was beyond me and I had not solved it when on the journey home we entered the mouth of the Klagan river on the last lap to Klagan. Suddenly I remembered that we must pass Bukit Mendagu (Mendagu Hill), a slight elevation on the true left bank of the river, which was reputed to be haunted.

In fact so great was their fear of this place that natives generally avoided passing it, preferring to make a long detour round another river rather than risk the anger of the evil spirits that made it their home.

But as we were pressed for time Sabtu and the crew had silently, though fearfully, conceded to necessity, relying no doubt on my presence to ward off any evil that might happen, for they knew that some months previous

I had explored the hill and even breakfasted upon its summit and still was alive to tell the tale.

As we neared Mendagu all the tales I had heard about it came back to me. How that at times fish with no flesh, but only bones that glittered with a blue phosphorescent light, were to be seen swimming about. How that at times a storm would arise and part the water on either side, leaving a dry wide channel along which, like the Israelites of old in the Red Sea, one could walk from bank to bank, while at others the water was fathomless and of immeasurable depth. How a wonderful brass spear-head of utterly unknown workmanship had been found by a starving Dusun on its summit. How he had kept the spear for many days, and each night dreamed so terribly of hideous grotesque forms that sought to clutch at him and kill him till in desperation he sold it to a Chinaman and so obtained release from his nightly horrors. How the spear had come into my possession, and, because so many coveted it, as a work of supernatural origin that had dropped from heaven, I had slept with it under my pillow for fear of theft. How sweating, trembling in every limb, I had awakened in the pitchy darkness—my lamp having burnt out—a cold, gripping fear at my heart. How I had tried to sleep again and how nightmare after nightmare had haunted me, till I could bear the darkness and quiet no longer, so fearfully called for my "boy" and bade him light the lamp and make some tea. How that at times a noise like deep rolling thunder was to be heard rumbling in the bowels of the hill—a sign of dire and untoward happenings.

All these stories I remembered as we approached the hill.

And the sky was cloudless; the sea calm, the river

almost without a ripple, and the breeze blew lightly from astern.

Yet the laughing chattering crew of a little while ago had become strangely silent, and Sabtu's face wore an expression of sombre anxiety.

Suddenly the air felt cooler. The crew huddled together. A shudder ran down my spine and a creepy, prickly feeling reached to my fingers and toes. My flesh was turning goosey. A feeling akin to fear was reaching out and enveloping me ; almost I could feel—— Then with a start I shook myself, cursed myself for a fool. Afraid ! Of what was I afraid ? There was nothing to fear. A hill on the river bank, a collection of fish-wives' tales of ghosts and evil spirits ? Spirits ! I was becoming a superstition-ridden fool. I would break the spell here and now, lay the ghosts of Mendagu once and for all. And I started to sing, but the look of horror on Sabtu's face froze the words on my lips.

" Tuan ! " he began in an awestruck whisper but I broke in, " You're an ass, Sabtu ; all of you are asses. There aren't any ghosts or fleshless fish. I've climbed old Mendagu and fed on his summit. There's nothing—absolutely nothing—not a spirit to be seen or heard. And even if there were I'm not afraid of them. We'll call there now and cook our tea on the great bare rock that overhangs the river and you shall see, there's not a single spirit and nothing, absolutely nothing will happen."

" Tuan ! " The word was one long shudder of horror.

Then It was upon us—a great cloud that blotted out the sun and spread and spread over the heavens—a mighty wind of icy coldness that blew straight down from Mendagu and lashed the river into " white-horses " which quickly grew into angry, leaping waves. A rending tear and the sail went streaming in the wind torn into a dozen tattered pieces—a stay-rope came hurtling aft, missing my head by inches and left a vivid weal on Sabtu's face. Three blinding streaks of purple lightning—three deafening peals of thunder—a storm of hail descending, whipping our faces like the thongs of a knout.

And then—it was over. Quick as the dart of an adder's tongue had flashed the anger of the outraged spirits, leaving us stunned and maimed and chastened.

"Coincidence?" I hardly dared to think the word, and yet what else could it be?

"Ikan berhantu!" (Spirit Fish). The words gasped by a boatman, who sat with bulging eyes and pointed with shaking fingers, broke in on my reverie. I followed his sign. And there swimming around the boat were the fleshless fish—or so it seemed, for their bones glittered with a blue phosphorescence and it was as if they were devoid of flesh and skin.

Even as we gazed they disappeared; just for a moment we saw them—then, with a movement of lightning quickness, they were gone.

And once again the sun was shining; once again the sky was blue and the surface of the river calm. Then we hauled in our tattered sail, lowered our mast, and to the chugging of the Evinrude went up-stream to Klagan.

As subsequent days passed in uneventful sequence the influence of Mendagu began to wear off. The sun shone with continued tropic fierceness and, as Hari Raya approached, the minds of all in Klagan returned with enthusiasm to the coming sports which were to be held in honour of the Festival. It seemed as if ghosts and superstitions were things of the past; as if we had dwelt for a time in a night of terrors and emerged at last into the light of day; as if we had been wandering in the trackless jungle and suddenly stepped out into an open plain.

And then the spirits of Mendagu spoke again !

At dead of night in my house I heard their voices ; anchored out at sea off the mouth of the Klagan river Sabtu and my boatmen heard them ; in the shops at Klagan the Chinese were awakened ; at the office the sentry on guard caught the distant rumbling ; in the barracks the sergeant was aroused from his sleep. Yet, strangest of all, across the river Aji Pati and his people heard nought at all.

It was the eve of Hari Raya. There was no thunder in the air ; the night gave no promise of storm—a cool clear night with winking stars and never a cloud in the sky. I was fast asleep. No dreams or nightmares disturbed my slumbers.

Yet I awakened with a start and for some reason listened. There was thunder in the air or else . . . From far away came a muffled rumbling, like the distant detonating of a mighty gun. Six times it sounded and was silent ; six times I listened, then heard no more. And something indefinable told me that no thunder claps had rent the air. Whence then came this noise and whence this mystery ?

The opening of a door broke the silence, the patter of bare feet came sounding down a passage, then halted outside my room.

" Tuan ! " My " boy " was calling and fear strove with wonder in his voice.

" Tuan ! " The call was repeated with fear as its dominant note.

" Yes ? " I answered.

" Ada dengar bunyi bunyi macham meriam besar." (Did you hear the noise like big guns ?)

" Yes," I answered as I opened the door and stepped

out. " Yes, I heard the thunder ; but why disturb me, Amat, at this hour of the night ? "

I spoke with an assumed severity I little felt, for just as a mist comes stealing in through open windows, so cold fear came creeping into the house. But before Amat had time to answer we were joined by my frightened cookie and almost gibbering " takang ayer."

Then down a path that led from the barracks, past the office to my house I saw a lamp come dancing with wavering, uncertain gait. Someone, probably the Sergeant, was coming and the lamp jerked in unison with his unsteady steps. It had almost reached the office ; a little more and it would have passed.

Then, " Halt ! Who goes there ? "

The challenge, flung on the night in a high-pitched Murut voice, came with a startling suddenness that made me jump though I had been sub-consciously awaiting it. And he who carried the lamp must also have been startled, for with a rattle the lantern fell to the ground and went out.

Out of the darkness came the answer and I recognised the sergeant's voice. " Friend ! It's I—Sergeant."

" Pass, Friend," the Murut policeman gave the counter. " All's well."

But was it, I wondered ! If so, then why all this disturbance in the night ? And I waited. The flare of a match, the lamp relighted and the steps came nearer and nearer. Then they halted outside the house.

" Naik, Sergeant ! " (Come up, Sergeant !) I called out, and went to meet him as he climbed the seven steps up to the verandah.

" What is it, Sergeant ? " I asked him, as having saluted he put down his lantern. He looked at me with wonder staring eyes, then passed his gaze on to where Amat stood and for a second was silent.

Then regardless of discipline and manners they both broke out, " It wasn't thunder, Tuan, it wasn't. . . ." Then they stopped as a long low rumbling sound came stealing through the night. Then silence, save for our quickened breathing.

From across the river came the barking of a favourite hunting dog of Aji Pati's ; the homely ordinary sound broke the tension for a moment, just long enough to set my brain in action.

" Sergeant ! " I said, " go across the river. Ask the Pangiran if he heard the—the rumbling, and enquire if he knows what it is."

" Tuan." The sergeant saluted, turned on his heels and departed.

As he receded into the darkness, and the light from his lamp grew smaller and fainter, a curious sense of the smallness of humanity, of the utter insignificance of our comprehensions stole over me, and the necessity for human company compelled me to keep my " boy " in purposeless conversation, while cookie went to make some tea and toast.

Then once again we saw the lamp approaching, and the sergeant came up the steps.

" Neither the Pangiran nor his people, Tuan, have heard the noise. They were all sleeping when I crossed the river and I had to wake them up."

" Sleeping ! but you saw the Pangiran ? " I questioned.

" Yes, and he had heard nothing. He seemed surprised. Then, as I described the noises, how you had heard them, and I heard them, and the sentry too, he looked most serious."

" Yes ? "

" And said, ' Tell the Tuan it is Mendagu and it always spells a warning. It was so before Mat Sallel's time, before the smallpox and the Musah raid. But that for three months there is no need to fear: after that things will happen. Tell the Tuan to-morrow morning I will visit him and will he excuse me to-night on account of my age? ' "

So the rest of the night passed in idle speculation, and never was I more thankful for the returning light of day.

In the morning Sabtu met me; straight from the river he came to my house. But with a gesture I silenced the words that were breaking from his lips.

" I heard it, Sabtu," I said. " I know. It was thunder."

He shook his head. " The spirits of Mendagu, Tuan, are very powerful and I am much afraid. For they speak with a voice like thunder, which is the same and yet not the same."

I looked closely at him and saw rings of sleeplessness under his eyes.

" You'd better have a rest," I said, " for if you don't your boat won't win the paddling race this afternoon and you'll be beaten by the police, those kapirs of Muruts and Dusuns, who eat pig and worship spirits at the top of Kinabalu! "

The jibe was meant and took effect, for the rivalry between the police and boatmen was generally friendly and always keen.

" Jangan susah, Tuan," Sabtu answered, " anak klassi musti menang." (" Don't you worry, Tuan—we boatmen will win all right.") Then with a smile he saluted and went as I bade him to rest.

But in the Sports that afternoon the boatmen did not

win, and were beaten by at least a length by their rivals the police.

Then two months slipped by in quiet routine and day followed day till the third month was nearly at an end. And this month died and the fourth was born and had grown to half its age when the first happenings began.

A Chinese coolie on Labuk Estate, tormented beyond endurance by a tandil (overseer) and another coolie, tried to hang himself and failed. Then, sick with his failure and tired of life, he wounded one and killed the other of his tormentors. Thus death though from the gallows came to him as he wished.

At the Suruan timber camp three Chinese were returning in an open boat from their work in the jungle to their " lines " at the close of a strenuous day. As they turned a sharp bend in the river the boat capsized. One of them reached the shore, but two were drowned.

At the same camp a Chinese coolie, goaded into fury over some fancied slight, suddenly one evening seized a heavy chopper and attacked his companions. In the ensuing struggle he was overpowered, but as the night was too far spent for the Assistant in charge to send him up to me for trial at Klagan, he spent the night handcuffed to a post. The next morning under the care of four coolies he was sent up the river. During the journey he complained of sickness and so lay down in the bottom of the boat, and as a protection from the sun his companions covered him with a kajang (leaf awning). In due course the boat reached Klagan, but when the rowers pulled off the kajang the wretched man was dead. Was it fear, or had his hands and legs been bound too tightly ? I did not know and had no means of finding out, for the nearest doctor was eighty miles away in Sandakan.

On the Sugut coast, in an isolated position, was a shop

in which dwelt two Chinaman and the little son of one of them. To them, in broad daylight, came a " dapang." In it were four Obians. They were in search of rice and tobacco of which there was plenty in the Kedei. But a Chinaman likes to be paid for the goods he sells and an Obian likes to take what he wants regardless of a Chinaman's wishes. And so two cold, stiff Chinese corpses were discovered on the floor of the shop ; and fifty yards away among the tall growth of ubi-kayu lay the blistering body of the little boy. The gaping wounds of each were terrible to see.

As this sequence of untoward happenings unfolded, like the chapters of a novel, with ever increasing intensity, one curious fact came gradually to be borne in upon me. In every instance the *dramatis personæ* were Chinese. Why? Had they and they alone incurred the wrath of the Spirits that dwelt on Bukit Mendagu ? Was it because in their trading activities they were keener and sharper than their opponents ? Was it because in the country of their adoption they lived an alien life ? Was it because ? . . . But why continue conjecture ? For an event that swept the district from end to end, leaving in its path a trail of loss and desolation, of poverty and blasted hopes, a plague and a legacy of swamp and sand was nearing its due date of fell accomplishment.

Never shall I forget January 1918 and the " Great Flood," as it has come to be called. Never in the memory of any living man in Borneo had such a flood been known. From end to end of the territory the rivers rose and rose bursting their banks and spreading wider and ever wider, till the country, save for the hills, seemed one vast sheet of water.

For one whole month we in the Labuk and Sugut never saw the sun. For one whole month each day the rain fell, till on the 28th my rain gauge was washed away.

Fifty-six inches, and still the rain was falling, still the waters rose!

There was no island of Klagan—it had ceased to be—only a few buildings which rose stork-like out of the madly-swirling water.

Two houses had been washed away; the water spread to the floor of the boatmen's quarters, to the floor of the barracks as well. Each building built on piles stood five feet off the ground, but the water rose without ceasing, covered the floors, then crept up the walls with slow persistency, driving the inmates out to take refuge in the office, the only building left that seemed to promise safety.

Yet I was scared. For though the office stood some feet above the ground, it was built on insecure foundations and I was afraid it might not stand the strain of the mighty volume of water, that, sweeping among its piles, bore huge trees and solid islands of uprooted earth out to the sea which daily grew muddier and muddier.

So, to my house, which though low was stronger built and stood upon some slightly higher ground, I brought them in a vain hope born of desperation.

The odds, however, were against me, and at 2 a.m. on the 29th there were three feet of water over the floor while the kitchen and servants' quarters, which were built level into the ground, were almost completely submerged. Only the office remained as a refuge—a modern Ark amidst the waste of waters.

So, like Noah of old, I collected my people around me, leaving the World as represented by the Chinese and natives to look after itself. There was nothing I could do for them which they could not do for themselves and my first duty lay towards the Government servants under my care who looked to me for help and guidance.

Three times my boat, laden to its utmost capacity, made the short perilous journey from my house to the office. Every minute was fraught with danger and unforeseen possibilities, yet I can remember no more exhilarating moments in my life.

In the bows stands Sabtu ; the helm I hold myself. Two words of command " Let go ! " the twist of a paddle and the boat is in the raging torrent, tearing with unbelievable rapidity towards our goal—a solitary, ancient rubber tree that grows close to the office. Closer and closer we are approaching—God ! can I make it or shall we rush by ? No sound in my ears but the roar of the waters, the beat of the rain on the swift-running tide ! With all my strength I push the tiller hard over, leaning with all the weight of my body against it. Thus released, I make a funnel of my hands. Closer, closer ; just a second longer, then " Backwater " I yell with all my might and four oars strike the water, eight arms strain with all their strength to lessen the approaching shock. Just for a second we seem to tremble, pause and steady in our mad flight—just for a second but in that moment I find time to yell " Hold tight " and Sabtu, reaching to his utmost limit, seizes a branch of the rubber tree.

Just as the strength of a chain lies in its weakest link, so for a moment our future hangs on Sabtu as with a sickening jerk the boat, checked in its mad career, spins round and, rocking, swaying, points its nose up-stream.

Over the roar of the waters my voice rings once again. " Daiang " (row), and the four oarsmen strive to their best endeavour to lessen the strain on that one frail link.

I cannot bear to look at that solitary form straining,

straining, till it seems his strength must break ; just for a moment my eyelids fall and a fleeting prayer ascends to Heaven, to God or Allah, call him whatsoe'er you will : just for a moment the balance trembles, then—gradually inch by inch we are moving forward : slowly the branch comes nearer, till over us all its leaves are rustling and willing hands reach out to grasp it, seize it and hold it, granting us respite, while in the bows a form lies panting, heaving and laughing with hysterical delight.

Yet we have still to reach the office, still one last effort before we are safe. Can we, can we do it I wonder—and hesitate to make the attempt. Just a few yards, but the swirl of the water ! And if we fail ? God knows the result !

" Jaga, Tuan ! " (Look out, Tuan !) From the office, over the raging water comes the cry with startling suddenness, and hard upon its heels follows a rope flung by a Dusun sentry, who has seen our peril and, acting on blind instinct, has solved the riddle of our approach.

But no sun shone down on the morning of the 30th. Only the pitiless rain continued and the water ever rose. The office rocked and swayed to every footfall. There in our midst—among the policemen and the boatmen and their wives, among the prisoners and my servants and our cats and dogs and monkeys—the sergeant's wife gave birth to a still-born child.

The pity and the horror of that day will always haunt me. The ceaseless rain, the rising water, the swaying office ; the babel of voices, the smell of cooking, the stench of humanity, the barking of dogs ; the groans and cries of a woman in travail ; the tears of a mother whose babe is dead.

That night I made a decision which I communicated to all.

If on the morrow there was no abatement, if the rain, still fell and the water rose I should send the women and children under Sabtu's care in my boat to Tetabuan. There was a risk I knew, yet it seemed the lesser of two evils, and to give them a better chance of safety than waiting for the ever rising of the waters and the certain collapsing of the office. It meant food and drink for them, whereas, if they stayed, in two days' time our stores would be depleted. And having landed them at Tetabuan Sabtu would go on to Sandakan to tell the Resident of our sore straits. And perhaps—though the hope was faint and trembling—a launch might be sent to us and we be rescued from a watery or starving grave.

And as I wrote my letter to the Resident I pictured the launch striving to make headway up the swollen, maddened river ; caught in the swirling eddies, twisted and turned first this way and then that ; twisted and turned till broadside on she was caught in the terrific current and swept back, the while from the office we watched and waited, counted the inches untouched by the water !

Cold and grey the first faint streak of dawn came stealing through my office window. I was cold and shivering ; even the hot tea that cookie brought me failed to give me any warmth.

"Your wife is ready, cookie ?" I asked him and passed out to the verandah. I did not wish to see the misery of parting in his eyes.

I went straight to the office steps. One look, then—"Sergeant ! Sabtu ! Cookie ! Amat ! God, the water hasn't risen ! Hasn't risen since twelve last night ! !"

My voice went pealing over the office, and as its echoes died away a mighty cheer went ringing round the rafters and the office swayed most fearfully as with a rush the police and boatmen and their women gathered round me in a frenzy of relief.

As we looked and measured carefully, slowly realising the tremendous import of this fact—that the water had not risen, hadn't risen since twelve last night—a tiny shaft of sunlight came stealing through the branches of a grand and ancient rubber tree, kissed its leaves and then stole onwards, till it rested gently, lightly on the third step of the office, the step from which the water hadn't risen all the night !

" Then we needn't go to Tetabuan, Tuan—at least not yet ? "

The question came from the pretty newly-married wife of a Dusun policeman.

" Don't you want to go ? " I questioned. For answer she shook her head ; then, shyly looking at her husband, she once more shook her head, as two large tears rolled down her cheeks and splashed the floor.

In the days and nights of horror she had been the pluckiest of them all. Always cheery, and singing ; always nursing other women's babies, and cooking for her husband ; always mending and sewing and never repining. Yet now she wept ! In some small way this brought home to me the knowledge that not I alone had suffered during these last few days, not I alone had played a part, nor carried, locked in my heart, thoughts that I did not dare express.

" And the water hasn't risen since twelve last night ! " My own words came back to me as I gazed upon the little crowd that pressed around me, waiting anxiously for my decision.

It hadn't risen—then perhaps it would rise no more—perhaps the flood was over and the heavens held no more rain ! What if I ordered the departure and the flood had reached its limit ? What if I bade them stay and the water rose yet higher, and the rains came on again ? I, and I alone, must make decision.

I turned to Sabtu and the sergeant :

" Tell the women to eat now. They can wait till 8 o'clock—we'll see what the weather is like then—but they must be ready at eight—in case—I have to send them down the river after all. Two hours will make no difference and perhaps . . ."

Somewhere in the office someone started singing, in a high-pitched treble voice. It was the little Dusun wife, who but a moment ago had been crying out of sheer relief.

Suddenly I too felt the great need of relief :

" Cookie," I yelled at the top of my voice, " Cookie, you scoundrel, bring me some breakfast ! Porridge and kippers ; then curried eggs and rice."

. . . . . .

The flood had reached its limit. The heavens held no more rain. The grey clouds slowly passed leaving an azure sky, and a golden sun looked down upon the vast and turgid waters that went racing by in angry frenzy, hurrying to reach the sea. It was as if they were ashamed, frightened of confinement in the river-bed and so they hurried out to join the ocean, lest in the days that followed they should witness the scenes of desolation they had wrought.

Sand and swamp and flies ! Crops ruined and buried ; houses washed away ; homes uprooted, hopes devastated; the work of a year blotted out in a night. Homeless and foodless the natives came to me, came to me out of the night, and I—what could I do ? What was there to do ? They had no food, no implement, no pans or pots—all had been washed away, carried to God knows where and buried under feet upon feet of sand.

Sand and swamp and flies ! Such is my recollection of the district during the year that followed. Of the measure of relief and reconstruction, of the death of Aji Pati and the appointment of a new chief ; of the departure of the old Resident and the appointment of a new one ; of the work at the timber camps ; of the daily office routine ; of new policies and innovations I have my recollections. From the storehouse of my memory I may resurrect them, may find them worthy of recall. For the moment they seem forgotten. It is as though there was nothing—only sand and swamp and flies.

CHAPTER VIII

LABUK AND SUGUT (*continued*)

COLONEL Cobb, when Principal Medical Officer in Borneo, held that on account of its unhealthiness and isolation no European officer should be stationed for more than eight months in the Labuk. There was also an unwritten law which, for these very reasons, allowed an officer to take long week-ends in Sandakan every three months.

How strange a thing is the personality of a place! How strong it is! How potent in moulding the lives and characters of those who live in it! Surely in the building of towns, in the opening of ports in our far-flung empire this personality should be considered!

The Labuk!—encircled with swamp and jungle, traversed by rivers, bounded by hills and sea. It is as if a soul were imprisoned within those mighty barriers; as if a slow, long, lingering tragedy were being enacted, as if through the years and years of the past and through the years and years to come this soul were striving for freedom, to reach the light of the sun. So over the district there broods a spirit of sombre sadness, which touches and dwells in the hearts of its men.

Jesselton!—a strip of sand bounded by the restless sea and stony hills that slowly rise, as the rungs of a ladder, to the topmost peak of Kinabalu, who stands a rigid and immovable sentry guarding the gateway to the land of Sabah (native name for B.N.B.). A gateway through which one passes to enter a realm of cold formality. And, having entered, the door is slammed behind one. No passing in and out, no meeting others of the wider world outside ; only a slow absorption into a life of conventions, bound with red tape and mutual admiration.

From Jesselton to Beaufort and thence to the far Interior this spirit of self-satisfiedness can roam, but over the boundary of Kinabalu's impregnable barrier there is no passing. So back it comes to Jesselton to rest and find a home. A home, not of its choosing, but of necessity, for as the mountain guards one border so does the sea shut off all hope of escape. By the World unknown and lying off the beaten track, no steamers call, no tourists' footsteps tread the streets, no travellers stay in the one hotel. Its isolation is complete and Jesselton becomes a Parish Pump indeed.

Sandakan ! The Perfect Bay. A natural harbour, where the steamers of the World can meet. From Australia, from Manila, from China and the Dutch East Indies they come. And their coming brings a presence, breathes a wider, freer life that is felt in every corner of the town. One forgets that Europe is 9,000 miles distant or that one is living in a little known tropical Protectorate under the autocratic rule of a Chartered Company ; or that the sea is full of weird delicacies beloved by the Chinese and the jungle is inhabited by elephant and rhinoceros and pig and deer ; one forgets that the population is mostly native, that an " amok " may occur any day ; one forgets that letters come five weeks late, that papers bring stale news which the wireless has forestalled.

BUFFALO.

SANDAKAN FROM THE HILLS.

p. 242

These things sink into insignificance, become not a constant thought or reminder of what many call exile, but just a subconscious background, a kind of stage setting to the life of the world—that world of which Sandakan feels itself an integral part. Here to-day and gone to-morrow : a traveller of repute, a famous missionary, a noted financier, a great journalist, a naturalist, a bioscope operator, an opium smuggler—they all pass through, all come to the club ; they tell their stories, and shed their personalities, leaving behind them some subtle contact of the world—the great big World that knows not Jesselton, passes by the Labuk, yet embraces Sandakan, bequeathing to it a tolerance and sympathy and hospitality all its own.

Such were my thoughts as the " Petrel " steamed slowly up the Labuk on the evening of the day I left Sandakan. For a little while I had been in the World and of the World ; touched as it were the fringe of the World's garment—and now, only eight hours later, these last few days seemed a dream—I was back once again in a world of my own.

As I pushed off from the launch—anchored in mid-stream since the floating wharves had been washed away by the great flood and not yet rebuilt—I could see the sergeant waiting on the bank to meet me, and I knew from the way he stood there was something on his mind. At the foot of the office steps the guard were turning out to give me the salute ; down the path from my house three dogs came romping, barking their delight at my return ; from out of a shop hurried cookie, disturbed over a game of cards, running home to prepare me a meal ; from the sand piled high in front of the house the gardener picked up a chankol (large hoe) and made pretence of cultivation ;

inside a battered fence, that once enclosed a spacious vegetable garden, some half-dozen prisoners quickened their languid digging ; from across the river came the beating of gongs ; from the tops of the coconut trees came the cooing of doves ; in the west a blood-red sun was setting.

This was my world, which in a way contented me. For in my hands were all its tangled skeins gathered ; the unravelling and straightening out of which was my daily task, and having accomplished which there still remained the weaving of a harmonious, composite pattern to occupy my brain.

Yet somewhere in the world I'd left behind me nations in arms were fighting, thrones were tottering and republics springing into growth. This much I knew and remembered for the night before some of us in the club had talked the War. But now, as I stepped ashore and met the sergeant, fondled my dogs and took the guard's salute, I wondered ! For Sandakan seemed a dream, the world a thing apart, the War but a nightmare of some troubled sleep. Only Klagan and the Labuk existed ; only the district and the natives, only their lives and hopes and fears were a reality ; there was nothing, nothing but the jungle and the rivers ; nothing but the sand and swamp and flies.

Such is the potent spell a place can cast upon a man.

In the months that followed there was much to do and I was very busy. So, though Press telegrams reached me by post and mails arrived bringing news and letters, the world still passed me by. It was as though I read some history, skimmed it and gleaned it and—then forgot it. And all the while events were happening ; climax would follow climax with bewildering rapidity, and the great World watched with tear-dimmed eyes.

How strange and almost incomprehensible it seems here in England, looking back over a lapse of five years, to think that a great event can happen and the news of it remain unknown for weeks. Yet, in the by-ways of the Empire such may be the case and moments of delirious joy pass quite unknown.

I had been travelling for eighteen days round the district, and by chance had left Klagan before the mail came in. On my return journey I decided to visit one of the timber camps. Apart from official duties—an evening with the Assistant would be a pleasant change.

As my boat drew alongside his wharf I hailed him but no answering shout came from the house, which seemed wrapt in silence ; some clothes, however, drying on a line, spoke of someone being in residence. I clumped up the stairs, my footsteps sounding unusually noisy, and so on to the verandah. Yet no one came. I waited, but all was silent.

" Boy," I shouted, and my voice went echoing down the passage that ran the length of the house to the kitchen at the back. " Boy—mana Tuan ? " (Boy, where's the Tuan ?)

Still no answer. Only a creaking sound from a room behind the verandah which I knew was the bedroom. Then a door opened—the bedroom door—and a woman's head appeared in the opening.

" Siapa itu ? " (Who's that ?) the head asked sleepily.

" Sahaya " (I), I answered. " Tuan Cook."

The door opened wider and the woman—half Chinese and half Suluk—the Assistant's native " keep "—came forward rubbing the sleep from her dark brown eyes. A smile broke over her face as she recognised me and putting out her hand she murmured, " Tabek, Tuan " (Greeting, Tuan).

" Tabek, Mary " (for so she was named), I answered, then enquired the whereabouts of my friend.

From her I learnt that he was in the jungle, superintending the laying down of a rail for the purpose of getting out some felled timber, but that he would be back about 4 o'clock.

" You will stay the night, Tuan ? " she asked me. I nodded and for a little while I could hear her moving about the spare room. Then she came back bearing in her hands a tray on which were whisky and soda.

With a smile she put the tray down, picked up a glass, poured in some whisky and looked at me.

" Say when ? " she murmured, for she spoke a little English.

I let her fill it ere I stopped her.

" Well, Mary," I said as she passed it to me, " what's the news ? "

" There isn't any," she replied, " at least nothing that I can remember. Tuan, manager of the Timber Company, was here two weeks ago and the motor boat is out of order. There is a biawak that is stealing our chickens and—and—— "

" Nothing else ? " I questioned idly.

She shook her head, then added in the most casual tone in the world, " Tuan tahu prang sudah habis ? " (You know the War is over ?)

Speechless I gazed at her. The greatest news in all the world and she had said there was no news ! Oh the wonder and the glory of it ! The War was over ! Oh the pity of it, the damned pity of it ! That I should learn the news like this !

I raised my glass and drained it. Then pushed it across to her. Suddenly a question came hammering in my brain. I flung it at her.

" When ? When did you get the news ? "

" The news ? Oh you mean about the War ! " I nodded. " Not last week—no, the week before—Tuan Manager brought it—yes it was on the 10th."

The great moment of the world, when the nations of Europe were delirious with joy, when England from end to end was one loud shout of thankfulness and praise, when the cables and the wireless were flashing the tidings to the Empire's furthest corner, when Sandakan and Jesselton and Kudat were as little towns gone mad, when the clubs were full to brimming and the champagne corks were popping, the Great Moment passed me by and I learnt the news a fortnight late, in a wooden house on the banks of a sluggish river that carved its way through the jungle and the *nipah,* from the lips of a half-caste native woman who ransacked her brain to remember if anything of interest had lately happened !

Thus 1918 drew to a close and even we in the Labuk felt the note of hope and promise. All over the country efforts were redoubled to make the forthcoming " Our Day " the greatest of them all. The War was over ! In our thankfulness we must transcend our former efforts. Each Residency strove to reach a higher figure than the one attempted last year ; each district strove to beat its former best. Till in the end the country's total was surprising and Sandakan stood out first upon the list.

Turned into pounds, dollars and cents it may seem a trifle, but when I handed in the Labuk list, nearly double what it had been the year before, I could not help a thrill of pride which ran right through me, when, remembering all we had suffered—the Flood and Influenza—in the year now drawing to its close. I looked upon this widow's mite, so gladly given by " those damned, illiterate natives " dwelling midst the sand and swamp and flies.

For to them the War, so far away and incomprehensible, spelt hardship. The hardship of high prices and poor markets. No flame of patriotism or devotion could burn in their breasts, no seeds of moral right quicken their imagination : they only knew their unseen Rajah was fighting ; was hardly pressed by his foes ; that both the combatants were white men. To them the Armistice brought no sacred or sentimental emotions ; but it brought a hope which they at once expressed : " Now that the War is over perhaps prices will go down." And of this hope they gave their contributions to the " Our Day " Fund of 1918 in a glad and willing spirit.

How badly that hope was realised is now a matter of history all the world over, but as the old year died and the new came in a Merciful Providence gave no warnings to us in the Labuk of a tragedy that soon was to be enacted, the horror and magnitude of which would ring from end to end of the country.

Rumours of " leave " had reached me and, though I loved my work and still felt well, was still prepared to " carry on," I realised that England called me, that the last eight years had claimed a toll. Yet somehow the idea seemed fraught with strangeness. England ?—What was it like, I wondered, for I had almost forgotten. Pals ?—I hadn't any, for the War had killed them and the few left I knew were married. From somewhere in my brain I conjured up pictures of my people—Father and Mother,

Sister and Brother—pictures as I knew them when I had left home in 1911. Then I looked at the photographs they had sent me. The same and yet . . . What would they think of me ? How should we agree ? A youth of 20 had left them, a man of 30 was returning. Could life be picked up where we left it ? Would the intervening years be bridged ? An English lane and garden ; a village church ; the winding Thames ; my old school ; Trafalgar Square ; the Empire ; Prince's ; even Pinoli's passed in pictures through my brain. Passed and faded, giving place to Kinabalu, to the island of Danawan in the pale and silver moonlight, to Bungaima wracked with cholera, to the little dancing maiden, to the storm of Mantanani, to a filthy Chinese brothel, to Mendagu and its spirits, to a mighty swollen river, to a rocking swaying office, to the harbour of Sandakan, to the bright and brilliant sunshine, to the heavy tropic rain. . . .

" Tuan ! Haji Noir wants to see you." My " boy's " voice broke in upon my reverie. With a start I awakened from my dreams.

" Tell him to come up, Amat. Then bring in some coffee and put the cigarettes on the table near my chair."

Something told me that Haji's visit was of importance else he would not have called at so late an hour, and a curious sense of foreboding stole over me as he climbed the stairs and entered the house.

" Tabek, Tuan Haji," I murmured, and waved him to a seat.

He sat down and I pushed the cigarettes across to him. Absent-mindedly he took one, rolled it between the palms of his hands, put it in his mouth and forgot to light it. As I watched I knew my fears were well founded for as yet he had forgotten to give me greeting, and in matters of courtesy he was always most punctilious.

Amat came in with coffee, set it beside me, waited while I poured it out, handed a cup to Haji and then departed. Still my visitor did not speak.

" Well, Tuan Haji, what is it ? " I said, breaking the silence.

With a jerk he put down the coffee cup he was holding and looked at me.

" It is about . . ." and then he hesitated.

" Yes ? " I encouraged him.

" It's about the Tuan Manager, Tuan," Then he became silent again and nervously twisted his cigarette.

A native is always diffident in talking to one white man about another, moreover I knew that Haji was aware there was no love lost between the Estate manager and myself. Thus it behoved me to walk warily for some sixth sense told me that Haji was in deadly earnest.

The surest way to get a story from a native is to let him tell his own tale in his own way. It is a long and circuitous method, garbled with much irrelevant matter, but the story is there for anyone who runs to read and with a little patience the wheat may be sifted from the chaff. Any other way spells chaos, for a native becomes hopelessly muddled under a fire of cross-questions and resents too close an examination. His mind does not easily seize upon essentials and, if shorn of the trivial incidents attached to any sequence of events, loses its thread of remembrance in an utter maze of conjectures.

Haji was educated for his race. He could read and write. He was the successor to Aji Pati, now unfortunately dead—yet I knew his limitations.

" I think, Tuan Haji," I said, " you'd better tell me

your story. I'll listen. But remember you are talking of a white man and a manager of an Estate."

"Tuan ; but he's not of your bangsa" (race). "He's an Orang Blanda" (Dutchman) "not an Orang Puteh" (Englishman ; literally White Man).

"True," I broke in, "none the less he's a white man, Tuan Haji ; remember that."

"Tuan !" Then Haji began.

"You remember, Tuan, the lake on Labuk Estate, that piece of water near the new main road and edged on its further side with jungle ?"

I nodded. "It's haunted, isn't it ?"

"Yes. Years ago there was a village where the lake now is. The headman's daughter was being given away in marriage. All the village were gathered together to attend the feast. Several buffaloes had been slaughtered and eaten ; many jars of Tapai had been drunk. The feast and merriment were at their height. Suddenly into the midst of the revellers someone pushed a dog, dressed in a coat of painted bark, with a necklace of human skulls hung round its neck. There was a shriek of laughter. Then someone caught it, poured Tapai down its throat and released it. As the fiery liquid burnt its throat and the potent spirit went to its head, the poor beast drunkenly staggered round and round, the while it uttered plaintive howls. But the assembled company only laughed the louder, careless of impending fate."

Haji paused to relight his cigarette, which had gone out during his recital.

"You know, Tuan," he continued, "no animal must be ridiculed. Even the monkey, who apes the man, must not be jested with. They have their place in the scheme of Life and belong as much to Allah or the spirits of the

Dusuns as we ourselves. To make a mock of them, to mark them for unseemly mirth is to incur the anger of the Power that rules the world. In the Tuan's land it is so too, is it not ? "

" True, Tuan Haji," I answered. Then he continued.

" And this poor beast was a hunting dog, the fastest and bravest in the village. To him had fallen a dozen pig ; many a stag had felt his teeth, and the fierce Tembadu knew him. Him, out of all the pariahs that scavenged round, these drunken revellers fixed upon to hang their ribald jests ; at him they shrieked their senseless laughter, making of a king of dogs nought but a starveling tukang lawah (clown).

" Like a flash of lightning the wrath of their outraged Gods descended. There was a sound like the distant roar of breakers ; the ground quivered, the houses shook and trembled. Then the earth opened and all—save one—were swallowed up. In the morning this solitary survivor gazed upon a slimy, sluggish, bottomless lake.

" 'Twas he who brought the story to my father's father's father. 'Twas he who was the progenitor of that accursed race—the Dumpas—found only on the river near the lake."

Haji paused and I could see that he was strangely moved as he related this ancient legend, yet I knew we had not reached the crux of his visit.

" Since then—" once again Haji was speaking—" the spot and all around has been ' Berhantu ' " (haunted). " The soil close by is fertile, the jungle thick, the undergrowth impenetrable. But this one spot is swamp and in its centre rests the lake which has no bottom. No one must live too near to it, or plant too close to its confines.

To do so is to court disaster—disease or fire or, possibly, death.

" Some years ago—before the Tuan was old enough to come and rule us—there was a tobacco estate on this land. For years and years this spot was never touched ; all around it lay the plantation, but never a tree was felled, never a rotan taken, nor the surface of the lake disturbed. The plantation flourished ; the crops were good ; the company made much money. Then a new manager came, who heeded not the superstition. He only laughed, saying he had no fear of ghosts, that he needed the land for his tobacco. So trees were felled, the rotan taken and his Chinese coolies bathed in the lake."

Haji paused again and looked questioningly at me.

" The Tuan knows the rest of the story I fancy ! How the Chinese coolies burnt the Estate to the ground ; how they attacked the Europeans and drove them off the Estate till they were forced to flee to the Government station."

I nodded assent. The record of the event was among the files in the District Office.

For a little while there was silence between us. Then our eyes met and I swear the same thought was in our minds. In a flash I understood the reason of Haji's visit. For since the days about which he had been talking a new Estate had opened on the old land. The manager had been twenty years in the country and yet I was afraid. Would he learn from the past ? He was not the type of man to set much store by a native superstition. His tobacco and commission interested him much more.

" Is that all, Tuan Haji ? " I asked, but as I spoke I knew there was more to come.

" Not quite, Tuan. There is just a chance—but the

Tuan has given orders for some timber to be felled and the rotan to be collected. And on the edge of the lake he intends to build a kongsi " (coolie lines).

" How do you know ? " I questioned.

" Landau, the Sungei, who works as a mandor, told me. It is he to whom the Tuan gave the orders and he is afraid."

" So ? . . ."

" I have come to you, Tuan, for I am afraid also."

Long after Haji left me I sat in my chair thinking. Dinner grew cold and when I tried to eat it I found my appetite had vanished. Far into the night I sat thinking, for I too was afraid.

All was not well on Labuk Estate I knew ; yet there was nothing I could actually lay my hands on : nothing on which I could take action. I had reported my fears to Government and talked the matter over with the manager. There matters must rest for after all it was his business. Yet . . .

Perhaps the story got into my blood ; perhaps I am a superstitious fool. Anyhow a few days later I made a point of visiting him and brought the conversation round to the haunted lake.

" I know what the natives say about the place," he answered, " but I'm going to plant right up to it all the same. There's heaps of good rotan there that I want for my drying-sheds, and the Chinese coolies can bathe to their heart's content."

" Look here——" I began.

" Damn it all, man," he broke in hotly, " for the Lord's sake let me run my own Estate. I'm sick to death of these blasted superstitions. You're worse than any native and pander all day long to their whims and fancies. Do what you like in the district, but on the Estate—well, damn it, let me alone."

I said nothing for I had failed; all that remained was to wait, and wonder whether history would repeat itself.

Nearly a month passed, then on the morning of Chinese New Year it happened.

Curiously enough I was at that very moment relating to my friend of the timber camps who had come up to me for the night, Haji Noir's visit, his fears and my own pleadings. I remember remarking that I was particularly anxious, as the launch bringing supplies and stores was some days overdue. I recollect commenting on the fact that a large batch of new coolies, men disbanded from the Chinese Labour Corps in France, had but recently arrived on the Estate and that their behaviour in Sandakan, even under police control and supervision, had been most truculent and exceedingly insubordinate.

Even as I was speaking my worst fears were realised. Hurried uncertain steps approached, the sound of unusually hard breathing reached us, the high pitched voices of excited and exhausted natives broke the quiet, and before I could look over the verandah to see what caused the unusual stir the manager of the Estate staggered up the steps of my house and gasped,

" My God—they've killed him—killed the Assistant—they've burnt the Estate—they've got rifles—all the rifles—they've attacked the Head Tandil (Head Overseer)—they nearly shot me—just missed . . . My God—it's awful."

Then he sank into a chair.

Quickly I turned to my friend from the timber camp.

" Get him some brandy," I cried, " a strong dose ; I must turn out the police. When he's better, if I'm not back, both come to the office." And I left to set about giving instructions to the Sergeant of police, the issuing of ammunition, the preparing of boats and collecting of coolies for our transport up river.

Hardly had I completed my instructions when the other two came in. The manager, revived by a stiff brandy, was calmer and more collected, and able to give me a coherent account of all that he knew.

"My God, Cook!" he cried, "it's awful, and but for chance I too should now be dead. I took an unusual walk, the day being as you know a holiday—and on my way back to the house heard sounds of firing. I thought for a minute some of the natives had shot a deer—but the noise and firing continued. I hurried on my way and met two of my old Chinese coolies. They were terrified and running away but stopped long enough to cry out 'Run, Tuan, run for life—the new coolies have all risen—they've killed the Tuan Kechil (Assistant). They're shooting the head tandil and others are looking for you. Fly for your life,' and with that they continued their flight. I ran to my house as the noise and firing increased. I seized my shot-gun and was about to rush out, when my housekeeper and her little girls appealed to me for protection. I hesitated. The noise grew nearer. A local native ran in—he had seen the body—the poor fellow was dead—killed in his bedroom. Nearer came the cries and the firing continued . . . What should I do? The woman and children? To stay was to be killed. They seized my arm and dragged me to the river. I pushed them into a sampan (boat) and sent them off with a couple of boatmen; into another I tumbled and followed just as a dozen or so Chinese came rushing to the water's edge.

"I travelled faster, and on reaching the lower landing-place got out as I could see coolies running madly to try and cut us off; I fired but missed—the coolies fired but they missed me! Then a great shout went up and I saw flames leaping up from my house. The coolies on the river bank yelled with delight and in the confusion the other boat slipped by; then quickly I followed. As we paddled down-stream I could see the flames spreading all over the Estate. My God! but it's awful!"

"You are certain your Assistant is dead?" I put the question curtly.

"Certain—the man who told me is reliable and he's chief hunter," he answered.

"How many firearms had he—three or four?"

"Four: an elephant gun, a Winchester repeater, a shot-gun and a snider—also a revolver and heaps of ammunition."

"How many more are on the estate?"

"The head tandil has two, the shopkeeper two. They are all by now in the hands of the rioters."

"Are your Javanese to be trusted?" I then asked. "Will they help?"

"No," he replied, "they're all sick with influenza and the biggest funks in the world—as I left they were bolting into the jungle."

"Can you trust any Chinese—your old coolies?"

"There aren't ten on the Estate I'd trust—the rest are all new men."

"This is no faction fight—you're sure?"

"Quite—there's no quarrel between the Chinese and Javanese—they're out against the management only."

Then for the first time my friend spoke.

"How many police can you take up?" he asked me.

"Six," I answered; "not including the Sergeant."

"And the Chinese number?"

"Two hundred and seventy," blurted out the manager.

The only reply was a long-drawn-out whistle, and for a moment there was silence between us. But in that moment my mind was made up. Rightly or wrongly I had come to a decision; weighed up the position of affairs, the probable course of events, the chances of successful intervention; and my calculations included a knowledge of Chinese character.

The silence was broken by the manager.

"When are you leaving for the Estate?" he asked rather diffidently.

"I'm not going," I answered slowly. "I shall sit tight and wait for reinforcements from Sandakan and then . . . G——, you've come up on your motor boat?" He nodded. "Good! Then you'll take in a letter for me at once."

"But surely——" broke in the manager.

"You're safe and sound here," I interrupted; "your Assistant is dead, you're certain of that; your head tandil is a Chinaman; your Estate is in flames! I number six rifles. They total eight. I have to collect and go up the river in open boats, they remain under cover and command all approaches. I see no single circumstance or factor that would justify any precipitate action. Can you name one?"

He was silent, so I continued.

"There's no white man to be rescued, no faction fight to be quelled, no property to be saved, and by the time I reach there evening will be coming on! The trouble started at six this morning. I can't get there before four this afternoon! What would be the object of my visit? The quelling of the riot, the arrest of the ring-leaders, the sending them down here under escort, and guarding of the Estate and maintenance of order till help comes from Sandakan. Can I do this with six police? I might! If the coolies were unarmed, possessed no firearms, there'd be more than a chance of success; as matters are the risks are absolutely unjustifiable: the rank elephant grass along the river affords excellent cover; every unused and ancient drying-shed on the estate is a potential ambush; a couple of lucky shots—and . . . No! I'll wait for reinforcements, trade on the Chinaman's own nature, and then strike a full and certain blow."

Such had been my decision of a few moments ago and in less than half an hour the motor boat was chugging downstream on its way to Sandakan, bearing my brief report and request for help.

Then followed what will always seem to me the two longest days of my life—days of waiting—during which, though I was certain I had acted rightly, my mind foresaw the inevitable verdict of 'coward' pronounced upon me by the great majority of Europeans in the Territory.

Every now and then an odd coolie or so would come in, having fled from the Estate, bringing a wild tale of terrorism and debauchery that fired my blood and nearly broke down my resolve of caution and patience till close questioning proved the story a gross exaggeration, the fantasy of an excited and overwrought brain.

One move, however, I made. The same night I despatched Haji Mohammed Noir, the local headman and chief, on a reconnoitre. He collected four or five of his personal entourage to accompany him, but on my suggesting that I should also be of the party he flatly refused to set out if I persisted in my intention. The enterprise, he stated, was hazardous enough, without the addition of a European—and his Tuan to boot ! So as I badly wanted news of happenings on the Estate I had to concede the point.

Very early next morning (Feb. 2nd) Haji Noir returned bringing a tale that coincided with and amplified the manager's report. Quietly as his party moved, he said, whenever it tried to land and move about the various dogs on the Estate would detect the sound and give alarm. Immediately shouts would be heard, whistles blown and lamps or torches appear. In their glare many coolies would be seen running in the direction from whence came the barking ; shots were fired and bullets whisked around, one of which actually tore the gunwale of the boat.

The news was meagre, but confirmed my opinion of the situation and proved beyond doubt the conviction of the belief that the riot was one of unusual organisation and only to be tackled by an adequate force.

So the 2nd and the morning of the 3rd passed in waiting and perfecting plans for action what time the reinforcements arrived from Sandakan.

Two o'clock had just been sounded from the District Office when an orderly came running to the house to report, simultaneously as I myself heard it, the sound of a launch approaching up-stream. In ten minutes I was aboard the s.l. "Petrel," as she dropped her anchor amid stream, and a few seconds later had met and was imparting my story to the Sub-Commandant of the Constabulary.

He had with him fifty police-Sikhs and Pathans, and was at first all for immediate progress to the Estate, but, as the situation was unfolded to him and he acquired a knowledge of local geography and conditions, he revised his plan and readily adopted the idea of postponing his attack on the rioters till the next morning, by which time and unknown to them we could, by a night march over an old and disused road, guided by two hunters who had just reported, arrive at their rear and catch them completely by surprise.

Thus no start was made till 5 p.m. at which hour the launch steamed slowly up-stream, her engines running slow and her funnel smokeless. At some considerable distance from the Estate wharf anchor was dropped and we again waited—this time till 10 p.m.—when we transferred into open boats (dug-outs) which we had towed up. Thus unseen, and we hoped almost noiselessly, we arrived on the Estate.

The Sub-Commandant—being my senior in the Service—was in command, and made the following dispositions. His force of fifty men together with my six native police he divided into three sections. No. 1 section was under his command; No. 2 under the Sergeant Major, and No. 3 under the Corporal. A body of fifty free natives, whom I had collected with difficulty, were placed under me. They were armed with spears, parangs (swords) and an odd rifle or two. My orders were definite up to a certain point. After that my actions were to be of my own discretion.

The force disembarked from the boats about 11 p.m., and in almost utter darkness we marched in single file as silently as we could along the old unused tobacco road. The long lank grass and lalang reached up to our waists and soon we were wet through.

But that was of little moment as by 1 a.m. we had to ford the Labuk river. The hour was a matter of importance since the river was tidal and at 1 a.m. would be at its lowest, but even so the water reached to my arm-pits

And then commenced another long and cold wait, for we were by now only an hour from our point of attack—the rear of the coolie lines—which had been fixed for dawn, between 5.45 and 6 a.m.

An advance guard consisting of a native corporal and three police had been sent on ahead to take up a station on a bridge that crossed a small stream and dissected a cross road to that on which we were to march. This precaution was justified as they captured a solitary coolie who might easily have reached our halting place by the river unseen by us and returned to give the alarm to his fellows.

At length, with a sigh of relief, our leader gave the signal, and snake-like the force commenced to wend its way along the road to the longed-for scene of action. In a few minutes we passed a smouldering ruin—it was the Assistant's house, burnt to the ground.

I knew that soon we must pass some more houses and kongsis (coolies' lines). Would they be burnt too, I wondered! Suddenly I bumped into the man in front of me—one of my own police—and a second later Haji Noir bumped into me. The line had come to a standstill. A whispering broke out and came floating down to me. The Major wanted me, so I quickly went to the head of the line and there saw the cause of our halt. A hundred yards away was the blurred outline of a house; from its closed windows and door came puny streaks of light. Cautiously the Major and I, accompanied by one of the guides, crept up. Our ears to the cracks of the door and windows we listened. No sound reached us. We moved to rejoin the line when the Major slipped. In an instant the dogs inside gave tongue. Breathlessly we waited. Nothing happened. Either the inhabitants slept soundly or ignored our presence. Quickly and under cover of the barking the column passed the house and progress was continued.

I turned to speak to Haji Noir to give him an order to pass down to my free natives. But there were only five of them left—Haji Noir and his personal retinue. The rest, scared by the barking of the dogs and possibly afraid of passing the haunted lake that was close to the other house, had slipped away under cover of the darkness. They never reached the scene of action till 11 a.m., by which time all possibility of danger was over, but the possibility of loot most probable.

In the East the sky was slowly lightening. Dawn was about to break. Silently we marched on. Suddenly as the head of the column rounded a bend in the road the line halted. A message came down to me to go forward to the Major. I obeyed. And then an extraordinary sight met my gaze. A little ahead and to the left of me were two long lines of kongsis, facing each other. Throughout the whole length of their verandahs were placed lamps, torches, and candles, the effect of whose flickering lights was weird and unusual in the extreme. But from the kongsis themselves no sound emanated. Those kongsis, I knew, were the Javanese lines.

Further on and almost right ahead of us were two more large kongsis. These—the Chinese quarters—were also wrapped in silence.

The Major was in a quandary. Our captured Chinese coolie stated the Chinese were in the lines nearest us ; the guides stated the further kongsis were those of the Chinese ! Did I know ? Who was telling the truth ? Was the whole plan to be ruined by the lies of a Chinese coolie or the stupidity of a native ? The Major became angry, and as his anger grew, regardless of the need for silence, his voice rose in a crescendo.

The lighted Javanese lines and the gloomy Chinese quarters certainly provided a puzzle, but in the end the old plan of attacking the Chinese kongsis was adhered to. In fact the necessity of so doing was quickly realised by the Major when I pointed out that in the Javanese lines there would be at least some forty or fifty women and children. It was impossible to think of subjecting them to a cold blooded volley from our police !

So the column crept on a little further, while an uncanny silence brooded over the coolie quarters. Cautiously each section took up its allotted place. Quietly section No. 1 drew the bolts of twenty Lee-Enfield carbines, inserted twenty .303 bullets and almost as quietly shot home the twenty bolts.

The edge of the sun just glinted on the horizon. The Major stepped two paces to the front, as he stood at the side of his section. He raised his hand. Twenty rifles smartly pointed at the kongsis. Twenty fingers caressed their triggers. But the signal to fire was never given. Instead a look of surprise spread over the Major's face and following his gaze I saw the head tandil emerging from one of the kongsis. With his hat in one hand and the other raised he came towards us crying out, " Don't shoot, Tuan, don't shoot ! The coolies wish to surrender and ask me to plead for them."

" Hold fire ! " The order came from the Major, but in the tension of the moment was imperfectly heard and a ragged volley of shots rang out.

Then pandemonium broke loose. From out of the Chinese lines came pouring the Chinese coolies, talking and gesticulating wildly, while from the Javanese kongsis emerged women and children, Javanese men and some Chinese too.

" Ada Prentah, ada Prentah, ada Tuan ! " (The Government are here ; the Tuans are here !) was the cry taken up and passed from throat to throat.

The Javanese huddled together ; but the Chinese in their terrified guilt tried to scatter. Strenuously the Major, the head tandil and I strove to make them understand that they were to collect in rows on either side of the road and that if they did so and were obedient there would be no shooting. Slowly they grasped our meaning and hestitatingly began to line up, but even so it was necessary to send my native police and free natives to round up, at the edge of drawn parang and spear, the more terrified or recalcitrant.

At length order was established and the Major and I, with the help of the head and under-tandils, were taking a roll call of the coolies present. As we did so I was mentally congratulating myself on the turn of events, for, though greatly disappointed at the absence of a fight, I felt my diagnosis of affairs had been more than correct and that the coolies who on February 1st had been intoxicated with success and the lust of murder had, as I intended they should, in the meanwhile been so puzzled by the Government's seeming want of action that wonder had deepened to fear and fear to a realisation of the power of the Prentah.

My reflections, however, were rudely shaken, for suddenly, just as the Major and I were at the end of the lines of squatting coolies a shot rang out, followed in quickest succession by three more, and four bullets whizzed past our heads—two actually passing between us. They came from a little house on a small hill about a hundred yards away. In an instant No. 1 section, at a command from the Major, had doubled along the road and taken up a position in front of the house and about fifty yards distant.

No sound came from the building. On instructions the head tandil called out in Chinese to those inside to come out or remain at their peril as disobedience would be met by a volley from the police. A face appeared at a window and then withdrew. The head tandil repeated the command and warning. Still no response.

" Fire ! " the command rang out and a volley was poured into the house. At the same time my small force rushed the hill, the police and natives yelling with delight at the prospect of possibly using their parangs. In the vegetable garden which surrounded the house we captured a Chinaman who turned out to be the *de facto* leader of the riot and the actual firer of the shots at the Major and myself.

At the steps of the house we met a woman with a baby in her arms and two children clinging round her. All were weeping, and no wonder ! for the husband and father had been killed by our volley and lay in an ever-widening pool of blood. There was one other casualty—a man shot through the arm and side, who died that same night in the Estate Hospital.

Thus ended the riot on Labuk Estate—the biggest and most serious affair of its kind that had ever happened in North Borneo. But though the riot was quelled, my work on the Estate had only just begun and all chance of " leave " vanished. That afternoon we buried the charred and burnt remains of the poor Assistant, reading over him the Anglican Church Burial Service and placing a wooden cross at the head of the grave. Thereafter for many days, among the smouldering relics of the manager's house and fermenting shed and other buildings, the preliminary enquiries dragged their interminable course. Then, duly committed, the accused came before the Sessions Court. In the end some five or six out of nearly fifty coolies were condemned to death ; a few more received sentences of ten years gaol and under ; but the majority were released. There was so little evidence—only that of a few frightened Javanese coolies, whose memories could not be relied upon—on which to convict.

Yet such is the justness of the laws in Borneo, so carefully is the sacredness of Life regarded, that although all who had taken part in the riot and dacoity and murders, even to the smallest degree of being one on the edge of a crowd, were legally guilty of the offences committed, still only those against whom the actual perpetrating of crimes could be proved were sentenced.

Among the released coolies was one who carried in his heart a secret, whose face was ever an impassive mask. Never by sign nor word nor look throughout the preliminary enquiries did the faintest breath of suspicion touch him. Right through to the end of the trials in the Sessions Court his record appeared to be blameless.

What were his thoughts as he heard the death sentence passed on his comrades ? How could he keep his face as their eyes met his ? Never an eye nor muscle twitched as gaol was sentenced upon the rest.

And they whose days were numbered, who could count the suns they knew each day would rise, would they keep silent ? Would they take their secret with them to the grave ? We wondered ; for we knew that somewhere in the background dwelt a master mind ; we knew that these wretches upon whom death had been so justly sentenced were but instruments after all.

The days of grace were passing. The day of execution drawing near. Still no word : no sign of betrayal. But one more day remained ! Lingering in their cell awaiting the last dawn their eyes would ever witness, something snapped within them. It was not fear for they knew that they must die. It was not hate for they were past all feelings. Perhaps it was a sense of justice ! If they must die then why not he, the author and the instigator ? So they spoke, and gave his name and number (registered Estate number) and described his face. They also told us the story of the plot ; how every Chinese coolie had put " his mark " to a document, swearing to kill the Management and ruin the Estate.

A trial followed. Then a conviction. In silence the condemned man heard the sentence and passed out ; only the days of grace remaining, remaining to him of life.

. . . . . .

The gaol square is filled with coolies, Chinese and Javanese—the remnants of the sacked Estate—squat on their haunches, waiting with eyes that are fixed on two wooden doors. For these doors will soon be opened and within them hanging from a rope will be a writhing, twisting, turning corpse.

Six measured beats strike on the quiet of a fair tropic dawn, then quiver into silence. The door of a cell—the cell of those condemned—opens. A warder and two others enter. One word is spoken. The hands of him whose earthly life is closing are tied behind his back ; his feet are linked together with a chain that yet enables him to walk. Over his head a large white hood is fitted and tied with strings beneath his chin. At the back of the cell another door is opened. Through this door the hooded man is led, then along a short and narrow passage into the cell of execution. To the middle of the floor he shuffles. Then is turned right about to stand upon a crack hardly perceptible that stretches from left to right. Motionless he stands, without a quiver. Even his breathing is not heard. But the hood is faintly beating to each muffled respiration. Over his neck a noose is placed, then drawn tighter and the knot is carefully fitted on that one frail place. By a lever stands the executioner ; his eyes are waiting for a signal. Just for a moment I glance at the doctor ; then my eyes pass on to scan the face of the Gaol Superintendent. Like an alabaster figure, like a graven wooden image he stands ; the might and majesty of Law personified. Just for a moment I catch my breath and my eyelids flicker. In that moment the signal is given, the lever pulled, the trap doors parted, and I look . . . Only a yawning chasm, only a rope from the ceiling dangling, dangling down into the pit, and that rope is twisting, turning, and at the end the lifeless figure of what was once a living man.

CHAPTER IX

LOCUSTS AND LEAVE

THERE was sufficient time I reckoned for one last trip round the district before I went on leave ; that is, of course, unless anything unforeseen occurred to once again prevent my sailing.

Who was coming to relieve me, or the actual date of my departure were facts quite unknown to me. Yet it was with a holiday feeling that I set out on this trip.

To Annai at Trusan, to Panglima Mait at Tetabuan, to Hammid at Telupid, to Salleh at Lingkabak ; to Boji at Meridi, I had said farewells. Good fellows all. They were not brilliant but they did their best ; always cheerful, always steady. Always did they make me welcome. Their work was not hard, but then their pay was little.

Mingled with my farewells was a warning. The scourge of locusts was over the country. In North Keppel and Marudu the plague was devastating the crops. Watch must be kept ; word sent to the utmost ends of the districts to warn the natives. At the first sign or suspicion report must be made.

I travelled on to the Paitan to spend a last two days with Haji Abubakar, of whom I had a high opinion and still higher hopes, if only he would curb his infatuation for keeping female slaves disguised as junior wives.

On a patch of gravel in front of the barracks someone was dancing to the beat of gongs slung from the rafters of the barracks' verandah. From the river bank came a stream of natives intent on paying their last respects. From up the river came the sound of paddles ; others were coming and would not be denied. The barracks, and the square in front, were crammed to suffocation—yet still the crowd congested, packed itself a little tighter, squeezed in here, expanded there. Still the gongs continued beating, still the dancing figures swayed and the moonlight shed its silvery light over the jungle and the river gently rustled between its banks in seaward flight.

Suddenly there came cessation, just that pause as in a dinner conversation, when speech is silent for a fleeting moment and the air seems heavy with some unspoken thought.

In that silence from across the river comes a voice. " Boat ! " it calls, and yet again.

" Boat !—ada surat sama Tuan surat deri Lingkabao—ada susah di—Lingkabao—ada susah skali." (Boat !—I bring a letter for the Tuan from Lingkabao where there is great trouble.)

On the opposite bank is standing a policeman. The moonlight glitters on the numbers fastened on the front of his small round red cap—glitters on the brass buttons of his tunic, flits to the buckle of his belt then passes, pauses and then winks and glitters on his silver-mounted parang resting in its wooden sheath, hung with coils of human hair, that is fastened round his waist. In his hand he holds a letter.

Six strong strokes and Sabtu has reached him ; six more and he has reached our bank. Through the crowd he quickly presses, mounts the barrack steps and stands before me. Then saluting hands me the letter.

"The news came in about eleven—three hours after the Tuan left. Salleh at once wrote the letter and I have come straight through."

"Good going, Tuah," I answered, looking at my wrist watch, then I dismissed him and opened the note.

It was from Salleh, written in Malay, and told me that the locusts had appeared in the Ulu (Source) of the Lingkabao river.

That which I was dreading had happened. The plague had crossed from Marudu into my district, where the Indian corn and sugar cane and rice were ripening.

Silently I handed the note to Haji Abubakar. I felt too knocked out to speak. Surely the Labuk and Sugut were accursed. Last year the flood and influenza!—now the locusts' plague was on us—all the crops again to be ruined and starvation once more to stalk the land!

For a moment I sat huddled in my chair, while the natives looked and waited. Then two large paws rested on my knees, a cold nose rubbed my cheek and two dark brown eyes—those of my woolly sheep dog—were gazing into mine. Mike sensed my trouble, and strove to comfort me the only way he could.

"Michael, Michael," I murmured as my arms went round him, "Michael, old dog, we'll best 'em yet." Slowly his tail wagged; his wet red tongue lightly licked my cheek. A moment more and he was peacefully sleeping, curled up like a ball at my feet.

He was a dog. And yet he knew. He was an animal, yet he had comforted me, given me strength. Had spoken in the only way he could; had spoken and said he

A DUSUN SEPULCHRE.

MENGKABONG.

p. 272

trusted me ; trusted me so that in the face of trouble he was content to lie down and go to sleep.

From Michael, the sheep-dog, my eyes wandered over the crowded, expectant natives, dressed in their finest and best, assembled in this small outstation to do me honour, to say good-bye and wish me luck on my homeward journey. In the months to come what would their fate be ? I wondered. Then I rose to my feet and spoke.

I told them how I was going to leave them ; how that perhaps the locusts might detain me ; how that if another came to succeed me they must always give him of their best, trust him, please him and obey him. How that the Rajah thanked them for their presents to the " Our Day " Fund ; how that the War was over and the German foemen vanquished. How they must continue to plant their foodstuffs ; build strong fences against the pig ; how that the Prentah really loved them, thought and planned always for their good. How that on the morrow I should retrace my steps, cut short my visit to Tuan Haji and return to Lingkabao ; go up the river and find the locusts—see if they were fliers or hoppers, do all that I could to prevent the plague spreading ; how they themselves must watch and guard and at once report their presence ; how that each man in a village had his duty to his neighbour ; how that far across the water I should think of them ; how that when my " leave " was over I should return to my adopted home ; how I valued their affection, how I strove to win respect.

It was a halting speech, and at times the Malay was bad for the words I wanted would not come and thoughts tumbled out so fast they would not wait to be expressed. Yet they understood and as I sat down there was silence —the silence of comprehension—for a minute.

Then from the crowd came the quivering voice of a frail and aged Chinese trader in whose house and shop, far up a small and little-travelled river, I once had spent a night—the first white man he had seen for eight years.

"For over thirty years I've lived in the country under the shadow of the Prentah and what the Tuan says is true. The small-pox came and the Prentah cared for us; Mat Salleh rose in rebellion but the Prentah fought and killed him. Musah raided the Paitan, but the Prentah was merciful and forgave him, for his offence was the outcome of fear and ignorance. Many Tuans have dwelt among us: some for a year or two, some only months; some have travelled the whole wide district, others were content to stay in their house. But this Tuan—in my house he spent a night, dandled my children on his knees, watched by my wife when dying of fever. To Tagypil and Tigabo his boat is always sailing. At Meridi on the Sugut, at Telupid on the Labuk his voice is known and loved. I am old and very aged. I have lived beneath the Prentah, I have sometimes met the white men that the Prentah sends to rule us, but never, never . . ."

His quavering voice broke under his emotion. He struggled but could not continue. From the packed crowd arose a murmur, growing stronger, ever louder. "Betul, betul, Tuan, Tuan." Through the crowd a tiny girl wriggled and twisted till she stood before me. In her hands she bore a complete set of three brass trays, black with the dirt of ages, lost midst the cobwebs of years. With a shy smile she curtsied, then, in a piping voice, "Father gives these to you as a keepsake," and she pushed them into my hands. Swiftly she turned to leave me, but, swifter still, I caught her hand.

" Minang," I answered gently, " say thanks for me to your father for his gift, which I greatly prize."

" Tuan," she hardly murmured, and her great shining eyes met mine. She was a child of nine or ten yet for a moment she typified the country, the district and the people. Her little hand lay in mine, cool and trusting, yet through her parted lips her breath came quickly, her unformed breasts, too, quickly rose and fell. She trusted me amidst her new and strange emotions, just as the district learned to trust the Prentah midst new laws and policies and plans.

From my pocket I drew a clean silk handkerchief, flicked it into a triangle and laid it lightly on Minang's shoulder. It was a sign of betrothal, a symbol of love, this giving of a handkerchief by man to maid. A mighty shout went ringing up to heaven from the assembled crowd. There was not one present who misunderstood my meaning. It was my message to them all, my dedication, my promise of return when " leave " was over.

In the East the dawn was breaking ; slowly the sun cleared the tops of the trees, but the gongs went on for ever beating. Across the river my luggage was borne. Along the narrow, winding trail the coolies bore it, up steep hill and down the other side ; under the leafy canopy of Billian, Camphor and Selang Batu (names of trees), through small swamps, over tiny streams till at last we reached Sungei Sungei, where our boats were waiting for the long hard pole and paddling up the Sugut to the mouth of the Lingkabao river.

Here I stayed for a night and found a letter from the Resident informing me that during the next ten days or so my successor would arrive in Klagan and that after handing over the district to him I was to proceed to Sandakan and go on leave.

Was I pleased and delighted ? I hardly knew. For now that "leave" was becoming so close a reality I began to feel the sting of parting. One thing, however, was quite plain. I must go up the Lingkabao to gain the fullest knowledge of the locusts.

So the next morning we started and poled and paddled up-stream for four days. In many places the rapids were so steep and rocky that we had to disembark and unload all the luggage before we could drag the boats over the great boulders. Then in the afternoon of the fourth day as we were gliding along on a smooth, deep reach, whose banks were thickly covered with bamboo from out of which every now and then peeped little grassy patches, suddenly from afar a dim, whirring noise reached us.

With paddles poised in mid-air the coolies waited, listening, wondering. Nearer and nearer came the noise ; slowly it grew louder and louder. In the sky the sun was shining—a flaming ball of brass—no cloud flecked the azure heavens—the water of the river sparkled—in its depths the shadows played and the tall bamboo was mirrored—not a ruffle on the surface. All was peace, the peace of a perfect tropic day. Only that strange, unearthly whirring ; ever growing nearer, closer.

Then It came creeping over the water, turning its face of sparkling beauty into a dull and dirty grey. No longer danced the shadows in it, no more the bamboo nodded to its own reflection. In the heavens the blue was fading, as when a cloud falls lower and lower, and the face of the sun grew hidden, blotted completely out of sight, leaving only a musty yellow-brown reflection like a November fog in London, pierced by a myriad electric lights.

In our mouths and ears and faces flew and flopped the hungry locusts. The air was full of them ; the boats grew full of them ; the grassy banks, and the bamboo were full of them—crawling, flying, eating.

That night, since the villages were in the hills, for the fourth time we camped on the river bank, building kajang shelters as protection from the dew or rain. The next day I spent in visiting three villages where fortunately the damage done was not as yet very great, for so thick was the luscious vegetation of the river that the locusts had no need to wander far afield.

In reality there was little I could do, for it is a hopeless proposition to try and cope with locusts in the flying stage, so I concentrated on teaching the natives how to look for and destroy the eggs ; also I detailed Salleh to go up to the farthest boundary of the district, visiting each village en route, to collect statistics of damage done and to continue the work of extermination.

That night as I looked at the holes in handkerchiefs and vests, made by the hungry locusts while the articles were drying in the sun after being washed, a full realisation of the possible damage the plague might effect was borne in upon me.

What if they spread down the Lingkabao to its confluence with the Sugut ? From there went down-stream to Sungei Sungei and Trusan on the coast ? What if they went up the river to Meridi or crossed the rentis to the Tungud and down its stream to meet the Labuk ? Here to separate, to track its source or find its mouth ? What if from Sungei Sungei they crossed to the Paitan, found the Kanibongan and Kaindangan rivers, found them and followed the length of their streams ?

From end to end of the district there would be no

rice, no sugar cane and no indian corn ! Only the ubi Kayu and the sweet potato would remain !

Sand and swamp and flies ! And now the locusts !

Clinging to the mosquito net of my camp bed I could see them as I fell asleep to dream of England.

Two days later I reached Lingkabao office. Two days more and I was " home " in Klagan. Here a mail was awaiting me. From it I learnt that rice was so scarce in the markets of the world and the price so high that a Food Controller had been appointed ; that rice would be sold on a ration system ; that subsidiary food crops must be planted ; that every care must be taken to preserve the district's rice ; that every effort must be expended to increase the food supply ; that . . . I read on and on— things to do and things not to do ; they were interminable, they were sound and necessary forethoughts, they were wise and able precautions of administration—yet in the Lingkabao there were locusts ! And if they spread, if this ravenous, all-devouring army started on its march . . .

I turned to another letter. It was from my successor. He would be arriving three days later ; he would take over all the stores in my godown ; he hoped there weren't any damned locusts in the district ; he trusted there was a large and well-filled vegetable garden.

In disgust I threw the letter on one side. Locusts— well the damned things were in the district, and somehow it seemed to me as if their presence were my fault, as if I had been guilty of some act of gross negligence. Vegetable garden ! There had been one once. Now there was only sand. Feet upon feet of sand ; the fault seemed mine. There seemed no excuse. All I could say, all I could ever say, was " There was one once but . . ."

I picked up another envelope. It contained my " leave " papers. Would I sign in a certain place ? Would I fill in a certain date ? Suddenly I felt an over-mastering need for leave ; to get away, away ; away from the sand and swamp and flies ; away from red-tape and cold officialdom ; away from the burning, blistering sun ; away from the cold pitiless downpours ; away from the jungle and creeping rivers ; away from the sea and twisting bridle-paths ; away, away, away !

I seized my pen. Then, " Damn them," I cried, " if they don't know the dates in their blasted file-stocked offices—why should I ? It's their beastly work to get these papers ready—not mine. To hell with them all. I just won't help them. It's always the same, you do the work and they get the praise."

Away ; away. To a land where snow was falling ; to a town where the streets were paved ; to a garden that grew roses ; to a church where walls were old ; to a house where the servants were maidens, where the grooms and gardeners were white ; to a dinner where one ate mutton ! I'd go—I'd go—" leave " papers or no, I'd go, just jolly well go and blast them. I'd missed the War—they'd kept me in the country. I'd missed my " leave " and given 'em eight years of my life and now, just for a paltry signature, just for a rotten date, they were going to start a quibble.

" Dawn is breaking roseate o'er the sky."

From the boatmen's quarters the song came stealing. The voice of the singer was ragged and untuneful yet the familiar song, with its fascinating lilt and cadence, soothed me. Almost unconsciously I hummed the second line with the singer—

"In the trees the birds are carolling."

The "leave" papers dropped from my hand and I sat down at my desk.

"Love is ours and it can never die."

I found myself gently singing this last line.

What did I know of Love? In the last eight years I'd met two unmarried white girls! When I left England in 1911 I was heart-whole. Love had not entered my life! Then why did the song so strangely move me, why did it soothe my jagged nerves? I pondered, staring straight in front of me, seeing nothing but the opposite wall of my office.

"Sahaya punyia Tuan mau pergi chuti." * The words, high-pitched in execrable Malay and with a mumbling accent, were spoken by my cookie to a friend as they were walking past the office.

Suddenly I knew; suddenly the great truth burst upon me: I was in love; hopelessly, utterly, absolutely in love. For eight years I'd been in love and never known it. Every day and every night I'd never realised it. I was in love: in love with life, with Borneo and its people—in love with "my people, and my district." I was "their Tuan" as they too were "my people."

A heavy paw was scratching at my leg; a woolly tail was thumping on the floor. I looked and saw old Michael. He knew. The excitement in the house, the empty walls, the piles of half-filled boxes, the matless floors, told him

* "My Tuan is going on leave."

the old, old story—another move. His head came up to me and rested on my chest.

" Michael, old man," I whispered, " it's a long long move this time and one I make alone. You'll stay behind, Michael, you'll stay and guard my ' home.' You'll be my ' ganti ' (substitute), Michael, till I come back again."

Into the office walked Haji Noir, splendidly arrayed in a brand-new suit of clothes.

" Tabek, Tuan Haji," I cried in a voice that belied the moisture in my eyes. " I've just been telling Michael he's to be my ' ganti ' while I'm on ' leave.' How goes the Tamu ? Are there many people ? "

" It's only the third Tamu, Tuan, but there are many people present. They are full of the idea. It was a great notion of the Tuan's to start this Tamu. But when the Tuan goes will the new Tuan keep it up ? "

" Of course he will," I answered, " but it's up to you and the people to make it go. You can make it or mar it just as you please. If you don't want it, there's no need to have it ; if you want it, why let it drop ? I only thought it would make things easier, level up prices and give everyone a chance to barter. That's all. Is Tamu opened ? "

Haji shook his head. " Not yet. I thought as there were many people in Klagan the Tuan would address them on the food shortage and the new rice restrictions. It would be better to talk to them before the Tamu opens ? Shall I bring them to the office ? "

" Yes. It's a great idea of yours, Tuan Haji. Bring 'em up as soon as you like."

With that he left me and in a little while I heard the shuffling of many feet and the babel of many voices on the long verandah outside, which also did duty for a Court House.

I looked up from the report I was writing to find the office orderly standing at my elbow.

" Well ? " I asked.

" Tuan Haji says ' all is ready if the Tuan is ' ! " he answered, and went out.

Slowly I followed him, but when I reached the verandah I faltered. It was full from end to end ! Chinese, Tidongs, Dumpas, Dusuns, Bajaus, Suluks, Sungeis and Javanese ! All were present ; all were wearing their best clothes. Mingled among them were the policemen, the boatmen, their women ; the clerks and their wives. On the face of Haji was the broadest of smiles, for I had so easily fallen into his trap.

Flight was my only escape and flee I could not for the only exit was blocked by that vast crowd. There was nothing for it but to mount the dais and sit down at the table from which I had so often given sentence.

For a moment there was silence ; and I was still trying to get my breath when I realised that Haji was reading from some paper in his hand. What he read I never heard nor understood for I was struggling for control. But the document signed by all present and by many more besides is in my keeping. Still I listened, uncomprehending, with a brain as dead as dough ; listened while the faces all around me became blurred and fainter ; listened while I heard my own voice speaking and found myself standing ; listened as I heard their footsteps descending from the office to the Tamu ; listened while I heard the cries of barter. And all the time there was ringing in my ears the great love song, the Salamun—" Love is ours and it can never die."

" God ! " with a start I pulled myself together as three strident blasts from a steamer's syren smote the

Dusun Woman.

Bontoc Woman.

p. 282

air ; then round the bend of the river came the " Petrel " bringing my successor.

As I went to meet him I kept saying, " Another day and two more nights. Another day and two more nights. Another day and—— "

" Cheerioh, old thing, and how are you ? Lucky devil to be going home on leave."

Clambering out of the boat he had grasped my hand ere the echoes of his salutation died away. His coming was as a gale of summer breeze, his presence comforting and warming as the sun. He was big and bluff and hearty.

" Another day and two more nights ! "

" What d'you say ? " he questioned.

" Nothing," I answered as we mounted the steps of the house. " Nothing of any importance. Have a ' stengah ' " (whiskey and soda) " ' or a gin pahit ' " (gin and bitters).

. . . . . .

" Good night and good-bye, Mem. And thanks for all your kindness. Good-bye, and cheerioh. No, thanks ! I'd really rather go aboard alone. Cheerioh and tons of thanks."

I had been staying, while waiting for my steamer to Singapore, with the Commissioner of Excise and Customs and his wife, who were one of the cheeriest and most hospitable couples in Sandakan. The previous night they had given a dinner-party of intimates to speed the parting guest. But this night of departure I had begged there should be no festivities. I wished to go aboard alone; steal quietly, as it were, from the country.

Down the winding path from their hill I stumbled,

with not so much as a lantern to assist me. I reached the bottom and turned for a last look at the house. Save for their bedroom window it was now wrapped in darkness. As I looked this light went out.

Past the recreation ground and a solitary Dusun sentry; past the huge offices of Harrisons and Crosfield; through the small door in the big Customs Gates; down to the wharf. At the foot of the gangway my " boy " was waiting.

" Everything is in order, Tuan. Your two big boxes in the hold, your cabin trunk and suit-case in your cabin."

" Baik, Amat," I replied and put out my hand.

" Salamat blaiar, Tuan, dun jangan lama; lakas pulang." (Bon voyage, Tuan, and don't forget us; return soon.)

" Salamat tinggal, Amat," I answered, " salamat tinggal! " I mounted the gangway; he turned from the wharf.

Eight bells broke the stillness of the night. From the bridge a voice came booming—" Stand by! " The telegraph bell was rung. From the bowels of the ship came the hum of engines; fore and aft the winches groaned. " Let go for'ard! " the voice cried, and a rope splashed into the sea; the aft rope followed suit; the telegraph bell tinkled again. A widening patch of sea grew between us and the wharf, which seemed to be slipping by for its red light was now abaft our stern. Up on the hill the town lights twinkled; twinkled and faded one by one.

We were moving, slipping forward; we were passing the barracks and the houses at Fort Pryor. Out of the darkness loomed the great, twin peaks of Bahalla—the island of the lepers. We were in the open sea. Somewhere on our port lay the Labuk Bay and the mouth of the river ; somewhere in the distance lay Klagan wrapt in slumber.

From the bridge two bells were sounded. The steamer was wrapt in sleep. Slowly I went to my cabin and switched on the light. In the lower bunk a rather fat man was snoring. Slowly I undressed. On my bunk my boy had laid out my " sarong " and " Kabaiah " (sleeping garments). One foot was on the fat man's bunk ; my hands were clutching the edge of mine. The fat man turned and muttered in his sleep. Then came a longer, louder snore ; I switched out the light and went on deck.

. . . . . .

Singapore was full to overflowing, with its hotels crammed with husbands, wives and children who had been waiting months for steamers to take them home.

To the Passage Controller's office, where from among piles upon piles of papers I dug out the august official.

" Have you any papers about you ? " he snapped rather wearily.

" I'm afraid not," I answered sadly ; " but I'm nearly dying and must get home."

" Dying ! You look the picture of health ! Where are you from ? "

" Borneo."

" Been there long ? "

" Eight years."

" God ! Then we'll send you home ! "

He gave me a pass and a letter to the steamship agents, which in the end I did not use, as I travelled with a party of friends on a Russian boat, which crawled along, but eventually landed me at Marseilles, into the middle of the dock strike.

Paris! Boulogne! A mad rush through the Customs; a scrum to crowd on to the boat; the pulling away of the gangway; the gliding out of the harbour; an icy wind; a grey sky; a rough, choppy sea.

By my side, well forward, was a pretty French girl. The wind and spray were whipping our faces, but we enjoyed it. Then as the sea grew rougher I noticed she showed signs of distress.

Hardly were we out of the harbour when—

"What are those cliffs in front of us?" I asked, for we seemed to be heading straight for land.

Just for a moment she looked at me—then—"England, mon ami," she answered, and staggered down below.

England! My hand tightened on the rail and I held my breath.

Folkestone! A rush through the darkened countryside; the lights of suburbs; the lamps of slums; the glare of a mighty station; a crowd of willing porters; a seething mass of detraining people. Victoria! London! England.

I spent that night in Town. The next day I called on my Father in the City—just dropped in as if back from a week-end. Then down to the silver Thames, where my sister met the train in; then on to the house where my Mother was waiting in the garden—the garden that grew roses.

England! Home!

THE END

PRINTED BY THE ANCHOR PRESS, LTD., TIPTREE, ESSEX, ENGLAND.